"Willis Barnstone has a [...] ed as a writer, he is also dazzlingly prolific—a combination which has caused some distress among his fellow poets and some critics. But it's time we faced life, and this rare phenomenon: everything he writes, from his invaluable *The Other Bible*, a compendium of holy texts no writer should be without, through his brilliant translations and beautiful poems, up to this new collection of 501 sonnets, *The Secret Reader*, is a breathtaking achievement. Buy this book." **—Carolyn Kizer**

"An amazingly original and profound poet offers a sequence that draws you like good fiction . . . The eagerness, love, and metaphysical tension to join and recognize impossible solitude go through the histories." **—Ruth Stone**

"The stunning scope, their wonderful irreverence, their slangy, antic humor, their stark realism, and their brave confrontation with the ultimate questions all combine to bring us a worthy lifework that is bound to be recognized as a masterpiece." **—Philip Appleman**

"Who isn't pleased to be given a bonus? There are bonuses in the work of certain poets. One of them is Willis Barnstone. His thought is of course the core, but with it come tones and overtones, undertones even, from the poets whom he has so brilliantly, so sensitively translated from many languages. Their voices are there with his, with the poet who has such an ear for language that no subtlety escapes it." **—James Laughlin**

"Willis Barnstone is an American original whose recently completed collection of sonnets is a classic. A great achievement, reflecting a lifetime of commitment to the act of literature. It is filled with lyricism, passion, meditative wisdom, irreverence, blasphemy and unflinching compassion for the human condition. Clearly a tour de force." **—D. M. Hertz**

"In the sonnet form Willis Barnstone has discovered a beguilingly flexible means of casting material usually reserved for the memoir and the prose essay. Those who have known him mainly as a translator, Spanish scholar and Bible editor, can now share his vividly personal secret, this summa of 501 amazing sonnets."

—Edwin Honig

"An important collection by one of our most exciting poets."

—David St. John

"If sonnets were windmills, give Willis Barnstone a knighthood and a horse with dreamy eyes, not for his victories alone, but because something in this book helps us get up out of the snow and ice of our lives."

—Stanley Moss

"Through the lyricism and urgency of these 501 sonnets, something terribly human rises again and again, assuring us it is impossible to keep Willis Barnstone's *The Secret Reader* secret."

—Yusef Komunyakaa

The Secret Reader
•
501 Sonnets

The Secret Reader

·

501 Sonnets

Willis Barnstone

University Press of New England

Hanover & London

University Press of New England,
Hanover, NH 03755
© 1996 by Willis Barnstone
All rights reserved
Printed in the United States of America 5 4 3 2 1
CIP data appear at the end of the book

Some of these poems have appeared in the following
publications:

*Agni, The American Scholar, The Antioch Review, The Arizona
Quarterly, The Bestiary of Bishop Theobaldus, A Book of Women Poets
from Antiquity to Now, Boundary 2, The California Quarterly, The
Chicago Review, Correspondences, CutBank, The Denver Quarterly, The
Dream Under the Sun: Poems of Antonio Machado, Exquisite Corpse,
Five A.M. in Beijing, From This White Island, The Formalist, Holiday
Magazine, International Poetry Review, In the Midst of Winter:
Selections from the Literature of Mourning, Kayak, The Kenyon Review,
Laughing Lost in the Mountains: Poems of Wang Wei, The Literary
Review, The Massachusetts Review, Modern European Poetry, Modern
Poetry Review, The Nation, New Letters, The New Republic, The New
York Quarterly, Nimrod, The North American Review, The Northwest
Review, The Partisan Review, The Poems of Saint John of the Cross,
Poets at Wesleyan, The Prairie Schooner, Sappho and the Greek Lyric
Poets, The Sewanee Review, Six Masters of the Spanish Sonnet, Southern
Poetry Review, The Southern Review, Sunday Morning in Fascist Spain:
A Memoir, The Tar River Review, Times Literary Supplement, Voices
within the Ark: The Modern Jewish Poets, The Wisconsin Review.*

"Lapland" first appeared in *The New Yorker.*

Dry brush drawings by Willis Barnstone

My thanks to Ayame Fukuda for
her crucial readings of these poems.

for Sarah, Helle, Aliki,
Robert & Tony

Everyone is a secret reader. Every book is a secret reader too. And even in those apparently barren and lone caves at Qumran, hidden words on a papyrus apocryphon waited, as we all wait, for eyes to discover and decipher them. So, by accident or luck or the begrudging indulgence of time, the secret reader may find the secret reader.

Pierre Grange, *On the Dead Sea Scrolls*

Contents

HISTORY I

Gas Lamp, 1893

The Good Beasts

Contents xi

HISTORY II

Solitude of Planets

My Heart Is in the East

HISTORY III

Gospel of Clouds

HISTORY IV

Kafka in His Small Room

Kafka in His Small Room

HISTORY V

To Find You at the End of Our Strange Walk

A Chat with the Reader

One morning in a class given by Louise Bogan in 1956 at Columbia University, Miss Bogan (as she wished to be called) ordered her students to write a sonnet. We were lucky. An external command is sometimes a liberation, the ego ceases to contend with itself, and one can act. I also welcomed the assignment because I liked the dramatic breath and short short story I saw in the sonnet. Before Louise Bogan started something that was later to lead me into eighteen years of vice, I'd written only one sonnet, a bad, stilted piece published when I was twenty-one in *Nine*, an English magazine. In the intervening years in Greece and Spain, however, I was reading and rereading the extraordinary sonnets of the Spanish poet Miguel Hernández (1910–1942). Possessed then, as now, by Hernández's poems, I borrowed his spirit and speech to write the class sonnet, whose title I think was "No." Bogan's order was ignored after the first show, however, and two decades went by sonnetless except for three orphans in my 1959 book *From This White Island*. When the "do a sonnet" order came again one November night, it was a compulsion, its source in me, and nothing it seemed could shut it up.

The specific preparation for my eighteen-year drunk on the sonnet took place in Argentina, in 1975 and '76, during the "Dirty War." I was living on Paraguay Street, a block from Jorge Luis Borges on Maipú, and began to see the poet regularly, to read to him (he had been blind since his mid-fifties), to travel with him into the interior of the country, and to translate his sonnets. I read my English draft, then the original Spanish. Borges heard his poems in his own tongue (he had not heard them read aloud before), sat back with his immense smile, and the lines in Spanish he liked he repeated sternly and melodiously in his deeply coarse milonga voice. "*¡Qué lindo!*" – How beautiful!" he said spontaneously. It was tremendously moving. His innocent cheer of self-praise contrasted with his public tenor, which, with his "mighty club of modesty," was always to put down "this minor South American poet." A few months after our initial collaborations, *Holiday* published six of these profound, Socratic, resonantly passionate sonnets in English version, sending me $600, which I handed to him. I remember Borges's mischievous laugh when he took the check and said, "Let's split it."

I had been trying to persuade Borges to publish a collection of his lifetime sonnets in Spanish through Carlos Frías, his editor at EMECÉ, but was getting nowhere. In the poetry books of his middle and late years, at least half the poems were sonnets. I guess that Borges knew he had not completed his life cycle of sonnets and that each batch was a developing spell leading to his final illusions. He was right. His sequence of sonnets was completed at his death. Now, when the complete sonnets appears, it will be a unified, major publication, a history of the poet's portraits, dreams, meditations, nightmares.

In those months in Buenos Aires of evening bomb blasts and kidnappings, I often worked through the night on new sonnets from a book Borges had just brought out called *La moneda de hierro* (The Iron Coin). One day a decisive event took place. Late in the afternoon, while English versions of those poems were still spread all over my living room floor, Carlos Frías knocked at the door of my apartment. "Borges has a message for you about the sonnets," the editor said.

"What's the message?"

"In your translation of the Whitman poem 'Camden, 1892,'" Frías said discreetly, "Borges thinks your rhyme in the last couplet is incorrect."

I wondered why Borges hadn't called me himself. Why the messenger? I began to fumble with words, defending slant rhymes, saying how modern poets in English liked to use muted assonant rhymes, how . . . .

"Borges thinks you should try a little harder," Frías coldly interrupted.

So I tried a little harder. I discovered it was not much harder to make rhymes perfectly consonant. And this achievement had advantages beyond that of euphonious final vowels. Each new formal obstacle orders the imagination to look a little farther and opens escape from the trap of the literal and the obvious. The experience of translating some thirty sonnets by Borges, followed by twenty-four from the sixteenth century French poet Louise Labé, was my training for *The Secret Reader*.

The itch to turn emotion and thought into cadenced lines comes at any time into any solitude, even when one is steering a car. On a fall evening I was driving north from Bloomington, Indiana, to West Lafayette. I had recently bought a midget tape recorder. In the solitude of night driving, I spoke two sonnets into the gadget. I listened to them and heard a rhythm of verse drama and let myself enjoy it. In those two hours I *believed*—a feeling I've usually had about writing (never about religion) ever since I woke up in the middle of a freezing night in Maine and scribbled the first few poems. When I reached Purdue University, near midnight, the voice was still on the tape and I typed it out. The date, November 13, 1977, I remember because it was my birthday, the one saying I had just finished wasting half a century of the planet's oxygen. In the days that followed I wrote more sonnets with ink. I made a habit of reading each new one into my gadget and listening to it in the car as I drove around town. To hear that other voice say my words gave me distance. It buoyed me especially to hear the dramatic lines spoken by the other speaker, and I could hear what was wrong. I'm sorry I gave up and forgot that pleasant way of measure and change.

In the first days when it looked like the swarm of sonnets might become a fixed book, I padded that hope with sonnets translated from Spanish, from Francisco de Quevedo, Sor Juana Inés de la Cruz, Antonio Machado, Jorge Luis Borges, and Miguel Hernández. Then, as more poems came I threw out the translations from the body of poems (except for those poems and fragments, in translation, used epigraphically on section pages). I like to think all originals are translations, all translations originals, yet now I was trying for my own unity. I aimed for fifty poems, which soon were seventy-five. When I hit one hundred I felt a sense of closure. Indeed, as I moved slowly toward each round number, each poem carried, I thought, the weight and worth to be the final poem. That notion of finality was to continue until 501. Given this habit of imparting a climactic importance to each supposedly concluding poem, it's a wonder the book is not a colossal bore. In defense of this quirk, however, after the first four hundred I floated, and very quickly, through the last century. It was as if I had discovered the secret of flight, how to let myself go with faith, fear, and all the forces I could summon up to intensify the clarity of the moment. Then, the effort part faded and I truly floated. I turned into a passion and metaphysics machine, and this mechanical trance at the end felt secure and unworried. The last hundred was a gift to a scribe. I made it 501, rather than 500, for many reasons, not the least being its suggestion of Sheherazade (Shahrazad) and her 1001 nights of narration. As long as she could address and captivate the sultan of Samarkand, she would remain alive. I identify passionately with Sheherazade's survival talk to a secret listener. More, the number "1"—a beginning, a unity, an oddity—would allow me to stop. And it's true. I became instantly desonnetized, and every impulse to revert I've been able to convert into other things in life.

As the book grew, so did the number of books it contained, from *Gas Lamp, 1893* to *To Find You at the End of Our Strange Walk*. My son Tony said that "books" was not a good subdivision for the five parts and suggested "histories." So we have five *Histories*, implying some public history and private biography. As for the title *The Secret Reader*, it came only after I was ten years into the obsession, although the poem "The Secret Reader" was early. The original title was *A Rose in Hell*, lifted from a sonnet by Borges, which had the phrase "an angel in hell." I wrote him, confessing my theft. He replied that he was pleased, saying "a rose in hell" sounds better than a more expected "angel in hell," and anyway my phrase had given him an idea for a poem. My daughter Aliki loved and still prefers my Baudelairean title. Mark Strand (whom I first knew in school as a painter) said he didn't care for it and thought *The Secret Reader* was better. All this ruminating, verging on family gossip —which is our poetry—may upset you, the secret reader, whom I need to love and keep. But since we're chatting, each adding something and sizing up the other, I think it best to level with you about something as essential as the title that has your epithet in it and might not have. Being a poet is to define, to choose among possibilities often of equal worth. Being greedy, I'd like both titles,

A Chat with the Reader

since both are right. Being an artist means to choose and enjoy gambling with loss.

Sappho wrote that she couldn't hold the sky in her two arms. That impulse to hug what circles us outside and the illusions and futility of doing so is what defines us. This colloquy is my one chance outside of verse to speak to you, with the hope it's not one-sided, that you'll yap back, give it to me, proving you're there. I ask a favor. If you have the time, don't fish in the book. Read it. Maybe one history at a time. After a while, you'll forget the form, the sonnet, and take a changing snapshot of a me, your secret friend. Then we can merge. Don't worry about a lot of darkness in many parts. As a vagabond I don't know where I'm going and so fall into dimness, but even the darkest, despondent poem has a laugh to it. I don't know what I am but know that many poets make a poet. I'm their secret reader. Especially the Greek, Spanish, and Chinese nail me, and I read them often and steal from them. Among American poets I'd like to have the haunting narrative flow in poems by my daughter Aliki, who makes bright snow the sun's twin. Likewise I'm renewed by the disciplined Rabelaisian exuberance in poems by my son Tony. I'm lucky. They are relentlessly good teachers, letting me get away with nothing cheap.

I hope you, reader, will like this gossip in verse. If I were dead, I'd have to quit this habit of filling time with would-be art. Since life has no absolutes, the door is open for me to play with time, to assume existence, and to recall the surprise of you or me. I also recall how dull windows of black eternity stand on both sides of our few decades of consciousness. So with happiness and puzzlement, I say hurray for *words,* these ink shadows of shadows as Plotinos might have said. These shadowy squiggles of thought are imperfect and changing, but their very inadequacy makes them alive. Words hang around, and because they are things, sometimes they hang for a long time. They talk for a while from me to you, and then out to eternity where they are properly lost.

As I pause at the end of this strange walk, the screen goes dead. Then I read, SUN AT NIGHT IN THE TOWER. These words on the screen-saver comfort me. Though I live in Indiana and like it, I live essentially before this screen in a huge concrete tower where for two decades I wrote in sonnet form about things elsewhere. The

Chinese say the Tang poem "dances in chains," which can be said about the sonnet, though both forms know how to forget chains and voyage far. It is lonely sitting in this building, especially on weekends when my friends the night janitors, with whom I share words and coffee, are off. But if I am dispirited at times, there is you the secret lonely reader and the screen designed to keep SUN on it at night. Sun is the poem. I'm lucky each time I work and play with it. I'll be more than lucky if it gets to you. When I'm dead (and maybe when I'm dying, which must be worse), I'll feel exhilarated and warm with love because, pardon me and my lies, I may be sharing light with you.

February 1995
Bloomington, Indiana

A Chat with the Reader

HISTORY I

Gas Lamp, 1893

He Enumerates, with Proper Terms,
the Mishaps and Miseries of Life

A life begins with tears and turds. Then come
the gurgles, mamas and the bogeyman,
followed by smallpox, drivel, snot and scum,
then rattles, spinning tops, a noisy can.
Grown up he finds a girlfriend to seduce
with whom he gluts his crazy appetite.
As a young man he feels his words are trite
and every declaration a mere ruse.
As a real man he is a hopeless pest,
a bachelor chasing every hooker in
the street. Married he's cuckold in his nest.
As an old man he wrinkles, dries up, grays.
And when death comes, upturning all, he pays
for gurgles, girlfriends and each groaning sin.

Francisco de Quevedo (1580–1645)

The Secret Reader

I write my unread book for you who in
a life or day will find it in a box
or cave or dead man's pocket or the inn
of mountain light where we awake while cocks
of twilight scream our solitude. Our fate
is to be free. No public ink. No hot
or cold inferno of the private wait.
Just this apocryphon which I forgot
for you, the secret friend. You are like me:
one soul fleshed out for ecstasy and night,
this planet's only birth and death, unknown
like everything. Saul lied about the light,
for no one rose again. We are alone,
alive with secret words. Then blackly free.

Gas Lamp, 1893

Camden, 1892

The smell of coffee and of newspapers.
Sunday and its monotony. The morning,
Some allegoric verses are adorning
The glimpsed-at page, the vain pentameters
Of a contented colleague. The old man lies
Stretched out and white in his respectable
Poor man's room. Then lazily he fills
The weary mirror with his gaze. His eyes
See a face. Unsurprised he thinks: That face
Is me. With fumbling hand he reaches out
To touch the tangled beard and ravaged mouth.
The end is not far off. His voice declares:
I'm almost gone and yet my verses scan
Life and its splendor. I was Walt Whitman.

Jorge Luis Borges (1899–1986)

Gas Lamp, 1893

In brownstone Boston down on old Milk Street,
up two gray flights, near the gas lamp, the tailor
waits glumly for the midwife. August heat
has worn the woman out. Amid the squalor
she looks around the bed, clutching a cape
she brought from London as a child. It's dawn
and dirty. The dark tailor wants to escape
to his cramped shop. The woman's sheets are drawn
below her waist. She isn't hollering now.
Her eyes are dark and still; blood on her thumbs.
Her name is Sarah. No. I'm guessing. How,
untold, am I to know? Hot day has worn
into the room. The midwife finally comes.
Grandmother bleeds to death. My father's born.

Grandfather

Born over there, in mist, not even God
or Germans have a record of the house
or village outside Vilna. Here, the old
poor tyrant snips a cloth, stitches a blouse
or shirt, and finds a black woman to live
with when his wife is dead. His smart son sells
papers in Boston subways, won't forgive
the tyrant fool for whipping him. The smells
of steam and cooking mix with yellow cheeses
when suddenly the wrathful tailor seizes
a belt and flogs his son for rotten grades!
Last drama. Twelve years old, my father leaves
his home and school for good. The tailor fades
from all of us forever, stitching sleeves.

Mother Writes a Book of Breath

In innocence I piss and scream and wake
from belly-roaming seas, and pre-sperm death
is nine months gone! My first practical joke
is peeing on a nurse's face at this day-birth
of sleep on earth. That's life. My shit and stars
are all about, but arms of love sweep me
from loneliness. Mother removes the bars
of dungeons lost inside, kisses me free
of knowledge, free from the first union of
the blood. She writes a book of breath, page one.
I cry and she is near throughout the night
of infancy, feeding this alien love
with woman's milk. But now her breath and sun
are gone, and she moves into unknown light.

Mother

While you are lowered in the clay
we weep under the summer sun.
The rocking of the coffin done,
our meager party goes away.
You left so quickly for the night
almost no one on the great earth
observes the moment of your death.
We few who knew your quiet light
try to remember, yet forget,
and neither memory nor talk
will bring you sun once it has set.
Your life was brief—a morning walk.
We whom you loved still feel an O
of quiet absence in Maine snow.

Father on Glass Wings

Death calls from Colorado spring. The phone
tells me you jumped: angel with dizzy stone
arms, floating on glass wings. But you don't land.
Childhood. We're selling watch straps, store to store,
sharing a shabby Greystone room. The floor
is spread with schoolbooks. As you take my hand
we ride downstairs for papers: SNEAK JAP PLANES
SMASH PEARL HARBOR!! I've got Latin to do
but we walk Broadway. Dropping through spring-blue
sweet air (I was in Brunswick's tedious rains),
you shattered in the gutter. You'd be gray
by now, I guess, and coming up the stairs
is my young son I love the same old way.
He can't see you. I won't know his gray hairs.

Bowdoin, 1948

Hawthorne once had this yellowed room. We share
the morning gloom of alcoholics or
nocturnal masturbators, north and nowhere,
too isolated for a date or whore.
Were you a grind like me? A dreamer slob
and weird? I sleep, the window open to
the black Maine snow, hearing my roommate throb
and scream, an epileptic getting through
another siege. He's a philosopher;
I'm lost. But he was born a bastard, he
says bitterly; my origins I shirk
from. Worst (or best?) I doubt there is a me
concocting words in terrifying blur
within. Dream, Hawthorne. Words no longer work.

Tropical White Pajamas

In Mexico in a poor village near
the live volcano with its summer snow
and smoking heart, the Quakers settled here
and I dug privies in the mornings. Oh!,
one evening in the streets of Vera Cruz
I danced, wore a green mask; we heard the wild
huapango song, big stars cooked us. Those loose
tropical white pajamas and the mild
faces of Indian friends soothed us. We went
back to our room, our bed, took off our clothes,
both innocent as Eve. The *patrón* laughed
at us, smirking. Dawn found our bodies bent
for the surprise and birth of light! Who knows
your name? We fished through white night on our raft.

Nostalgia for a Chinese Commune
and a Mexican Work Camp

In China on a tea commune the room
where workers eat has its big photo of
the Chairman. Sometimes in her blue costume
a worker hides a novel. Word from above,
lessons, Mao's poems and correct thought. I am
brainwashed and thrilled.
                                        Younger in Mexico,
we sit together ethically with jam
and flies and Quaker books. I feel the flow
of William James' *Varieties,* and fall
in love with Lola as we meditate
in our work camp. I'm awkward and believe
utopia is our clinic. On our wall
Viva Zapata stares, hero who ate
the traitor's bullet. China's up my sleeve.

Rocking on the Queen

Deep in the hold we have no porthole, yet
I gaze, X-raying whales and a green squall.
The pitching of ELIZABETH has set
the tables rolling, banging wall to wall.
I push up to the deck and wait for France.
At twenty I'm a character whom Plato
might keep for lunch—yet the Greek's reasoned trance
is not my Bergson dream. I'm a potato-
head says my Marxist pal. Norm's blind but grins
at me. Naive! As Europe nears, wet shade
washes my eyes with reverie. I dry
my face. Europe is full of women. Inns
of smart delicious lips. We dock. The maid
at l'Hotel Flore pinches my pants and tie.

La Rue Jacob, 1948

War was fun for Guillaume Apollinaire,
sending letter poems from the trenches, yet
a bombshell came, gravely combing his hair,
but Guillaume healed in Paris, a cigarette
like a love ballad in his lips. I spied
life from a hotel room with a red rug,
hot water in the corner sink, and sighed
happy when the street singers used a jug
to catch the hailing francs. The courtyard reeked
with rising fumes of piss when evening rain
fell from the wine-blue clouds. Our sheets were far
too short. *Fin de la guerre.* Spanish flu creaked
into the poet's brain. We were young, zan-
y like Guillaume! who croaked with *La Victoire.*

In a Paris Faubourg

My Polish classmate at the gray Sorbonne
loves the romantic poet Bécquer. She
wears heavy wool, is Chopin-thin and fun
in Paris rain. One night she secrets me
off to a grim Free Polish Army party
up in an orange room. We're comrades and
march behind banners down Boule Miche. Hearty
and generous in bed, she takes my hand
a Sunday morning; we go to a faubourg,
a sleazy house. I don't guess why. "It's clear,"
she says. "I'm pregnant and abortion's not
a legal act in France." Up in the morgue
the foreign doctor cuts her up. "So, here
is your chef-d'oeuvre," he tells me. We are rot.

Going Muleback in the Snow on the Holy Mountain of Athos during the Greek Civil War

Going muleback in the snow to the mon-
asteries on the holy peak, I see
some rebel *kleftes* hiding from the drawn
weapons of the soldiers. When they spot me,
they fade. The forest groans. Once with the monks
they give me vinegared wine, bread, a bed
of straw on wood, and guide me to the crypt
where oil lamps by the icons show the blood
of converts sworn to parables and script
about some Essenes from the wilderness
who scorned the Roman weapons and were drunk
with faith and towering awe. Light gilds the hair
of one young beardless monk whose gaze and dress
call ancient zealots to their rebel prayer.

White Island

My first day at the school for Constantine
I meet a peasant father with two hooks
(wounds from Albania) and the German Queen
of Greece who loans me her blue *Faber Book
of Verse*. But soon I'm fired and so begin
to loaf and write on islands. Mykonos,
the iceberg. I'm the only *xenos* in
the village, living with a Greek, and close
to getting jailed for working without papers.
The ship comes twice a week. Down at the pier
we all watch who comes in, but lemon vapors
of broiling fish seduce me. One white night
Captain Andonis slaps his heels. Austere,
he teaches me to dance, to live on light.

One Andalusian Winter

It's early Franco Spain. Hunger of serfs
and fishermen like insects sleeping on
the sand under their boats. When morning surfs
into the village we pick up fresh prawn
and goat meat. Justo's all upset. They caught
and killed some *rojos* in the hills, and threw
the bodies over horses which they've brought
into the plaza on their way up to
the old Phoenician common grave of Jews.
Our farm—with sugar cane and orange trees,
with snow magnolias—is a paradise
almost for nothing. Lorca's a man of vice,
un loco to his fascist cousin who's
our mayor. Laughing I grieve by these old seas.

A Blonde in Tangier

Sean is an Irish Jew crossing on the ship
from Algeciras. He's just dumped his wife.
He has a snapshot of a Seville whore he whips
out in a flash, "She loved me." His bum life
with his old bag is over when her father socks
him. "No more fried-egg suppers." Sean pops by
one famished evening, saying, "Buddy, shall we wet our cocks?"
We go. A new moon stabs the virgin sky
over the Zócalo. Veils and kif fan the air
as we stroll eager through the Casbah streets.
Stores wide open. A narrow parlor jammed with Berber men
on *azulejo* benches smoking dope. The whores next door
    sit marketed on chairs.
"You first," says Sean. I choose a blonde. She treats
me fine. She's knocked up. Sideways I plop in.

A Tower in Tangier

Some place among onions of pain I lose
my nerve. Gone is the table in that tower
on the west coast of Africa I used
to climb to in the afternoons, where hour
on hour I'd smoke, sip tea, and look at ships
fall off the glass of fire into a throat
of stars. Back in my room a bone rat slips
along the walls, singing the infant note
of swallows as I boil the milky smell
of oatmeal on the green alcohol flame.
The green casbah moon floats over the square
like a knife patient in the dusk. I came
to climb jail steps to you. The Moors in prayer
yell from the towers. I climb, crazed, infidel.

Hiding in a Wardrobe Closet from a Landlady in London of the Great Fog

Winter mornings. London is dark. The fog
comes in the common toilet window (which
we're not allowed to shut). I read and hog
the quarters on my freezing buttocks. Bitch
and scrooge, I call Mrs Brightbottom who
leaves me her nasty notes. My lovely Thai
friend will redeem the day. I'd like to screw
her royally (I confess, ashamed, since I
am also dreamily in love with her
thin smile, her wistful arum lily throat).
The fog has killed the bulls at Hampton Fair
and I can't get to SOAS. Through the blur
I walk to Oussa's sheets. The night we share.
At dawn I'm hiding in her closet coat.

Columbia Blues and Green Fires

I got Columbia grad blues. I'm just as blue
as I can be. I love my childhood city
(though after Maine) and nice to see kabu-
ki or flamenco at the Y. A pity
Lionel Trilling finds there is just one
good phrase in all my manuscript and Tyndall
spits, "You're no William Butler Yeats." Yet none
like Wells: "Good poets go to jail and mingle
with rats." Lorca was in his drama class.
Once Henry Wells at a home party had
Lorca meet Crane. Two green fires. Nothing came
of it, though lead and ocean would go mad
and murder both. The rats and subway glass
I glare at, rocking home, are my blue shame.

Boot Camp in Georgia

"Yeah," shouts the corporal, "all Jewmen fall out!"
A black kid and me, we go to pick up
our 3-day pass from Did. "What's it about?"
"Jewish New Year." They fly us with our pup
tent, boots and duffle down to Georgia where
still on the airstrip a white sergeant blurts,
"Sound out your name and race!" We're in the fair
sweet South. "I'll squeeze that bastard till he squirts
white piss," the black kid whispers. I get stuck
three days on K.P. God what grease! I feel
good here. No anti-intellectual crap
of campuses. I catch pneumonia but heal
fast and they treat me good. Have friends and rap.
I don't have to kill. It's peace. What the fuck!

Yale

Sterling Library is a confession booth
where Virgil hangs out on a shelf by stars
gold on the ceiling calm and beaming truth
and blueblood aristocracy. Guitars
are out. I haunt the books, reading Jack Donne
who kisses metaphysically. In class
I'm shy and tongue-tied among gentlemen
and lovely women scholars. What a gas
to eat at Louie's, peddle to East Haven,
play with my infant daughter now become
my lifelong sun. With stupid discipline
I race through (gone for good the wandering bum
of Europe) yet among my peers I'm craven:
no pilgrimage to Ezra in his loony bin.

Red Guard Beijing, 1972

Madness is in the air. There is a smell
of progress from the fiery factories and
from *hutongs* and mass toilets. The deathbell
of nightingales is heard throughout the land.
I wear my Mao button. At the opera
my comrade from Inner Mongolia informs
me that "this joint is really jumping!" Ah,
I am a fan. I catch the zeal. Reforms
have unbound ankles, freed the children hidden
in dark mills, cured the deaf. The once Forbidden
City is a museum. I'm at the zoo,
I boat romantically on the snow lake
where once the Summer Palace Empress threw
heads in a well. Red Guards keep death awake.

Sewing Up a Heart during the Cultural Revolution

Shanghai. I smell my fear among the smells
of medicine and patients in the hall.
The nurse ties on my mask, quietly impels
me toward the table, but I hug the wall.
Hard to witness the bloody cut mushroom
of a man's heart. The eyes are open as
he sips a bit of juice, and the perfume
of death drips off a nylon thread which has
repaired the shadow of a soul. His ear
holds one electric needle, quivering.
His eyes call out. I think about crazed Lear
carrying his daughter, drownings off Vietnam,
my coffined mother on the train. All being
is good. The dark and gentle night is sham.

Secret Meadow in Vermont

Vermont was made by Andrew Marvell when
his solitude was green with mountain night.
Yellow meadow lying under the pen
of twilight sun. Rays scrawl on weeds with white
of the astonished moon. Three stars persist
while crickets rattle on the phone of wind
to bugs. Birds call up worms. Deer feel the fist
of grass about them. Our goat Smoky grinned
at us last afternoon when he took off.
He's back this morning, trampling on a rug
of black-eyed Susans. Drunk, minus signs on
his eyes, he leads us with his mocking cough
up to the secret meadow. Marvell, gone
into green shade, is laughing in his mug.

Near Annapurna

We are still at cloud level. Beautiful day.
Thin air. Cold but our sweat warms us. The snow
jungle of rhododendrums weirdly gray
around the deadly trail. My friend starts to blow
up, bitching, "Don't come too close!" A mule went
over the ledge an hour ago. We inch
down a stone cliff. ANNAPURNA. Indifferent
white continent. I can't make it. I clinch
the ice, crawl the ravine. As snow turns to mud
I slide on my buns. It's raining. Beautiful
hot rain almost washes us off the top.
We find a smoky cabin. I'm full of blood.
Go in feverishly filthy, dirty wool,
drink a pot of hot lemon juice, and flop.

Fever and Carnival in Vera Cruz

I'm seldom where I am. Herons and snakes
color the forest of the pyramid
where the old sungod dined on hearts amid
the stains of human fat. We climb. It wakes
the bell of absence, yet those days are gone,
the carnival in Vera Cruz, the flame
of dancing with a lover in the zone
of jasmine through the streets. I'm seldom where
I dream. Off in the jungle, by a tree
waiting for revelation in the glare
of nature, till I wake to a simple cold,
a wobbly fever and the anatomy
of pain for being dreamy, empty, old.

Life and Death of a Jersey Rose

Poor fallen rose. She dropped from a bouquet
plop wet into the dogshit near the curb,
a yellow throne in Brooklyn, and the day
has frozen her damp lips like a sweet herb
entombed in glass. The author of her bed,
a lordly mutt, stands on his stoop and grins
stupidly at a Yemenite whose head
is colorfully veiled from desert winds,
at Vito spray-painting SKULLS on a door,
at Mark Stein, pharmacist, at Jimmy who
fixes TVs. The Jersey garden where
she grew ignores her and she's lost the war
of place to all things swallowed by the air,
fallen like Kabul, cold and winter blue.

The Camp near Kraków

Over the gate the sign ARBEIT MACHT FREI.
I guess my village outside Vilna, which
was razed, came here in cattle cars to die.
Today it's raining on the Kraków church,
its peaceful domes, and on the camp which is
a gray museum. I see the children's skulls,
the shaven heads of Jews and gypsies, Poles,
photos of eyes like prehistoric flies
stuck on the walls outside the shower room
in which the rain prepared the bodies for
the ovens and the sky where bodies bloom.
ARBEIT MACHT FREI. Auschwitz is mute, the war
already fugitive. The rains evoke
a Slav, black-hatted Jews, tattoos and smoke.

Inlight in Providence

Before the dawn in Providence, before
the crows, the garbage men step out. Their cries
crack the air like lone Basque shepherds. The roar
of stars behind the hills. Although my eyes
are closed, the providence of sleep is gone
and time hovers handcuffed to time. I'm not
ready to fade to opaque prison dawn
and wish to wade under the river, caught
in galaxies of kelp. The gas stove talks
to me, the wind gets up, my brooding locks
me on the lonely earth where I'm a dream
under a sky of mint stars. Garbage pails
are rolling down the street. In the extreme
daybreak I wake from waking. Inlight pales.

Recalling a Life with a Greek

September melancholy. You are there,
sketching the island of the moonhigh wheat
and enigmatic tides. The iron chair
out on the terrace with your form. You eat
the Euboian yogurt cured in sacks and drink
sage tea with honey which the hotel stored
for us. And sketch the chapel. As I think
about our hills, the cave and brook, the sword
of water glittering the pepper tree,
I sigh for us. A thousand years have not
erased your drawing. Hold the sun. The fall
of Thera and our ghosts are a white dot
before your charcoal eyes. Near that spring wall
we pause. You sketch the tombs of porphyry.

Theft of a Brother

My brother lives between Mobile and Gal-
veston, in a great villa like a rose
between two pumping oil wells. He's my pal
and by the pool we play at dominoes
and drink, gossiping until the garden trees
swallow the moon, the aristocratic plants
and poor bamboo, until the old disease
of love maddens our brains with jungle ants
biting the family blood, and we escape
by car and plane. I have gone back to Rome,
stunned by a grave of brothers and its rape
or rain chilling the plate of lentils left
for us, that hateful feast after the theft
of brotherhood. The rites have killed our home.

For Father Who Opened the Door of Misery
and Jumped to Extinction

Father, I loved you and I found
there was no logic to the heart:
it cared, it glorified, was bound
by every laugh. Yet you made part
of me and I too have the weak-
ness of your end—that I would ditch.
Don't make me jump. I love. The bleak-
ness of the road you took (or which
took you) made you a villain, for
you smashed the myth of happiness,
leaving behind a fake, and yet
my brother thought it real. The mess
of street blood I cannot forget
in me. I love, but close your door.

The Spring Afternoon Aliki in Her Third Year
Starts to Drown

No melancholy yet. You are a green
planet on which a darkness only lives
to obscure death. But no one sees you lean
over the pond. We all are fugitives
from our new haven, at a festival
of arts in the woods. For fun you toss a stone
onto the water. Suddenly, you fall
in it, unseen! Your gold hair sails alone
at the far end where you were playing. You
float, limbs spread like a leaf. One minute more
and you will be extinct. A painter spots
the passive form, dives toward it. I jump too.
We drag you out, pump air through you before
you enter myth, before your beauty rots.

While My Daughter Is Sleeping

Brooklyn. My daughter sleeps on the main bed.
I have a couch next to the books, and lie
slanted but get to sleep. I've cut a thread
holding a swallow from the wandering eye
of fire. Under God's foot the cyclamen
is raging. Suddenly, there is no wife
or brother, sister, house. Clean day. Again
I start. Seferis wrote about his life,
"Let me grow old and die in my own land."
Can I grow old or die? Is there a place
my own? Child of N.Y.? White Greece? Black grace
of Patagonia? For each continent
I ache or laugh, but choose the ghostly hand
of the wind. Words, like flies, become my tent.

N.Y. Heat Wave

The light is all around us like a black
burning flounder. Below it black kids work
the hydrants, gunning cars with booming flak,
and cool the poison fish over New York.
The light is also *in* us, Hasid dark
and blazing in our brains down to glass trees
with roots of dream. I live from a black smirk
of unknown light, the ghost who never sees
herself yet knows the unknown universe
pulsing with supernovas. Angels sweat
and their wings drip with oil and steam and salt
into those Village junkie mouths who curse
at walls and retch darkly into the vault
of poison day! It's hot till we forget.

My Brother Enters the Earth on May Day

Stillness inside the box where Howard lies.
Carrying you to the grave I hold the tree
as long as I can. Last weight of you cries
in my arms. If there is nobility
in suffering, you are the prince of pain,
yet I think of you laughing, crazy, a man
who loved to play, made others play. Insane
or wise, you chose the way our father ran
(too early) into peace. Your death is weird.
I cannot know whether you rob us of
belief or force us into light. Your glow,
your genius-quiet Rothko chapel, love
for the plain pine—your box of death—appeared
and now your laughter sighs. Slowly you go.

With My Redneck Sons in Southern Indiana

The pampas of America begin
north of our barn. Glaciers smoothed down the earth
for buffalo and corn, but I live in
the poor south hills where farmland isn't worth
the taxes, and the KKK comes out
of the wet Gothic woods. Our humpbacked barn
is rusty in the patient twilight. Scout-
ing the Blue River bendable as yarn
or glowworms, I am not quite Baptist red-
neck like my sons who often paddle through
the bluffs. But in a barn I placed a bed
and desk and dreamt the world. Gone from the coast,
I camp on hills of vanished Indians a few
calm nights and hear trees talk. I'm still a ghost.

A Midnight Son Calls. He Too Is
an Architect of the World

Rob calls. He dreamt that I was dead,
a dream so full of symbols it
was literature. There in his bed
he wept, first time in years. The pit
of anguish held him darkly in
its paralyzing walls. I taste
his pain—but I decide to grin.
Dying and death are such a waste
of time, and I am busy. When
death comes to talk I will be scared,
I guess, and maybe force a smile.
Compulsively I'll push my pen,
joke, jog to Paris for a while,
my architect, but won't be spared.

To Feed a Weeping World

Who loves the lowly pours an oil
of blessing on the lips; who sees
the poor and acts will never spoil
a kiss; who feeds a child can freeze
and feel no chill. I do not know
the ways to help a weeping world.
Outside I hear a scream of woe
and wonder what new pain has hurled
a monster to his knees. To give,
be kind—it's not abstract—and what
else can we do? I woke one day
with children on my knee. I ought
to shout at death. For love to live
dying children must eat and play.

Peddler and Tailor

My grandfathers come to me in an old film:
peddler and tailor going to the New World.
In the Old World the image blurs, unknown.
My bones, nose? I must be a bit like them.
Old photos say, look, here you were with a
black hat, white beard, dark faith in the one God.
But they stood dully in the light that day
in Lutz. They were despised. It wasn't odd
a century ago to flee. They wandered here
in steerage, climbing seven flights, and sat
in safety in their tenements. I hear
a plane, a wasp groaning under the sun.
Below I'm undespised and free: the son
peddling a soul and wearing no black hat.

The Blue Planet

The planet's young. And we who came
here for a while by accident
of sperm and egg, who are a flame
surprised by being, fatally meant
for one eternal, dusty night,
wander, wander before we sleep.
I woke and found a bit of light,
turned it to words. Had I been deep
I'd have a home in some old barn.
In Paris the blue planet stole
the dark. In London in the tram
I read my books. Nothing would warn
me that a Jew without a soul
roams briefly guessing who I am.

The Good Beasts

Oh here you have the beast

O here you have the beast that cannot be!
They didn't know it and it came by chance.
They loved its neck and wandering reverie,
the still light of its gaze, bearing, and trance.

Really, it never was. Yet since they loved it,
a pure beast came to being, and there was room
for it, always, and in that space it fit
brightly and loose; it raised its head to whom

it wished. Scarce need to be. They gave no corn
to it, yet nourished an idea it might
exist, and the beast took on such power

from its forehead it grew a horn. One horn.
It came to a young virgin, came deep white,
and was in mirror silver and in her.

Sonnets to Orpheus II, 4
Rainer María Rilke (1875–1926)

The Good Beasts

On the first morning of the moon, in land
under the birds of Ur, before the flood
dirties the memory of a couple banned
from apples and the fatal fire of blood,
Adam and Eve walk in the ghetto park,
circling a tree. They do not know the way
to make their bodies shiver in the spark
of fusion, cannot read or talk, and they
know night and noon, but not the enduring night
of nights that has no noon. Adam and Eve,
good beasts, living the morning of the globe,
are blind, like us, to apocalypse. They probe
the sun, deathray, on the red tree. Its light
rages, illiterate, until they leave.

In Gnostic Paradise Eve Raises Adam from the Mud and God Rapes Eve

The Tree of Life has clusters of white grapes,
its color is the sun. The other Tree
shines like the moon, its thoughtful dates in shapes
of angels. Eve finds Adam's corpse. Since she
is made of light, she pities him and breathes
spirit into his clay. But God comes near
and longs to cast his seed in her. He seethes
with lust—Eve laughs at his intention. Her
sheer light darkens his eyes and in a breath
she is the Tree of Knowledge. When she emerges,
the Primal Father, jealous, cursing, ropes
her and begets a son. The serpent urges
truth and defiance. Naked the lovers grope
with God who rings his Tree of Life with death.

Eve, Paying for Truth, Drops Dead into the Eternity of Rain

Eve, who eats mainly fruit, tastes the bad end.
She is the first to go under the dark
and fade, but cannot feel surprise or spend
one micro-second to report the spark
of dull eternity burning her face
and liver like that wait before her birth.
She doesn't cringe or groan, but with the grace
learned from the flaming sword, exile on earth
and thorns of motherhood, she disappears
like an old lady curved over a mop
who quits her job and sinks. Eve has no fears
of light or loss of light and cannot know
the way. She isn't poor, and like a drop
of dust, merging with rain, begins to grow.

Lucifer, Angel of Light

The Magi make a star. Their heavens are
a tower of fire signaling a safe route
to Egypt, and the frankincense and myrrh
along the way roam like an evening flute
into the windows of an Asian jail.
Magic lies on a deer of flame along
the lakes of wheat; it kisses air like braille
informing fingers of the blind with song.
But Lucifer, angel of light, is gored
before the tangle of doves descending from
the Boss. Though poison burns the angel's feet
(like beasts chewing a dream) and bloats him numb
with truth to free us from the tribal Lord,
his sores of banished knowledge ache with heat.

Buddha in the Twilight

Twilight. The Buddha smiles between the day
and dark. A million years of insects or
an ordinary fig tree shades the way
where Gautama sat down to think before
he organized a way to free the brain
of thought. He chose neither body nor god
but what is common to a star or grain
of earth or a Mongolian pony shod
with glittering iron: the atomic light
which each thing breathes inside. The Buddha smiles
and continents are vaguely false. His calm
obliterates a city. Before night
swallows the terror of non-being, he piles
a mountain in his hand. The empty palm.

Socrates in Jail

Rapping all night, corrupting you, my friend,
I wait for dawn. The Delian ship is back.
They've taken off my chains. Sly to the end
I call your comrades women for their black
rainbow of tears blurring the soul. And death?
Death is a king's unbounded star of sleep,
the good eternity, or the soul's deep
underworld ramble where she burns her breath
in happy arguments with Orpheus
and Sisyphos. At least in hell the swans
are safely in the trees and cocks are sold
for earthly gold. As Krito pleads and plans
escape, I hear the mystic flute across
the city, and stand lucid, turning cold.

The True History of Socrates and Jesus
among the Strangers

Why did the Greeks cook up their dirty plot
to zap the kindest man in Athens, who
urged us to know ourselves and be in thought
below our thought, who in his cell spoke to
the hemlock climbing cold, saw his soul leak
into the ghost eternity of night?
The Greeks killed Socrates who was no Greek.
The only Greeks in Athens were the white-
robed officers of the tribunal. There-
after, similarly in Jerusalem,
the only Jews in town were thugs who stilled
Jesus who was no Jew. He came from Rome,
they said. Poor Socrates and Jesus, killed
by Greeks and Jews, by strangers. Sad affair.

Long Ago in Palestine Came a Temple Child

A vagrant took the solstice for his birth,
a cool and fragrant time in Palestine
when fig trees think of adolescent earth
and patches of young sun. There was no sign
of crucifixion. Nasty gossip, yes,
because he was a "temple child," they said,
a euphemism for the fatherless.
Born homeless to a single mother, his bed
a stinking shed in the back streets of the
old city, soon he picked up Torah with
some Greek. He was a demagogue. In those
days of the Roman occupation he
talked of heaven, crossing green dreams with a rose
until Rome fumed and spiked him into myth.

Joshua the Jew

King of the Jews, the soldiers name me, and
they spit, lay thorns upon me, smite my head,
while mocking and saluting. As the band
of Romans strips me, roughs me up—not dead
but rotting on Bad Friday—other men
dream up a way to warp the story of
my life on earth. Light of the world, but when
I use my balms to heal or speak of love
they lie and have me walking on the sea.
My simple arts they call a miracle.
I'm Joshua and a Jew. They change my name,
hating my blood, choking my identity
as rabbi. While I cry for help, my shame
is I am still a Jew, not God, they kill.

Jeshua the Gnostic

I, Jeshua, hanging on the cross
cry a bit, laugh because I know
only the man is aching. Loss
of blood is mystery as I grow
almost as green as sleep. But soon
I dream of Egypt, of the days
of boyhood when I saw the noon
turn midnight, when I felt the craze
to be a street magician and
to tour. Good life. I was a friend
to many till somehow I saw
the alien God. In my young hand
the eyes of heaven burn me. Raw
with light, I laugh up to the end.

Jesus the Christian

Saul the tentmaker spread the word: The Jew
the Romans killed was God. He came out of
the desert with a mustard seed that grew
into a mountain kingdom. Poised above
Jerusalem (the word means peace), he said:
I am the shepherd. Peace. Believe in me
and know the morning of the world. With bread
he fed a multitude, walked on the sea
in ghostly afternoon, and animals
out in the desert sighed. They crucified
the shepherd, who embraced the dark and died,
wine under earth. Then in his altered name
his Jews were killed, hunted and slain like whales
for oil, and he was God of death and shame.

Jesusa the Woman

Some say it is a man the Romans tacked
up on the cross. A man with naked breasts?
And that he screamed in pain when they attacked
him with a spear. I haven't screamed. Their jests
and insults pierced me more than labor on
the wooden beams. They lie about my sex,
yet you believe a gospel decades gone
after they spiked me up? And they perplex
me with their lofty souls, granting me slime.
I am a whore or witch or mother—not
a priest. Even the Pope cracked his Pole joke
saying I chose the apostles male. So choke
away up there. Millennia in the same spot.
I'm sick of rotting. Take me down. It's time.

Wang Wei and the Snow

Although Wang Wei is peaceful looking at
the apricot, the sea gull and the frost
climbing the village hills, or feels the mat
of pine trees on the mountain sky, or lost
in meditation loses nature and
the outer light to sing his way through mist
inside, although Wang Wei becomes the land
and loitering rain, his mountain clouds exist
as refugees from thought and turn like mills
never exhausting time. Wang Wei also
was stuck in life, and from his hermitage
he tells a friend to walk the idle hills
alone, to swallow failure like the age-
ing year, to dream (what else is there?) of snow.

Li Po Whispering Poems

My comfort's in the windy moon too bright
for sleep. Finally, dead drunk, I lie down on
the naked mountain, dreaming I can write
my sorrow on the pillow of the dawn.
Although I freeze under the snow that fell
like egrets floating in the water of
this sleep, my sadness like a white gazelle
wakes by the lake. I'm ruined. I call to love
(I've heard her whisper several times) and feel
no shame for indiscretions. Since my wife
is hungry, I have sold my goods and kneel
under the mulberry tree, taking my knife
to cut my shadow from the dock. To home
I row. The sailor moon blows while I roam.

Li Qingzhao and the Moon

Reading the lonely poems of Li Qingzhao,
seeing her lying drunk, her hairpins on
the courtyard table as she mourns the bamboo
bed empty of her legal lover, gone
beyond the sky and her apricot tree,
I know those geese and bugles that explode
her evening in the late Song dynasty
signal her unique sorrow on the road
of the blue lotus. By the Eastern Wall
her lord and friend fell into mist. Yet in
that same small garden of their scholar's house
they'd shared a passion for old scrolls, and when
he went (turning her moon to ink), in all
the world her grieving happened only once.

In Málaga a Poet One Morning

Eleventh century in southern Spain,
a Jew scrawls a green poem, talks Arabic
in the white sun. No wind. With ink of rain
and lightning quill he storms the moon. Then quick
as his dream lover's hips of fire, he drops
down from the scarlet night to sun and white
adobe walls. Gabirol paints the crops
of lime and olive trees in Hebrew light
of old Jerusalem. Yet why scrawl in
that fossil tongue? For God who paints the soul
with glyphs? Solomon Ibn Gabirol
scribbles for God and us. All poets do.
Happy, cantankerous, he shares our sin:
he writes for Sol. Then maybe God and you.

Even Dante the Perfect Songmaker Ate Crow

The sound and tale magician got tossed out
of his own city. With good reason he
got shafted by the Florentines: without
cloying remorse he was and claimed to be
the god of holy poets. So he wrote
and had a bigger head than Virgil whom
he made his Lazarillo. His blue note
was song to ice Medusa, and his room
the wondrous wordshop for his dreams; and yet
he hung around his city walls, his kiss
and cantos jammed like sausage in his sack,
looking for readers. Petrarch never set
his eyes on Dante's page—not on that hack
of pious verse, a poet none would miss.

Dante and Petrarch Singing the Blues

Petrarch merged with the eyebeams of his muse
and moaned to her; Dante rolled in the light
of paradise, and while they sang the blues
they suffered for their thirst: not for a night
of perfect love or unseen God, but fame
of Homer, range of Timur or a king
of Alexander's resonance. Their name
would float like Jesus on the lake, a wing
for Eden. Yet was Laura a mere crown
of bay leaves? or the *Paradiso* just
a ship of death to make-believe? These poor
grand poets cared for light; they ached to bust
their balls for words, were paid like any whore
for solid work and sorrows of the clown.

Luis de León in a Prison Cell

Outside my Inquisition cell, the stars
and cypresses are gossiping. Castile
under the song of planets, of the spheres
climbing the night up to a sapphire wheel
of farther spheres. A week ago the mules,
farting, whining, carried me to the coast.
I suffer creatures better than the fools
who lied me into prison, who would roast
me for my Judaizing texts. Like John's,
whose cell is a cold sardine closet, who
inhabits dark-soul night, my night is day,
even without a candle near. White dawns
of night! I drink the Song of Songs the way
a bird escapes, painting my jail skyblue.

John of the Cross in the Spring

After the dungeon and the whips, the night
of the Toledo fish room where I close
my eyes and am a woman pierced by light
that kills and gives no pain, again I doze
here in Granada on the hill, a whore
of God. Illumination comes and then
I soar, leaving for days. Only the floor
of the old Moorish convent feels me when
I vanish, happy. Peak of happiness
in the Granada spring of lions! Snow
of almond buds and mountain herbs! The sun
cavernously inside! My secret NO
is holy, white, ineffable. I've won
from death a spring frozen in secret YES.

Saint John Laughed on the Stairs

Saint John laughed on the stairs, a mystic child
with sun waking the wine. When cancer woke
his ulcerous skin, he chose to be reviled
in Úbeda. Nothing could paint the smoke
of his one-candle dark. In his black cell
he drank the science of his obscure love,
who came, who joined him and serenely fell
with him untellably. The black above
the earth was daybreak in his blood. Saint John
sat on the floor, babbled, and lived beyond
the word. Felicitous. The abscessed flesh
was nothing. 1591. A pond
of light. He drank the body of love, its fresh
illusion. Until death he lived with dawn.

Francisco de Quevedo Walking in the Fields around His House in Castilla la Vieja, Brooding on the Brevity of Clay Wings

Pigs are conversing with the afternoon
and laundry strung from trees, the cotton sheets
of farmers of Castile. Under the moon
I think of Chinese emperors and their fleets
seeking the islands of eternity.
Abysmal waste of time! Obsessed with time
I feel its famished movement wasting me
without a pause. Life is less fixed than rhyme.
I am a *was*, a *will be* and a wear-
y *is*, and shit on priests, on Jews, on kings,
on whores, on God, and furiously on death!
Worming my heart, my small realm of despair,
I know how fragile, vain, how black are wings
of clay when darkness savors my last breath.

The Ghost of William Shakespeare Speaks
to His Old Body

The worms have fed on blood, the dust has dried
The canticles of flesh, and time has coughed
On the brown marble of my throat. I died
But once. In that deaf fall down to the soft
Ice of extinction or to excrement
In the earth's tripe and carbon where a smell
Of former spirit haunts a firmament
Of coal, I'm free of Shakespeare's body and
His world, of heaven his unnatural dream
Against biology, of phoenix blood
His talking ink, and hover in a land
Invented constantly like sun or hell
Or love. But I'm in you. Like new spring mud,
Alive in you who make my maggots gleam.

George Herbert

I wrote a letter to my Lord
But couldn't spell the holy Name:
"What can I do against the Sword
Lost in my flesh I cannot tame?"
The Lord answered (although I never
Posted my word to Him), and said:
"The Sword is nothing if whenever
You rave with Lust you let the lead
Of Heaven's glass be cut and crazed
So Light will magnify your Soul."
I sealed the letter and was dazed
Before my Lord who filled the hole
Made by the Blade with Angel Breath
And cured me with an early death.

Sor Juana Inés de la Cruz Who after Criticism Gives Away Her Vast Library and Tends Her Sister Nuns during a Plague until She Too Is Its Victim

When I am dead they'll say I was a muse
and praise my science and the poems condemned
by fulminating bishops who abuse
me as a bastard child, mestiza blend
of Indian criolla. Monks scrubbed the floor
two weeks to cleanse the profanation of
the prelate's house, for I (whether a whore
or nun), a female, tread his realm of love
for God. The same men beg our bodies, rage
if we refuse, and fume if we give in;
my secret love only in verse is heard.
They flattered me, painting me young, but age
is not deceived. Shade, dust, cadaver win.
Gone are the books, my loves and my stained word.

Daydreaming of Anne Bradstreet and Her Eight Birds Hatcht in One Nest

Anne Bradstreet and eight kids, your house burns down
near Ipswich, but with faith you bless the Lord
for each child he turns cold. Beasts cry concord
in the forests of New England, and each town
sings Sunday glory to white God. How far
we are this winter, Anne, domestic friend,
who can't know me or my three birds. I send
my admiration and a Christmas jar
of honey for your offspring (which you can't
accept, because of unresponsive time).
With all your books flaming in natural crime,
you sing of nakedness: an immigrant
to Heaven. I'm not reborn, but dream a plan
of forests, milk, and naked Mistress Anne.

Pascal, Inventor of the Bus

My sister calls me Archimedes for
my shrewd *Essai pour les coniques.* I was
only sixteen. She loves me for my fuzz-
y genius. She's a nun. "Absurd, a bore
to be irrational," I tell Jacqueline,
and so I prove that nature doesn't hate
a vacuum, build a calculating machine,
but one November I see Christ, my fate
and faith. Doubt, depths, despair and miseries
ravish my brain. "FIRE. God of Abraham"
I scrawl that night of joy. I hate the sleaze
of Jesuits and Jews. Man is the scum
and worm of earth. Pits. Jacqueline dies. Piteous
the poor, to help them I invent the bus.

G.W. Leibnitz and Sophie in Berlin

Leibnitz is happy with the infinite
and likes the labyrinth of zero space,
a small continuum where monads sit
filling a void with energy and grace
of God—who might be possible like 1
or 2—or different souls under 3 skies.
                Then Gottfried has some fun
                    and loads his eyes
                      with fiery 4
                  and Sophie on the floor
            on Berlin evenings. Yet because
            Leibnitz makes small infinity
                his earthly, chaste, efficient cause
of love, he calculates his life as dreary harmony.

Spinoza

Here in the twilight the translucent hands
Of the Jew polishing the crystal glass.
The dying afternoon is cold with bands
Of fear. Each day the afternoons all pass
The same. The hands and space of hyacinth
Paling in the confines of the ghetto walls
Barely exist for the quiet man who stalls
There, dreaming up a brilliant labyrinth.
Fame does not disturb him (that reflection of
Dreams in the dream of another mirror), nor love,
The timid love women. Gone the bars,
He's free, from metaphor and myth, to sit
Polishing a stubborn lens: the infinite
Map of the One who now is all His stars.

(translation from Jorge Luis Borges)

Billy Budd

Billy knew how to make the ocean ring
with cloud-birds or the humming monsters in
the deep. The Handsome Sailor, mimicking
the illiterate nightingale, climbed up to win
his supper from the stars, and sang. He sang
tunes he made up to larger seafowl scream-
ing near the foretop. Barely a child of time,
from the maintop the angel had to hang,
for gagged by lies he had no words when quick
as flame from a night cannon his right arm
shot out and Claggart dropped. So through the mist
Billy ascended, and ascending took
the full rose of the dawn. Wordless his charm,
sleepy, now oozy weeds about him twist.

Emily Dickinson Withdrawn into Her White House Takes a Ride

Caught in one room Emily Dickinson
scrawled in her cupola. Although the day
buzzed with blue flies and its revolver sun
shot blanks of light at her, she found no way
outside not to auction her soul for coin
and so she brooded, kept indoors and wrote.
A wild-night love outside she couldn't join,
nor see an editor. Her paper boat
swam on green ink in an interior port.
Confined to mere infinity, her hand
said NO to Master God, yes to consort-
ing with a Moor. Inside she rode a train
far down to bedroom death, on bottomland,
and chugged smartly about on luminous pain.

Chatting All Night with Dickinson in Her New England Room

A light exists, your poems in which we talk
till dawn. You're in a white New England room,
I'm in a plane hanging like a nighthawk
outside. Though time is hungry germs, the doom
of friendship, doomsday now, wiping the past
away each instant, I will not submit
to losing you. You don't know me but last
night, each in our chair, we chatted, your wit
against the stranger. Wonder of the brain
that knows a window closed at death, yet keeps
a room after that room, after the chain
of dust, so we can speak alone. Your sleep
is false (or reader, even talk with you
is doomed), and Emily and I are snow.

Walt, Foaming from the Mouth, 1892

Don't be surprised. I'm still hanging around,
talking to you. You thought me dead. I am
cheerfully in your room. I'm lost and found
and found and lost. A red-faced man, a ham,
and yet I'm laughing in the mountain air
out with my night bats floating. Don't be sick.
I failed. Emerson liked me, yet his care
cooled after one brave letter. Did he stick
by me? Why should he? Loudmouth, I contain
too much, embarrassing my friends. I shout
and whisper in your soul, and what you own
will rot, but not my words. When time speaks out
and death demands, do not go blank. The stain
of grass is deep. With me you're not alone.

Cavafy on His Own Bed above a Poor Taverna

The Jews and Christians of this city hound
me with their cults. "Despise those marble limbs
and worship the unseen." Bigots. They've found
an ally in Plotinos and their hymns
sing of a diamond heaven. It's no light
for my illicit afternoons whose sun
is candle weak, corrupt, and erudite
with kisses gambled on a strange bed. Son
of passion, I'm spent like burnt tobacco for
these nights of bloody thighs and lips. I use
a chaste demotic Greek and long ago
entombed my name in candid poems. I choose
the old city as my metaphor to know
rare limbs, old kings, and me, time's aging whore.

Antonio Machado in Soria, Jotting Lines in a Copybook about Leonor Who Died

Walking in Old Castile, a widower
and young schoolmaster in my dirty clothes,
I'm gravely recreating Leonor
who left me in the spring. I almost loath
the adolescent fields, merino sheep,
blue peaks, the first whitening brambles, plums,
your child voice in my ear, yet walking numbs
intolerable whispers of the bed. To keep
your face, it's best to learn to wait. I will
know victory (or so the proverbs go)
and see an elm that lightning might ignite
and char. Dry elm a century on the hill,
still graced with leaves, my heart would also know
another miracle of spring and light.

Antonio Machado in Segovia, Daydreaming as Usual of Soria, Baeza, and Sevilla

My window grins over the crypt of John
of the Cross's bones down in the cypress grove.
I'm living up the hill in a small room on
the Street of Abandoned Children. I keep a stove
under the round table, a blanket on my knees,
and each night scrawl till dawn, throwing away
the papers with their dream of orange trees.
The hunched lady scrubs my ashes off the gray
floor and toilet's red clay bowl. My cell,
the dream ground of a Chaplin-walking man,
has (like Saint John's cell) a cot, chair, and field
around for solitude. The Andalusian
fountains laugh blue. My eyes, a lost moonbell,
are grave and funny like an orphan child.

Anna Akhmatova under Glass and Artists
Everywhere Who Know Obscurity

Akhmatova looks at her graying hair
and tells the mirror how they cannot kill
her—though they try. Happy, rich with the glare
of memory over her bugged windowsill,
she isn't fully silenced. No one tries
to kill or silence us (such honor comes
like a red star only in the iron skies
of police states), yet some of us know slums
of quiet where our mirror reeks with van-
ity and self-hate, and a loser's cry
is rain slopping forever on a can
of trash. Akhmatova looks at her face,
still under glass: a florid butterfly
rich with the horror of its special grace.

Marina Tsvetayeva and Her Ship of Being
Sailing Even Now in Darkness

Strangely, Marina found her light
and death too early, and she left,
a hounded maid. Trains flowed at night
carting her exile and the theft
of her laughing, staccato knife
of words. Daughter of Moscow, who
hanged from her Russian rope, a wife
beyond the suburbs, floating to
her ship of death. Her ways are clear:
she stares from an Egyptian crypt
with guardian jackals. Her typescript
in braille illuminates a Peking
Man hunting deer. Her ship of being
is out of light, yet always near.

Borges

Old man from the North, immaculate liar,
your iron helmet and the deadened eyes
waken at dawn, and watch red spears take fire
and fade on Danish beaches. You despise
the lazy, learned man moving in gentle
amazement with a cane, who keeps a gold
watch in his coat so he can lose the mental
con game with time. You feel remorse for old
Jorge Luis Borges, outwitting God,
Persians, and the algebra of being. Both of
you hunt like madmen for a word. Your love
is hidden, though it burns behind the sword
of Norsemen and the cane. You are a fraud
and friend, a haunting brain and lonely lord.

Borges and His Beasts

Something is wrong with your face. No, it's not
an old man, but one who has not grown up.
Despite gray hair or one eye caved like a cup
and dead, and one eye that is a gray plot
of yellowish mist through which a white deer
leaps and fades or flashes blue in a dream
where you forgot your death, you longly scheme
the alphabet of light to fill the sphere
in your heart. Blackness gone, now you must smile
like a child. You relish an Old Norse word
offered the sky. But lonely and absurd
you know something is wrong. Face of a child,
laughing, tormented like a tooth, your eye
waters to know the panther who cannot die.

Gas Lamp, 1893

Dionysian Bucky Shoving Food in His Mouth

We wait for the late train at a fast food
Steak & Egg place, my sons, a teacher and
Bucky: sixteen years, autistic. Our mood
is goodbyes. Bucky, camera in hand,
shoves supper in his mouth, utters a bird
cry. He is my sons' age, but more like me,
bird shrieks and all emotion—yet no word
to clarify the spirit. I take tea
and steak. A cop at the vapory counter ignores
us. The waitress is perfect starch. You're Solomon
and fellow slob, and know the edge of wars
in Athens, Buenos Aires and Luzón,
my pal in the Manila jail. You're mild
and numb in public pain, animal child.

Bret Bare, Are You Alive?

Strange name. You were a big minimal man
who went through World War with black hair and blue
sea eyes, bastard son of a clergyman,
a combat rifleman who never knew
his secret genes were epileptic. Then
you came to do philosophy, and we
were friends. On crooked nights we talked like Zen
disciples living in a frozen tree,
over our dorm, up on the drunken moon.
You were depressed. I was a ghost inside
a ghost, looking for light. We left. I went
into a Paris flat, got married, tried
to write away my strangeness. Once, you lent
me ice, and split. If you're alive, come soon.

Larry Rothman, My Army Buddy

We all are drunk, happy and smart, and none
of us knows how to drive. Earlier this night
Victoria in Boston sang Ravel,
which we got into for a dollar on
the charm of Army dress. You have to spell
me, Larry, since I can't keep our damn truck
from bouncing off the road, and you drive worse
than me. But singing crazy, with our luck
we make it back to base. Later a curse
snakes through you. There by Mr. Ketcham's land,
with crazy Vermont birds over the wood
below our rocks, the carcinoma cell
squanders your liver. Earth conceived you good
yet let you rot. Death grips your yellow hand.

George Ballou among His Animals

Oldest pal, wild in your Chelsea mud hole
where I could always crash next to the beasts
and birds inhabiting your flat, your soul
got bald, it hurt your pride, but peaking priests
and brats of Salvador couldn't eject
you from your hammock in the jungle where
you slept and trapped your friendly snakes. You picked
a wife and two and three. They let you share
a child, you maddened them, they dumped you. Now,
leg amputated, books unpublished, friends
burnt out and you burnt out, you lie, a sow
among the roaches crawling on the ends
of rotting pizza. George, the ravens faint
in France. Remember rain, animal saint?

Late December, Where Are You, Robert Frost?

Where are you, Robert Frost? The first poems
I heard were yours which you recited on
the stages of my many schools. "Rough gems"
my teachers called them and called you "the con
man of the cracker barrel." Jealous snobs.
Plato wrote for the tomb of his ally,
Tyrant of Syracuse, "Honored by the mobs
of patriots—but I was one who loved you, my
friend Dion!" Once in Middletown, we three,
Snow, Frost and Stone sat down to eat a cold
lunch. Almost deaf you did the talking, told
how you read Homer only in the Greek
at Harvard, quit and hit the woods. I see
your face this morning, fresh, and winter bleak.

Ruth Stone on Her Cold Mountain

She lives in clouds on her cold mountain in
Vermont. Only Wang Wei has walked the mist
beyond her cottage—solitary inn
of winds snowing down from the Gap, a fist
of ice punishing deer up on the rim
against the stars. Ruth and the deer don't care.
They don't eat much in winter. But the hymn
she scribbles on a Kroger bag takes her
back to a day in London where a hang-
ing spouse allied her to a Chinese monk,
who sang for decades in her ribs. The pipes
are cracked yet flame grins through the owls. A long
murder made her nun of wind and windpipes,
laughing with ice and enemy of junk.

I, George Seferis, This Friday of Barbary Figs, Say Hello to Blood

Two horses and a slow carriage outside
my window on the road in Spetsai where
I walk when everyone has gone to hide
under the cypress shade of sleep. The air
is salt, a gentle wind of brine and smells
from the old summer when a woman said,
"I am no sibyl, but your asphodels,
Antigone and blossoming seas are dead.
So let's make love." I am a diplomat
and poet, taste the archeologies
of old statues weighing me down, yet think
before I'm under house arrest I'll chat
and sleep with her. Help me, cut me. The sea's
live blood is better than a glass of ink.

I, Vanya, Plot My Escape

Uncle Vanya peers through the window to
the garden. Moscow lies beyond the haze,
beyond the chitchat and the piles of blue
logs in the snow. Blue angels in a craze
are seething in celestial drapes. They want
escape yet I cannot throw off his old
impotent fuss. I understand but can't
bluster into the snow to take the train
to loneliness and gambling poverty.
The winter dulls. I move into the sane
prison of spring. And my epiphany?
My vision festers like a half-loved friend.
What good is boring truth in a household
I'll never leave? This play can never end.

God on Fire Gets Gravely Sick

Up by the moon, an astronaut or so
for company, a lonely man of means
yet bored beyond belief, God drops below
to his own Earth Lab. Camping on the greens
of Central Park, he sniffs the grass and herbs,
drinks the air sky, laughs full of his creation,
and slumbers in the spring. He knows his verbs
have made the day. A crack-gang on location
sees the old naked boss, bashes his skull
for fun until a cop comes by to nab
him for indecency. Using his pull
by spring he's sprung and gets the hots for girls
and boys. He'll try out fabled love and grab
some ass. So God gets AIDS, his pearl of pearls.

Keep Blabbing, Magic Johnson

Your hand was magic, Magic, but your name
was not a condom capping you from AIDS,
and now, with cheerful poise, you use your fame
for information. Blab loud. The word fades
in Washington. Its White House is immune
to dirty viruses. The President
is mum about the agony. The moon
and sun come clean. They show. How can torment
be cured in silence? Sick or well we know
how time gives life and death, and when its bell
begins to roar, it's time to hear. Magic
has left the magic city. He is sick.
Before the diarrhea and wasting hell
consume you, laugh and speak. And do not go.

Antiprayers

I was born a night when God was sick,
gravely.

César Vallejo (1889–1938)

God the Child

We are the same. Children. We both were born
in a dark sea, but I exist with warts
and wormy insomnia. God is a unicorn
chasing a mirror to destroy the quartz
precision of external time. I dream
a child's dream: both of us with sandwiches
and milk are wandering like an expert team
through cities of the pagans. Neither says
a word while blinded cows circle a well,
pulling up water. God tells me *he* made
the fields, the dust, the cows. I'm glad to know
someone like Einstein, warm and unafraid
to play with stars. Then back in time I grow
desolate. I made God who then made hell.

Portrait of the Lord as a Young Man

God is the science fiction hero of
old Persia. Floating out of Asia's eye
down to the Sinai, a whirlwind just above
the desert moonland, Mazda quits his dry
Medes of the Sun to be the glum one-God
Father commanding Jews who wait for a
messiah. Josh, his stand-in, pulls an odd
Houdini comeback miracle: a way
to life through death, offering white-cloud hope
or horrid fire. Josh is the rage in Rome
(while Allah trots triumphant on the sands).
Aloof to Galileo's telescope,
Reb Joshua of the Lilies fills our dome
with radiance of his face and punctured hands.

God in the Bathroom Mirror

Though I lay nine months sharing blood and food,
curled in my mother's sack, I quake alone,
and since my birth I've breathed in solitude.
In solitude I come on love and loan
my heart, wounded in solitude by love,
seeking oblivion, union, and the peace
of being found and lost, with logic of
a head drunk in transcendence or hot seas
of blood. God is my choice, though he is me.
I am a fool before my powers to fool
the mind, and weak before such ecstasy
of hope. Flat on the bathroom rug I scratch,
edgy while vapory God burns on the glass,
in solitude: a steamy, ticking jewel.

Rapping with God in the Kitchen

God blows into the kitchen. I'm undressed.
I've just dashed back from trying to sneak outside,
naked, to throw you off. "We will arrest
you for lascivious carriage," you tell me snide-
ly. I compose myself. "God, be my friend.
Don't haunt or dream me. I'm no punching bag
and yet your fingers whisper I must end
this whim of peace without you. Let's relax,
sit down, slug a few beers and chew the rag.
Maybe in nightmare you will drop your mask,
reveal your eyes, be gentle and be known.
You're all I have," I say in weakness, "but
for God's sake, show your face." At this, you cut
me off and fade. My lies work best alone.

The Watchmaker God

You save perfection for yourself. We are
the movements running down, the crooked wheel,
while you the maker are the awful star
in harmony with nothing wrong. I feel
insulted by your absence. Yet, if you
were real, I'd be diminished. I am I
alone in my glass world. I hurt, I cry
(humiliating act) and can't get through
with words. I fail repeatedly and lose
the face I love. The hands fall off! Just time
to shout. I hate your secret life and cruise
against a cosmic glass. I'd rather be
a mumbling imbecile than a dumb mime
of your perfection. I am spooked and free.

Lord of the Inferno

In making an inferno you conceived
a state as lonely as your own. You try
to make me ache in boredom, unrelieved
of the Great Wall of solitude, and lie
about yourself so I will leap with mad-
ness back to you, losing the circumstance
you lack: existence. Yet I watch a sad
black janitor, tall as a street lamp, danc-
ing up the stairs. I jog with a blind run-
ner and recall a cancerous child who saw
through a glass wall and smiled in peace while sun
left her on an ice hill. She was a rose
in the dumb corpse you made, and warm and raw
she sank in hell amid your hungry snows.

God in the Hay

I wish you were a woman. Sappho had
a friend and ally in bright Aphrodite
but you're a moron, a pathetic sad-
lipped thug whom I dream up. Goddam your flighty
and murderous moods! Your face is ocean black,
an octopus of hope, yet I can't find
your eyes, which like a negative stare back
inverted. So in sunlight I am blind
before their sexual glow, and inside they
are white like vision, escape my look, and dim
into eclipse. If you were a real lewd
woman, crude like me, I'd plop you on the rim
of the blue planet in some barn. Then nude
with grace we'd bounce in heaven on the hay.

God the Smoky Hero of Byzantium and Maine
Who Elicits Prayer

God is the hero of the soul, the Pan-
tocrator dominating domes of O-
sios Lukás. His Greek stone eyeballs scan
our fearful hearts; his anguished icons glow
in smoky mystery. I look up to search
his porcelain eyes in which the superbrain
of the Lord lives, as once I said arcane
Hebrew words over grave pits by the church
of the Maine Jews. Yet Mother never spoke
again and Father lies as spirit's trash
with no one to reveal his leap to dust.
A joke. God can't fly down a single crust
of heaven's bread. I peer into his smoke
and know myself unsaved, yet free to crash.

Guilty as I Feel, I See You, God on the Rampage, Knocking Off Gentle Animals

You trapped me, put me in a self, and walk
away the way a formal lion trainer
turns his back on sullen beasts. I talk
to you, but I'm an impudent complainer
or loudmouth pest to think I'm in the world
you think about. With your monopoly
on power, you soar while I am slowly hurled
from mountain hopes down to the infamy
of squeezing fleas out of my thighs. It's sad
to itch late at night, weeping like a child
ghost. Maybe I trapped *you*? And have I gone,
leaving you sloppy like a sterile mad
goldfish gasping in a tank? No. You're wild
and punitive and execute the fawn.

God in the Grave

Why talk to you? To one who won't exist,
who has no ears? I sit in bed alone.
No one is watching me or knows the list
of failures in my head. And if I groan,
why should the angels hear? We're all the same:
born howling, not to know, but made to die
and blur. I cannot know why being came
to me. It simply came and I was I.
But you came too, hovering with secrets and
revealing none. So hope for mystery keeps
us all inventing you, a coin for peace.
But I am dry. I feel a strange command
to bury you outside the universe
along with death, our other lonely curse.

God the Miser of Time

I do not love you, God. If you have ears,
record it: old mafioso bishop, lack-
ing decency, your power enlarged by fears,
dumb to compassion, deaf to justice, black
at night when darkness hangs on us, and white
against the sun, but never seen out there
or in the mind. You said "Let there be light"
and there was darkness, chaos everywhere.
Words and no voice. I do not love you, Lord,
for you, miser of time, do not love me,
never give back one look or holy word.
You'll never be, although I rant absurd-
ly to the graceless ghost. Ἄξιον εστί
the death in which I am already poured.

God Our Light

Like obscure poets in a Midwest town
whose voice will never reach the world, or in
the Zaïre courtroom where the judge puts down
his gavel, ordering death, and all eleven
young officer defendants jerk erect-
ly to their feet and then are shot that day,
their intellectual voices hushed, dissect-
ed from their hearts by fire, their obscure way
to fame some lead marks in the *Times*, so all
of us act out obscurely, with a flare
at times, a life alone, disguised by love
and every public act, before we fall
into the absolute ditch, seen from above
only by God—our light—who's never there.

God on Trial at Auschwitz

I go to God by slipping dimly crazed,
dropping through graves, and not a dream, and wake
from day, felicitous, roaring, amazed
by light. The Lord is lurking as the snake
of heaven and I know that death when all
surprise of solitude is gone. Some sheep
wobble on a blue meadow, on the tall
sunny blue Mosque where God has gone to sleep
it off, snoring, dazzling, and high. I see
his throne and chariot, parrot and the stars
consuming dream. But in his bed our God
is put on trial at Auschwitz. Now the scars
of tattooed numbers kill my ecstasy.
I bump lonely against the holy fraud.

God of the Gas Chambers, Where Are You Hiding?

Yahweh, what do you have in mind while Jews
drop naked in the chambers or the graves
they dig in Poland or Ukraine? Who saves
the souls of women, babies, when the ooz-
ing gas screams in their lungs? Or blasts of lead
lay them out under the non-mountain of
the night? When doctors die, when tailors spread
their arms, imploring you, where is that love
for us who are of mud like you? But since
you are like us, we are the lice of dawn,
floating in oily lakes while you, the prince
of darkness, drink our blood. Please go. I am
a cousin of the slaughtered, not the clone
of swine. Die off to keep alive the lamb.

Dr. God, Patron of TV Evangelists

Dr. God fumes and threatens to exist
in the unknown. I look behind my eyes
or rapid words or thought to zero mist
and nothing clear. Dreams, yes, but in the guise
of consciousness I feel mere dark. No source,
no core. No I! Nothing to hear or hold,
so death works easily, needing no force
to still what has no body. With carved gold
and hymns and glory, God worms in. It's odd
to know we are to be extinguished when
the center of our being is never seen,
yet sobbing Swaggarts chat with their man God,
cooking up harm. Doc grabs his righteous pen,
prescribing AIDS to torment the unclean.

God in His Cunning World

My act of faith does not lead to your sky,
your cunning world inside my world, to shade,
light or wherever you hang out. You made
the others and yourself perhaps. Not my
mistake of birth. My faith is vague and dark
like a small coin that may or may not be
in my pants pocket, that might buy me hope
of knowing who I am. So I can cope
with time, it buys me time. For ordinary
failure, gloom, half love, I wander a park
at night, making it glass to glimpse the Jew
you sent as a white Christ you murdered or
(if he was you) who killed himself. I want more
than our lone dust. I need another you.

God and the Hope of Infidels

I have not played with God. God doesn't need
my faith. The cello of the opal spheres
rebounds lucid and white for those who read
salvation in a gleaming dove. But no one hears
the unplayed chords inside for us who pray
to no one, who invent the soul, who know
our alien ghost is brain, fed by a ray
of air, and doomed. For *us* I have to grow
an alphabet of trees. So in this book
the past is born in black, the I of ink
remote from *you*, the empty page a white
promise of memory. For those who look
at God, my book is poor, a blurry wink
on earth of earth, a hope for earthly light.

When God Is Gone Comes a Ship of Light

The ship of light dips into clouds and burns
the evening firmament and human eye.
We sleep. The sailor star, all in white, turns
for all of us in prison. I ask why
the sky is full, self-moving. How are laws
of movement, music and imprisonment
devised? Why does an evening horsefly pause
on my nose, sniff my life? I can't invent
a system or trade off my ignorance
for punctured Christ and hints of paradise.
There is a paradise of love. Here. Dawn
wakes it tender with wind. It sails in trance
and drops through amber dark. Seconds suffice.
I'm reconciled to hunger when it's gone.

Spirit Has a Beginning

Advice

Learn to wait. Wait for the tide to flow,
as a boat on the coast. And do not worry
    when it buoys
you out. If you wait, you will know
    victory,
for life is long and art a toy.
And if life is short
and the sea doesn't reach your ship, stay
forever waiting in the port,
for art is long, and never matters anyway.

Antonio Machado (1875–1939)

The Whisper

Sometimes I'm happy. Then the yellow cry
of sun roams in my ear, especially
if I'm in a dark room alone. I see
loud light! I float. Sometimes I want to die
and dream that Plato will instruct my soul
with secrets of our being before that leap
when I have slammed the final door of sleep.
I'm neither beaming nor about to roll
over and croak. I am resigned. I'm not
nature or you, but just one mind confined
to ink, and even this typed page is signed
like a fake portrait. Now, my clumsy thought
uses your alien words as if I could
howl my whisper beyond this fading wood.

Goodbye to Flimsy Words

Tonight I'm almost old enough to die:
the manuscripts are typed, the phone bills paid,
enough friends care for me to have me laid
with pleasant dignity sad in the sky
below the Maine earth where my mother is
in an old box; my missing father waits
for one to move his ghost. The funny bus-
iness of my books is done. Let all the plates
be run through acid. Let me not lie hop-
ing for a visionary angel to pick
up those untalking poems, fat like fresh soap,
that are indifferent to the sink of slick
reviews. Tonight I flash a nutty grin
at death where unheard words won't flop again.

Loving and Surviving Winter

Zero outside. December, and I've lost
a glove back in the snow or in a hall
of dumpy Ballantine. Luis tried to call
about his red German Bug dead from frost-
bite, but garages leave phones off the hook.
My room is hot yet my ears throb and ache
with cold. At three a.m. I try to shake
ice off a cedar tree, a snow-masked crook
sticking me up in darkness. I wish light
would stick into my soul. I love despite
our mess and an infinity of non-
absolutes. Klondike air is colder but
we're vaster than Alaska in this hut
where we can hide, wake happy, warm, and yawn.

Terror in the North Room

Terror in the north room. I woke from night-
mares. Miles of anguished skin, I woke and saw
who I was. Wrong again. Heat from the white
register blurred my head. You went. The law
of solitude like a gold bell rang out.
You were all gone. I couldn't look at me.
How could my small eyes see themselves without
popping out of their head? And naturally
I hid that head under the sheet. The plane
took off without me. You flew to the East
and like a city disappeared. Insane
I looked away. You shone again. The beast
I was became an ordinary man
dreaming up ultimate words, bribes, a plan.

Hacking Away at Roof Ice

Icy Monday. I'm on the roof to chop
free the trapped water leaking through the ceiling.
I like to fight the snow. Drenched, cold, I hop
night blind and hack at the black ice. I'm healing
the house, but almost slide into salvation,
plunging to tears and pompous ceremony!
What a dirty fool life can be! My nation
is at each other's throats. O family, we
cannot make Friday. Friday will be rain
to warm the ice, free up our hearts; and slush
will free our wounded cars. I'm not insane,
I have no history of hysteria or
depression. Yet, I can't control the rush
of rage. Eyes freeze, and wanting peace I roar!

Rolling Downhill

All day I do bits of work. No real plan,
fill out financial forms and read a few
glorious pages about Cavafy in a new
book that oppresses me with hope. I can
see Bloomington, a city where glass walls
are secretly erected till one day
one hundred years have passed. There is no way
to leave. I get my gloves. Aliki crawls
into the car. The road is icy so
we creep down Hillside, but tonight we'll work
together. "Hi, sweet." I'm so happy. Slow
we drive, gab, joking. Sheet of ice! I jerk
the gears. The globe and wheels meander. Flash,
we spin and smash head-on. My nerves are trash.

Holy Logos, What Can I Do?

My daughter says she's not hung up on words
as I am (though she now is majoring in
semiotics). Holy logos! Patmos birds,
white like the island village, scream and spin
over the Cave of Revelation where John,
sleeping on a rock pillow, wrote his smoke
and fiery myth. My dream too: to live on
nothing but bread and words, maybe a coke
on Sunday, white walls of Lipsí across
the bay. I'm drained, so herbal tea. Then ink,
more ink. No stop! Are words more than the loss
of love? Than air? Than life? Can't even die
because I won't shut up. Here by the sink
by dawn my blood scribbles its sacred lie.

Any Island or Cave Will Do

Thirty years of poems on scraps and blue
books. Once on a Greek island I had no
paper at all, wrote on my arm and drew
twelve lines, then glided like a UFO
(filled with a troop of angels) to the beach,
jumped in the sea. Verse washed out. Any isle
or thing will do. And so I scribble each
odd revelation, stuff it in a file,
and host each visiting new poet star
who beams us with fair words. Since writing's far
from peddling art, I should dump vanity,
sadness and greed. Good to create alone,
pure as a germ! Do I hurt? No. I'll be
a will-less barn stone cool and on my own.

Who the Reader Is and Other Delusions

Of course I write this junk for *me*—because
I look for hills, for fragments of a wish
to glue like China or a star and pause
before, like sighting a gigantic fish
salted with fire, brooding over a cloud;
and live by it. Since I dump kerosene
on oysters, words are the mysterious crowd
of knives I use to slice my flesh and clean
blood from invading pearl, oil, moons. Of course
I write this junk for *you*. Yet with these lies,
am I a schizoid dreaming up the glare
of a warm woman's Captain Marvel eyes?
If you refuse me, well, drop dead, divorce
me. I'm a cryptic stone. More lies. I care.

Shaving in Mesopotamia

My bath is Eden. When I close the door
and lock my lover, Cairo, Buenos Aires
outside, I strip, do push-ups on the floor,
hop in the tub, dance in the Nile—Osiris
dreaming Isis—or read a Sufi poem
solving the riddle of the soul. I hope
no one breaks in. Shaving, I let the foam
paint me white as Apollo as I soap
a baritone you're lucky not to hear,
who is a secret pal of farts and steam.
The bath's a place to change a life, to cheer
the earth with reeking earth, to soak apart,
scrubbing with joy and meditative art
in gardened Nineveh, my tub of dream.

The Coffee House

Others are here for talk. I've come to find
salvation, so the coffee hardly trims
my arrogance. Sadly I suck the mind
of grounds for hints of grace. The napkin swims
bloated on hot tea spilled across the table
into my lap, burning me. The quick fix
of feeling, but I hold out for an angel
to float through caffeine vapor on its six
luminous wings. The waitress, circling by
the edge of purgatory, asks me what
I want. (To know the Book of Eve, I think,
or peel an onion down to its gray sky
of peace.) "A cappuccino, please." I shut
my heart and watch the coffee turn to ink.

Christmas Day

The snow crisscrosses down and flurries up
all afternoon, unaware it is snow
or some of us are desperate, or the radio
(unaware too) has Mimi drink a cup
of wine on Christmas eve. I work alone
in this dead building. Sons are sleeping. They
have thirty years before the middle way
of hell's dark forest. Don't give up. My own
nowhereness please forget. I go downstairs
for yogurt, smash the vender with my shoe
(it gypped me). *Buona sera, Mimi.* I'm through
with gray Bohemia. Resolute I stare
at junk and snow, and take a photo of
my heart, guessing at speed, focus and love.

Two Versions of Dying and the Aftermaths

I am too young, yet Gerry reads my hand
and sees the ruptured line. On the escalator
my chest breaks. The sun slips into Greenland
and drops. After they drop me in a crater
by my father out West, my city flag
droops limply for a day: *Arbeit Macht Frei.*
Or else, one evening in a cab I try
to squeeze my bursting plexus and I sag
against the door. Only my estranged wife
and children fly out to Maine. No one's sure
after a year what happened. Was it pure-
ly physical neglect? I took my life
in my own way. Now, quietly I reek,
and no one knows I'm still dying to speak.

Is God a Heavenly Bossman or a Bad Dream

Unlaughing God is sick, but he has tenure
in Saint Paul's or a Burmese hill with mist.
His whirlwinds on a desert mound resist
a carbon-14 test or laughing censure
by scientific children. God is grave
and makes us grave, and even me who can't
put up with him. He's passive like a plant
yet is the dark eye in the soul, who gave
the earth his verb. I also use the verb
gravely, yet spurt out blasphemies and try
to hear what he will not disclose: the heart
and light and echo of the silent eye
looking inward for another eye. I'm smart
enough to know I fail. Nothing is heard.

The Stranger in Southern Indiana

I must go. Not home. I live in an oak barn
in the woods. What better dream? The glass wall
lets sun or the full moon like a ghost fall
on a blue bukhara or a chair with yarn
and books. No chair of joy. Outside, in town
the teams, opera and friends are all remote.
I care for them. Only I don't like me float-
ing where there is no ocean. I slip down,
a dry ghost among ghosts. Where can I go?
Athens, Maine, NY? Roots? I'm everywhere,
and having no intimate love or face
to study, I've gone, yes, somehow I'm there
already in those woods where I efface
this strangeness. Where? I'm dead and cannot know.

Coffee in Predawn Buenos Aires

Depression is a sickness of the lips,
for words don't vibrate. Sleep hangs on the will
like months of blackness on Cape North, and grips
the pocket of the heart, squeezing, until
mere sleep is a food riot. But I don't climb
the walls. I'm low, not a mad bug. The wall
is an underworld city fog. Café time
before the dawn is for a hermit. All
the global light is out. I sip my blue
coffee mug, nursing the cool slop. The phone
and morning crowds uplift me from the slough
of solitary vision. When they're gone
I'm back in me, hanging in fog. Despair
and underworld I've earned as moles earn prayer.

Bed Visions on the Way Down

The sirens cough and flap outside the window,
impatiently. They want to flash their staff
of fire on me. Itchy, hugging the pillow,
I rouse the fleas of paradise, who laugh
at my incompetence. Why do I scratch,
debate convulsively? Even bugs sleep.
But I am hatching eggs of dreams, a batch
of iron coins to barter for a cheap
sea voyage to an African mud town.
On the ocean, love holds me for two days
conscious, jambs my eyes, prodding me to bite
angel worms nosing through the bloody brown
underworld. As I sink, the tossing maze
of shipwreck hugs the seabed, begging light.

Drifting on a Strange River of Milk

Why can't I sleep? My body's fine. I'm not
especially neurotic. Sad? Okay,
I'm down. Suddenly a strange river of hot
milk flowing between continents! The way
it curves on the horizon—five gold ships
and dolphins in the air—makes Yahweh warm
from a pig's navel to the stars. My lips
taste currants from a blue volcanic farm
and gossip with Seleucids bartering kings.
I get up itchy, wild, sipping hot milk.
Was I acting out a dream? Was I asleep?
Can I forget the melancholy leap
between towers, dangling from a single silk
thread? Months hum by. No sleep. The terror sings.

Since Death, That Callow Thief of Time, Is around the Corner, Let's Dance

Death is the thief of time, a wasting rest.
It honored Plath but froze her hand, yet some
fools speak of celebration. It's the test
of science, though the spirit remains dumb
and never can reveal where she has gone.
Socrates said, "I go to die and you
to live. Only God knows what's best." Each dawn
before my birth I can't regret or know.
Why fear the dawn of death? I'll never feel
its sky. Yet what gray fear not to know thought
or me or you again; to be red ants
eaten by ants and disappear! We're caught
like jumping smelts in a fire net of steel.
Before I am extinct I'll jump and dance.

A Little World Made Cunningly

El Greco walked the sea from Crete to Spain,
carrying inside his head an icon with its blue
and violet firmaments. He wore the stain
of foreigner. So did the doctor Jew
Cervantes and the mystics Fray Luis,
John of the Cross, Teresa, converts all
from Kabbalah to Christ or Greco's Greece
to cobbled hills of gray Toledo. Call
them Romans, Moors, burn some impure souls, curse
their strangeness. Spain got rich because
it mixed its bloods, got poor when purity
abolished wisdom. Memory heals the loss
of soul. It's best to laugh. In its old sea
of bastard blood is Spain's deep universe.

Romping for a Week in Xanadu, Ghengis Khan's Paradise City, Before Hopping on the Train back to Beijing

Your name is Finzi. Out of the black trees
of Italy, its garden mists, you came
with me to Xanadu. The Mongol Lame
Man rode his horse of slaughter through Tabriz
and Afrodisias, hot with oil and blood
smeared on his lordly face. But home was yurts
and golden ponies which he drove through flood
and walls to conquer China. Evening hurts
with carbon smog, yet in our bed we shine
as if the sun were stuck inside your cave
and my wild milk. Morning, we walk. The king
of Paradise is nothing now, a pine
that time can murder too. We kiss (and save
a hug for Ghengis), rocking to Beijing.

While the Planet Is Spinning without Eyes, Below We Dream of Milk and Cucumbers

Any time's good for sheets of love when love
is good. The planet's busy with its wind
and laws of turning; sex feels the roll of
raw time's eternal spin. Below we're pinned
in words, clothes, lakes of flesh bulging to flow
into each other. Come this morning. Why
care about earthly clocks? Blue rain we know
in our surprise of voyage. My friends die
with tumors choking time, Chopin today
again with rags of poison in his lungs;
we are surprise desire. I dream you sit
on me, naked with hips of milk. A ray
of spinning planet sweats along our tongues
like cucumbers. Our bodies drip and fit.

Sleep Talk

I was asleep. You overheard me say,
"I went down to the Dead Sea to look
for my father." I took
an unknown way
down to the deepest spot
on the earth. He was swimming in
the mineral sea to freshen
his body. He had that terrific smile, and not
a bit phony. I don't recall
a damn thing—only what you say I said.
Yet I saw him swimming frog kick, all
across the Dead Sea.
                    Half a century dead
now, he's still there, always in that
same acid lake, happy. We swim and chat.

A Winter on Mount Athos, Long Ago

Recalling Athos I am time's freak, one
who grabs the past and will not feel or show
his age. Outside Plato's cave the good sun
is drying off stunned hermits. Lilies grow.
Time hasn't wasted me that much. So far
I've copied memory's images, but lost
the words. Under the portrait of the Tzar
and the Tzarina, oblivious to the frost
on the great banquet table where the monk
left me black Russian bread and wine, I ate
my supper, happy and alone, and froze.
That happened in a monastery. Junk
I owned back then is gone. Cheerful, I wait,
remembering light outside the cave, and crows.

A Rose in Hell

After slopping through hell along three roads,
I stumble on a rose. Insane? A flower
in this dark land where we hop dark like toads
in darkness. Beasts. I hear Moscow's red hour
of revolt. No. I am too tired, too old
not to reform. Too much bathos of hell.
My tape plays old French songs. White rose. A bell
wakes the grand organ of the Tzar. I've sold
my house, bought an exhilaration shoe
to walk beyond the Caucasus. I try,
goodbye. I'm really well, and will fall on
a resurrection. Don't tell me I lie.
Can't I get out? I'm almost tunneling through
to ice, a secret rose, and blizzard dawn.

Spirit Has a Beginning

Although there's no Director of the Scenes
working especially for me, I bet
what happens is for good. Forgot my jeans
in Hong Kong; on a marble hill in Crete
I left a lens. Yesterday in Nepal
a boy got my glasses. Why do I lose
my things? Alms to the cosmos? When I fall
in love, it lasts a life, but I confuse
my lover, lose her, and walk for years
on fire. It's good. Rain will surprise my heart
one day before I die. Theologies
despise possessions, and I feel no tears
for things—though lost love replays death. Yet these
words come because I lose. Loss is a start.

HISTORY II

Maize god . Copan
Willie '94

Solitude of Planets

*He Points Out the Brevity of Life, Unthinking
and Suffering, Surprised by Death*

My yesterday was dream, tomorrow earth:
nothing a while ago, and later smoke;
ambitions and pretensions I invoke
blind to the walls that wall me in from birth.
In the brief combat of a futile war
I am the peril of my strategy
and while cut down by my own scimitar
my body doesn't house but buries me.
Gone now is yesterday, tomorrow has
not come; today speeds by, it is, it was,
a motion flinging me toward death. The hour,
even the moment, is a sharpened spade
which for the wages in my painful tower
digs out a monument from my brief day.

Francisco de Quevedo (1580–1645)

The Secret Hope of Me or Jacob the Tramp

I think this at the center of my life
(even a second before death seems mid-
way down the path): peace is a knife
removing guilty fat, but I won't rid
myself of the invisible deep rain
dropping on a white hut where I have gone
to be mild, lazy, far from murky Cain
or rage with Yahweh who has let us down
for now, for good. Wild Jacob by his lamp
is brooding about Esau whom he cheated
or an angel whom he fought, trying to grope
to heaven in a dream of ladders. Blistered
with pain, he scrubs his rags in wine. The tramp
cries out (like me) for peace. Dumb secret hope.

Solitude of Planets

To Her Portrait

What you see here is colorful illusion,
an art boasting of beauty and its skill,
which in false reasoning of color will
pervert the mind in delicate delusion.
Here where the flatteries of paint engage
to vitiate the horrors of the years,
where softening the rust of time appears
to triumph over oblivion and age,
all is a vain, careful disguise of clothing,
it is a slender flower in the gale,
it is a futile port for doom reserved,
it is a foolish labor that can only fail,
it is a wasting zeal and, well observed,
is corpse, is dust, is shadow, and is nothing.

Sor Juana Inés de la Cruz (1651–1695)

Genesis

In the beginning God made heaven and
the earth, which were invisible, unformed,
with darkness over the abyss. God warmed
the waters with his breath. Then his command:
"Let there be light." And there was light. He saw
the light, that it was beautiful. God's ray
entered the mire of light and through the draw
of darkness, and he called the morning day.
Then God said, "Let there be a firmament
amid the waters, let it grow between
water and water." In such way God made
and named a sky, splitting the waters laid
on earth from rains above. That boundless tent
became our heaven and its air was green.

Bloated with Light, Eve Faces Her Memory of God the Rapist

And darkness God called night. Yet that expanse
was weakness, thirst for an Edenic morning,
hunger for voyage in the south and trance
of reckless angels raping Eve. All warning
of their corruption went unheard. God held
to vision as he spent his rod, and never
fell into sleep. The fowl of the air yelled
into the face of the creation. Then, letter
by letter, texts of darkness cooled away,
and even during lunar eclipse, Eve found
no cliff of shadow. Nervous, sticky, sick
from God, bloated with light, she smelled the ground,
his sperm, his unkissed fire, and lit the wick
of memory. That brilliance God called day.

Tongues of the Deep

Sleep is not death, for blood is moving in
the deep like rivers under earth, and blood
is red with sun breathing under the skin.
And under sleep a city, white in mud
of darkness, wakes like sperm nearing the peak
of scream, says yes, I live. Sleep is not death
at all but wandering galaxies and weak-
ly clear to the deep brain. Sleep is the breath
of the creation blown into the lungs
of Adam, and his rib the wondrous Eve,
mother of milk and dust. Sleep is the star
below despair or Eden. Sleep is tongues
of an abyss in the magician's sleeve,
unknowable but there. The nightly scar.

Thunder

The groan of thunder is an earthquake on
the moon, lunar dissolution, a thread
tangling down with firebolts into the yawn-
ing face of a lotus pond. Thunder, spread
like honey on a muffin, drips through me,
dragging the ice rings of those planets cold
as fur on the Great Bear. The history
of thunder timing the cosmos is the gold
tip of a blindman's cane. But when my ears
erase the dream of drinking a white bullet
from the loud moon, the thunder disappears
like vision upon waking. Later it
will shrink to nothing but a silent door,
to grand illusion while my own stars roar.

Solitude of Planets

As Voyager sails close, hot Jupiter,
a million jungle clouds of gaseous rain,
turns its red eye to Earth, the gardener
of planets. The red eye's a hurricane
leering under the sixteen moons. The Sun,
Earth, and Jupiter roll alone and know
nothing of solitude, yet each is one
estranged, like us, in solitude, with no
way out of space. We think. And personally,
I am a floating record of one man
plotting to go beyond his solitude,
a shy bohemian waiting lustfully.
But like those Galilean moons, I brood
in circles back to space where I began.

When the Marble Dark Comes, Ink Will Boil

When I am signaled by the marble dark,
by gnats breeding like bloated cities in
the bones, or when that cardiac tool, the lark
turning the blood, wobbles like an old tin
megaphone, I'll salvage intricate nights
to write a log of life. Then day by day,
I'll etch the scream of dreaming Carmelites
in their moist convent, in their passion play
of climbing milky hills and lion caves.
At black noon of the flood, the scene will turn
poignantly clear—wisdom lips gone, gone waves
of carbon windflowers in your voice—yet on
my log the ink will boil into a dawn
of time where even flagrant words won't burn.

Antiprayer

I've never prayed and won't. But that weak act
fascinates me: to flop down and let God
kick my ribs, walk on my back and exact
the pleasure of blue wine; then hop up, prod
the Lord to hunt for a cheap bar and drink
ourselves into salvation. Soberly,
even if God has breasts, I'd rather shrink
my balls in alcohol than be a flea
biting the Lady's nipples. Lord, we two
are incompatible like green shampoo
and painted hair. At high dark by the vat
of death, will I crack? When those last dawn-pins
burst the horizon like a truck, my sins
and bones are mine, elusive like a rat.

Moon

The new moon is a dagger of salvation,
in time, a sunray curved like sorrow. I've known
you always as a friend. An aviation
profane with miracle. Your gleaming stone
came through a basement window when the leaks
were eating rugs or when I sweated in
the city park, deaf with remorse: the shrieks
of memory. Your ancient violin
rushed through my eyes. I'm sentimental and
my nuclear heart falls out. New moon, you're there,
as one night on a marble mountain when
I fell through fig trees by tubercular
children. Your tundra glared, saving me again,
till rain washed out the mirror in your hand.

Sun

Sun is the eye. Out there. A glaring, black,
impossible-to-look-at fire. It creeps
on insects, under water, in the crack
of falcon cliffs, on fuzzy eggs. It sleeps
on beads of planets strung on cosmic rings.
Its hydrogen explosions warm the flute
of rays poking through moonclouds, and its wings
of morning celebrate the garden fruit
with hymns of life. On gum and cinnamon
and every spice it heats the chlorophyll.
When Galileo looked through flaming glass
he told the truth and burned. Its miracle
alone makes light, the eye inside, a gas
of yellow worlds, the dark night of the sun.

One World

One world, here on the planet, and the stars
merely a glowing leopard on the night,
harmony for the mystic, but like Mars
just sand and gas and no heavenly white
reprieve from death. One flesh in solitude,
even from mind. One life whose great surprise
of being is wakening alone. I brood
on isolation, on one clock, on lies
of memory making us forget the clock
goes only forward yet is always now.
One world. One flesh. One life. One time. No way
of wobbling into light from this apoc-
alyptic loneliness! Dark, dark, somehow
in perfect darkness I want only day.

The Alphabet of Love

Sonnet of the Mild Complaint

I am in fear of losing the sheer wonder
of statue eyes, of your rare voice that grows
into my night through which it places, under
my cheek, your breathing's solitary rose.
I am in grief that on this shore I stay
a leafless trunk, and what I miss the most
is not to have your flower, its pulp or clay,
for my poor worm of torment, my poor ghost.
If you are now my only concealed treasure,
if you are dripping ache, my cross and quiver,
if I am just the dog of your high station,
don't let me lose what is my rightful measure.
Please decorate the waters of your river
with leaves from my autumnal alienation.

Federico García Lorca (1898–1936)

Reindeer

One night in Lapland I was in the street
with a young nun who held me in her arms.
The sun was weird and strong, washing our feet
with northern rays. We wandered to the farms
outside of town. She was a socialist
and French—so delicate. Two winters in
a   a sardine factory. When our spirits kissed
I blessed la Petite Soeur, feeling her chin
against my neck. Our union was a stain
of hope for both of us. I cashed a check
at Olaf Bull's and spent another week
with her among the fjords where houses were
uncommon dreams like us. We were insane-
ly stubborn, free—real reindeer in that blur.

Song of the Birds

After Pablo Casals had taped the Song
of the Birds, high on Canigo, we went
by foot, from the old French convent, along
the mountain rug of stars, down to the scent
of wheat. We couldn't see. You held my hand
because the trail was steep. Then in the grove
b   we saw ourselves. Naked. By the command
of natural soul, we lay down young and drove
our blood. Our tongues were water, our eyes huge,
earth an unknowing fire until the dawn
of cows and village children screaming led
us back. I loved you in our pure refuge
against the law. The night was sun. Though gone,
our virgin mountain is a lucent thread.

Daughter of the Sun

Last week another God showed up. She came
with proper attributes: the cosmocrator,
author of creeping beasts and clouds and flame,
the daughter of the sun, a poignant actor
in a rundown playhouse, playing her guitar
deep like the Red Sea. It was time for her
c to come since the old God was popular
so long but let us down. Much friendlier
and good to talk to, she confided in
me, spelling out the nasty facts I knew
already: love is real but hard to find,
our death mere oxidation, obscure mind
our only self. I wish I knew her true
white pit, her faithful teeth, her honest skin.

A Bus into the Moon

Tonight we walk across the border cool
as spies and take a bus into the moon
of time. To Eden south. We are the fool
of love—not holy like the Catalan
Ramon Llull—but with a toothbrush, a few
old shirts, some bucks for food, a pen and books—
d what else is there?—we doze and hang on to
the mountain village. There, amid the looks
of puzzled Africans, I chat in French
to get a room. But we move elsewhere in
the voyage. A gray hair (I pull out most
of them) lies on the sink. You jump and drench
your face in water; then eat, throwing the win-
dow open into the sun of time and toast.

Breakfasts

Our breakfasts are the deepest meal. We stop
at Rudi's. Tea and nutty junk. The sun
falls on the crumbs, on crowded food I slop
onto the *Courier Journal.* Just for fun
I poke your knees while you, quick reader, tell
me passionately what happened to the Poles
e or Cubs. We share everything. Milk, bill, smell
of goo and croissants, gossip, apple rolls,
and there is never time. So we don't think
a while. We eat and feel. Love isn't pain
but milky tea and voyage. And we go
out to the street, our bellies like a plane
about to fly to France in a great wink
of freedom, walking about exquisitely slow.

Jelly Will

Love is easy. You look
and suddenly you know.
Why do I know the book
of love too late? The snow
of tigers isn't bare
like me. I wake with shame
f and always wonder where
to lance the boils. I blame
the jelly of my will
on astronauts who went
out to the moon. But love
is sly. Let Job repent.
Not me. Ways of the dove
are mine. I never kill.

Theater of a Black Night

The going from a woman hurts.
On a stormy Paris day
of miracle maybe I'll find a way
to her on Cherche-Midi, but time perverts
my bistro hope
of sleeping with the woman
g I glare at who is gone. I grope
into a stupor of the gossiping sun,
and final loss
of pears won't pacify my appetite.
I never learn. In scratchy sheets I toss,
making up pillow scenes of love.
On this loner planet in my room I play the loner of
a whimpering black night.

Talking to You while Remembering My Friend
César Vallejo

Maybe you'll ruin me. How could I cope
with joy? My friend Vallejo and I were born
a day when God was sick—gravely—and mope
our orphan evening into a gold horn
of lamentation: Samson's howl, the streets
of rain, the meals alone. And yet like him
h (we're both mestizos) I could bear the whim
of just a cot, of hugging in our sheets
of sweat, then waking to a midnight meal
of beer and cheese pirogi. Any bed
or crummy couch will do. To be with you
on Brooklyn Bridge and say: here a Slav and Jew
stood happy gaping at this choir of steel . . .
César we dream. The phone is gravely dead.

Happiness of the Patient Traveler

I wrote a letter to the sun
to shine on us again for one
more life. Then begged him for the time
to let our tongues agree to rhyme
for one more year. And then I asked
for just a day, but he unmasked
i me with the alphabet of night,
and when I pleaded for more light
he spat on me with hours of rain
which finally washed away the pain
of time. I wrote a letter to
the sun and said I would let go
of love. He led me to a tree
inside, where I could hang and be.

Heron of the Night

Heron in mist. Friend in her bed,
aloof from sleep, curved in a womb
of whiteness. Solitary. Spread
around the mountainous globe. Her room
roams like a bird. Her eyes are large,
immaculate as hay and sad
j as iodine, her breasts enlarge
the sky, her palpitations add
memory to the glass moon, a flute
to grief. Her body is the heat
of Eve's intelligence. Far friend
of the tree. Night heron. Her sheet
holds us penetrating the end.
The heron heals; her fire is fruit.

Include the Rain

Include the rain in us. Outside this log
cabin big among dogwoods, let the rain
be in us where I cast a monologue
into the afternoon. One night in Maine
began my journey into solitude.
I've thought enough. Sometimes a Spanish book
k   or Chinese punching up a bus, the mood
of janitors on break, an Army cook
throwing a meat knife at a corporal keep
me happy and outside. I've known them on
my own. You slipped away. And so I'm drunk
on brandy in the rain. Being no monk,
in solitude I see your laugh, your yawn,
your toes. Let rain be in us while we sleep.

The Shingon Water Moon

After the sandwich we could still escape
for a few minutes, chastely in the street,
before the mammoth monolithic shape
of Cuzco's ancient buildings was to cheat
us of the rationed light of afternoon.
I held my belly (nerves or virus?), you
l   poked me again, and suddenly the moon,
the Shingon water moon which wasn't due
for weeks, was round and pure. I didn't care
about astronomy and laws. It filled
the sky supremely. Tender for your sake
alone, it washed a thousand rivers, stilled
the planet. When I puked you scratched its air-
less face. Moon gone, time gone, we fell awake.

Detained in Bucharest

When the Romanians placed us under house
arrest, I managed as your friend to find
a few hours in your bed. Then like a mouse
scurrying from light, our dread swelled. Streets were mined
with gray informers and the lines were cut.
There was a freedom in the dungeon, as
m   you called your digs, for silence sings (it's what
Pythagoras was hearing between stars)
and it prevented boredom in the night
of fear. Through absence we loved more. Your soul
of hunger fell, but a jail pipedream rose,
carting us over cities to a white
jade jaguar in a Maya village. Who knows
how we got caught? In dream we lose control.

Our Rain

After the auto wreck in which I died
I still felt stiff, but it was spring
and grass surprised us. Birches sighed
away the dark. Vicente couldn't see the king
and queen of Sweden but he walked
out of his house and wrote his unremem-
n   bered poems of sleep. And then you talked
to me. I got the car to work and mem-
ory of hurt was gone. Smooth as a knife
we drove to China, curved our lips to learn
the Uzbek words for tea, going as far
as Kashgar on a smelly plane. Red star
on us all night. I held you, back in life,
laughing, and paper rain began to burn.

The Tree of Life

Don't cry for me. The Tree of Life
is full of birds. When I was old
in winter, lonely as a knife,
and when my heart was blue and cold,
I fell in love. Don't cry for me.
The Tree of Life is lilac blue
o   and smells of May and poverty,
poor as an orchard of bamboo.
I fell in love when I was young
and now I'm crazy once again,
in jail with jasmine on my tongue
and in my heart a cyclamen.
Don't cry for me. I'm young again
and every spring is cyclamen.

Spring Is

Spring is. I guess my life is still
a glance at resurrection. I've had
my share of winter. With no will
or fear at all, I eased from sad
and hollow to your Burmese thighs
slender and frank like the new moon,
p   and wondrous. When I kissed your eyes
of darkness, I knew sun, a noon
of accident. We plan. Spring is,
though you have flown off to a cave
to look at paintings. "I will miss
you," and you went. A season gave
us life. I wonder—are we found
or lost? It's dawning underground.

A Crumb of Light

My own heart why such fear? (I'm borrowing
from Hopkins since he felt the most despair
or love.) He woke to fell of dark. The wing
of morning didn't comfort him. Yet spare!
There is one, yes, his roots found rain; he died
breathing "I am so happy." Hopkins, please
q forgive this mishmash of your words. I've lied
so often but your truth of grief, your breeze
of faith cooling down from your God, your com-
fortless, black wrestling with the terror of
your terrible Lord, all comfort me. I fear
and do not know my heart. It's gall, it's love,
and the confusion breeds a raging crumb
of pain! Fears seize. What light! I nothing hear.

Dungeon

I know the place of hell. I walk there though
it has no floor and wild sunbirds fly over
its perfect sky. Women like jasmine hover
in its night air. Orgasm of pain. So
in hell I dream. Quevedo dreamt quicksand
and wrote himself into a dungeon for
r four years; became a *was,* a *will be* and
a weary *is.* The Spaniard raged. To soar
he had to fall. Now morning lies above
my dungeon like a flower. My hell is vision:
we're in the shower, limbs hugging, we can't tell
the place. I'm lost in you. Why ache in hell
when grace is here? You smile, curing division.
But morning's gone, and dead in hell is love.

Under the Full Moon

Under the moon which doesn't rid the mold
or spiders from the house inside, we dance
a moment to forget, living the gold
of Jupiter, brightest of stars. The trance
is long enough. And through the woods the moon
is full is gone is solitary blaze
5   of union. Venus, crystal bird, is soon
basalt. My German shepherd chokes. And rays
of night, moonless, blow through a solitar-
y bed, blotch me sleeping on the dark side
of a half moon. What hell to be absurd-
ly chopped in half! No tongue, no cock, no hair
sweet in your thighs rolling into the ride
of the full moon. Spiders and crystal bird.

Trapped in the Cloisters of the Soul

en los claustros del Alma
Francisco de Quevedo

My orange room smells of the hungry sun,
and dawn is singing on the Roman bridge
in this old Spanish province. I take one
look at my watch, which tells me in the cage
of time how day is sweet is black, how you
and I are half moons twice alive but far
5   and wasting. So I let the dark turn blue
as corpses while I worm into the star
down in the cloisters where I'm feverish-
ly in you. Spain, my sister is the sage
of contemplation yet I smell the East,
a bookish dream of peace, the gibberish
of wisdom, wordless light. But I'm a beast
of time, a soul of terror as I age.

The Shower and the Bed

It is the first cool night of summer and
the extra bed was sold today. The hour
is bad—you leave at daybreak—and its hand
of truth already buries us. We shower,
forget a while (or do we wake?) and are
a Johannine sect, shouting, baptized with soap
u and protein rinse, arisen as a star
of watery raptured limbs, though no tin hope
deludes our kisses. I hop from the tub
to sort out chapters of my bible while
you skim a play. But soon you're half asleep,
cranky in quilts, and I, your belly scrub-
ber of the shower, become a plague rat creep-
ing into bed, dry on the flooding Nile.

Caught between Creation of a Moon Deity
and Torment of the Dreamless

My friend Matei says I'm a serious a-
theist. In Sumer you put your wise ear to
the ground or heaven. Is there any sigh
or gossip from Inanna that's not you?
Abandoned into being, given a face,
electric brain, a soul, you are a lone-
v ly figure here in holy godless space
and I create you seriously. You've gone
but with blue clay and paint and fire I make
you wondrous, and we leave the valley dust
to spend the night in villages. We wake
early to see the pomegranates bloom
and there we screw. Although I cannot trust
your lips, I must invent you in my room.

Inanna of the Holy Vulva

Nothing is lucid like the night we sleep
our hearts joined hand to hand. I stroke your hair,
your holy vulva watered with the deep
milk from a narrow boat while goats and deer
multiply in the forest. On your throat
a golden chain. Our nakedness is al-
w   ways new, yet even Inanna (less remote
than we) opened her arms and loins to all
the chatter of her shepherd. Daughter of
the Moon, lapis lazuli on her breasts,
she passed the gates of the black underworld
as perfect dust, yet wouldn't die. Hair swirled
around her head like leeks. Sprinkled with love,
she rose as food and falcon from the nests.

Drops of Night

Inanna howled and raced back to the sun
and fragrant boxwood where her prince was still
alive. She bathed for the wild bull. Yet on
the bed she stuck nails in her ribs. The will
to love returned her but the nights in hell
were jackals in her heart. All this occurred
x   in Sumer. Soon the Shulamite (her word
the drops of night, whose love was a gazelle
that vanished and returned to the cool
mountain of spices) knew the pits and day
of blood. I know these facts. The night is stark
with ancient underworlds. I'm in its school
of dingy walls, hugging scraps of the dark,
again alone. The sun has lost its way.

Letter to an Old Friend

A precise life. I think of you and write
letters and verse. These I drive to the post
office. The way back near your place—a rite
of history. Then I visit. You are host
and offer juices and we hardly know
we're strangers on a wharf. His things are here
y   and there—a shirt, book, Barbasol. I go
back to my janitors. You disappear
and I wait for a word, which I'll believe
a while. Miguel said not to look, it comes
when you don't look. Since I am short on hope
I'm thinking, yes, I've changed. You give me plums
in schliwowitz. We kiss like friends; you leave
for life. I'm with you in this envelope.

Nightingale

Patience. So many years of waiting wrong-
ly in a room with books. Doing this. Words
for every emptiness. Ecstatic song
floated over the evening gate—some birds
from the Pendeli quarries on the other
side of the mountain. Calm in the Midwest.
z   Gypsy my cat & Buck, dog, share another
forest, noisy, humid. We are beasts dressed,
far from the Mall, in nothing. I am ready
for you. An orange Karmann Ghia idles
out back. You smile into a bed. Already
we hear the nightingale. I didn't know
sun was so deep under the woods, or idols
like words so weak. I wait open like snow.

A Fly and the Darkness of the Sun

Without a field and with a field
to rest on—darkly with no ray
of light—I burn myself away.

Saint John of the Cross (1547–1591)

Season of Falling Out of Stars

Spring takes a year and then it hurts
because I'm incomplete, which is
how you feel too. I let my shirts
pile up, swear I'll wash them, yet fizz
away like coke, can't clean up. For
some other time, I say, and dive
behind a book down on the floor.
I flop but Oh you're still alive
and I'm alive. Blood on the snow,
car bombs and a Tibetan shot
mumbling a prayer, but you are not
a TV ghost. How prison slow
your coming was! My love for you
dresses a gulag in nice blue.

A Bell in the Deep Mountain

Dante was right to ignore heaven
and put Francesca in a hell
of doves, young and not after seven
decades. Love, being the deep bell
in the wood, only rings on earth,
our glory hell, not in the sky.
We feel an unseen love at birth.
Then walk a day alone, and die
to no lucent inferno but
to nothing. Dante envied her,
her paradise. I want that hut
of one shared universe, her fir
tree on a mountain. Cast in shade,
I cast for bells before I fade.

Life of a Fool

Since all my life I've been a fool (a fool
I'm told or tell myself), keeping a wife
in hell and me in feverish double life
or rather half a life, keeping my cool
at work, everywhere hanging on, how can
I change? A fool's a fool. I hear a voice
saying be free, like born again, a man-
ly surge! Helpless the fool. It's been my choice
to wait. Calmly I witness time turn yellow
on my photograph. I hear a voice, it's your
words like a marble poplar or a cello
or Attic walks at dawn. Athenian friend,
exile binds us. Was I a fool to soar
happy with you? Or free, at last, descend.

Sewn Up Tight

The doctor takes a knife and cuts my arm
and scoops out a sebaceous cyst of wax.
Going home I stop for donuts to disarm
the nerves. I'm sewn up tight, and to relax
I read the sports page, hop back in the car
and cruise dopey to my room where I can't work
between codeine and ache, winter and far
frosty spring. This is the first time a quirk
of wrong growth put me under knives. It is
a start. I fall in bed, resting on one
side. I'm between seasons. No place. The bus-
iness of my health is fine. I can't complain.
My arm is clean. The vulgar soul inane-
ly lies alone, hoping for sleep by dawn.

The Vagrant Soul Is Lobster Red

These nights of winter darkening the soul
are penal. Soul? Dead word? A candle guide
of noon? She shines like an abandoned scroll
in Hebrew, staring from a ditch outside
a Russian ghetto, washed with sun. I try
to yank her out. The coldness digs into
the flame pit. As I fade, all questions cry
for answers. Always the same. Nothing to do
but wait for some blue apple tree of light!
Soul is the battered child of Abraham,
hangman of God. She hides. She is a white
thighbone of winter sky. Surrogate lamb
on fire. The vagrant soul is lobster red,
is nothing, brooding somewhere in my head.

Circling into Rainy Dawn

Hunger but not for food. I want to know
the white viola pits of light that climb
over the termites to the burn and slime
of dawn. Rain. Rain. Mud is a drum below
the sticks of thunder. I am itch and skin,
another sleepless bed with me the bag
of mind, the pink leather manbeast. I win
against the darkness (ignorance won't sag
into sleep), turning around white peace,
the obscure moon inside. Hunger keeps me
awake, alert and brooding. For release
from nervousness I sound my thoughts. But what
hope in loud words? Or rain? Or you deep tree
of faith? I am the bush, the dwarf, the rot.

Astronomy of a Snowflake

Each flake lunges at the tower windowpane
like a starving dog with white eyes zigzag-
ing on the gale. Illusion of a brain
with icy blood and needle bones, a rag
of burning slush around a star. Inside
the astronomy of crystals is a sphere
of atoms charted and electrified
in its own universe, with the fused power
and primal majesty to disappear
and blow the earth apart. Each flake, unique
and free, pounding willfully against the tower,
over the moaning trees of ice, drops like
billions of germs or people drop. I'm one
of them yet think I'm Galileo's sun.

The Hills of Java

After the blizzard there is calm. Winds spill
snowbirds from igloo trees, who hop on snow,
probing the crystals for invisible
bugs. Now, snow roads are soup and I can't go
to run up your stairs, knock, kiss you tonight,
all night. And soon? If soon, why do I feel
rotten as if the blizzard will congeal
into a new ice age of beardless light
and ghosts? And yet I nightdream, daydream of
your lips and belly. We are in a plane
floating East. Steles glow. We're walking on
a bank where blood once filled the river. Pain
of serene Buddhas smashed like toads. Our love
is sun. Hills are a throbbing gamelan!

Floating after You

You call at four a.m. to say your car
broke down. The water pump. I swim to you
like an armed Chinese fish to insular
abandoned childhood, boil the Cuban shrew
who even now stifles whatever joy
a woman has. And you declare it's spring
but you are sick. I'll heal you. Poplars sing
in verdant wind. An old Mexican toy
of orange glazes whistles you to play
and glues me to your mystery. And so peace
is freeing me to float even to Greece,
Ohio or Oaxaca. I seek the way
of Daniel dreamer among lions, yet where
are you? I flop and angels glut the air.

Canticle of Loss

While I lie on your chest, while you lie on
my chest and we are happy in the weak
twilight, we know that sweetest art. Comes dawn
and the alarm! I put the last antique
clay goddess in a carton, and before
the mirror, under Asian necklaces,
we look at us. Bodies. Soon to explore
malignancy of time. And our last kiss
is gone (like Albinoni's heavenly horn
whose joyful *sphairos* sickens me!). We race
through lyric back roads, swear high vows, embrace,
dazed in a coma till the plane. Then born
to us is cowardice and loss. We freeze
like penitents. The plane takes off. Time grows.

When the Apricots Are Ripe

I know the garden. Deer eat there, are shot
and haunt us with their flight. And when I lay
surprised by wheat, under the apricot,
by the white pigeon tower, happy in our day
of kisses, hair, in our huge night of cries,
of loving screams while memorizing sweet
thighs pulsing, suddenly the animal
harries us with its blood. I'm at your feet
but you are gone. I call. Dead phone. I fall
in the same grove. And deeper in the wood
I call. How like a fool I shake! Your eyes
are olive on the olive mountains, of
course deeper than white night, now black. With love
nowhere, I rush on fire, frozen for good.

Fumbling Down a Shaft

Defeated I am groping in my head
for words that fell like Alice down a shaft
stored with pornography and an unread,
inflated dream-soul popping up: a raft
of starless revelation. And I'm look-
ing for an unmysterious face. On or-
dinary days she tortures me. The book
is an acosmic mountain on black fire,
stinking with smoke, but no poignant gold core
of letters. Frantically I drop a wire
of seldom wisdom down to the unknown
bottom where lightning bangs the inner cell.
I'm like an ape before a burning stone,
a grotesque by a simple rose in hell.

Loneliness and Dreams of Living on a Fig Tree

There is a loneliness of runners, sea-
worm, morgue and starfish, and I envy those
awaking lovers or a Greek fig tree
wrestling with crows and wind and drought, who knows
nothing yet dries to victory over sun,
who feeds on oxides and the rain she stores
deep in her hair. I hear your arms, throat, nun
and nightingale of love. Jealous of doors,
I crawl the ceiling of my one-room sol-
itude: a fly confronting lunar space
or amber pools. I'm free to buzz or fall
to glue. I buzz crudely. You shiver but
sun warms our globe. We could live any place
happy. In a wild fig tree or white hut.

Domination of Miracle

The boy, skating wildly on the North Sea
frozen along a Danish strand, goes home
after inspecting polar gulls. There he
studies the Book of Wonders: killer foam
in the Red Sea, an old man smiting rocks
for water, words the finger of God penned
on holy stone. But why must human clocks
tick only forward? Desperately a friend
asks me if I believe in reincarnation.
I don't. Anyway, we'd forget, I tell
her. Time is law. Even that boy's elation
on the black ice is my concoction. Yet
nothing but miracles. Love is our hell
and miracle, burning till we forget.

A Fly

On this hot day of shame my body walks
in sweaty clothes with cuffs rolled at the elbow,
dreaming beyond the view where my eye balks—
a fly, trapped, craving space beyond the window.
Apathy. Habitude. Even the weather
puts the fire out. And daily this and that
calms my hill horse, confining it in leather,
and tames the moon, the nightly acrobat.
This humid weather seethes inside my flesh.
I see no dome of light, no diamond beach,
no holy God to halt the minute gun,
yet like the fly buzzing against the mesh
my body feels the sky it cannot reach
and craves the darkness of the alien sun.

The Black Hill

There are two ways to fail. (And failure is
the providence we come to when in time
we tumble out of consciousness to mis-
erable extinction.) One way is to climb
inside. The hill is black on a plateau
where iron moondogs screech like cables. Light
can't understand that darkness, yet black snow
thinks, spreads like thunder where I saw a white
heaven of calm seconds. The other way
climbs out to you, gambling on bliss, begins
with a look, words, and our huge walk above
the city. We are drifting gulls, two pins
through a slow century. I choose the love
out there. Help me. To make the black hill day.

Looking for Moths or Planets

Long ago I turned my bed to the hill
to look for moths or planets, anything
out there not me. I looked for you to fill
the Book of Seven Words, the opening
of horror when I jump in a small pond
to keep from feeling nothing. Words will do
to make love good. I break a nightly bond
with suicide and set my watch to blue
sirens of the squad cars. From tenement
to barn, I go on turning in my bed
and hope your face will turn. When we relent
and live on the charred hill, we float like bread
on Galilee. Long ago the wait was brief,
holy. Now long. I live by no belief.

The Peace of Pears

There is a glory in the peace of pears.
No thought. Under the skin its fibers grow
in a wet cosmic ring, in light which no
one sees. It doesn't scream when a worm tears
a hole in it. I scream. I'm full of worms
and of course hide the rot. I want the pause
and peace of pears unconscious of the germs
of time. The miracle. But then the laws
of nature shake the second free of light.
I am depressed, tense in this room, hanging numb
to a white memory dropping like a train
through a black ocean. On this nervous night
I see a pear: maybe in northern Maine.
A glow. I want to live till it has come.

My Heart Is in the East

My Heart Is in the East

My heart is in the East.
I stand at the edge of the West. How can I taste
what I eat? How can I enjoy foods?
How can I fulfill my vows of return
while Zion lies in the domain of Edom
and I am in the bonds of Arabia?
I could easily leave behind
forever all the good things of Spain
 for the glory of seeing the dust of our ruined shrine.

Judah Halevi (c.1075–1141)

Nothing

Until our birth we are our mother's age.
Then zero. Time begins again. I'm back
to zero now. Not time, for I've a page
stained with four hundred glasses of cognac
I've drunk to sleep. My start is solitude,
the strange divorce from history of a life
and family. Even pills don't calm a brood-
ing storm of memory. What is a wife
and child to solitude? I hold my breath
to act (I can't look back), and take a walk
into illusion. From an unclean bed
I think of whiteness. Sérifos. Good smoke
of sea fish. Peace. A friend. The death of death,
for I can dream. Only my heart is dead.

Zero

Birth is a rupture from an older being,
the death of union. I was born alone,
naked and not again. Naked, the on-
ly way to sleep, to love. But secret meanings,
like Mahadevi's god-drunk walk through fire
withering her young and naked body, work
only for saints. Godless, I am desire
for time, not sizzling death, for any quirk
of revelation, for a pilgrimage
like Chaucer's talky gang—to hear a tale
and go. Where's God? I've known only one sage
and he can't see outside, yet covets union
with a word of sand. I go toward black confusion,
to zero. Huge. No perfect last white jail.

Archaic Faces on the Wall

On Saturday the judge will tell me: "Go
to freedom." (Santorini once was green
like glassy pitchers, but the lava flow
scorched and froze the island in an unseen
time trap where the hill castle's chalky steps
circle down to the port.) The day before
the legal end, I say: "Come, any place,
even a city room for rent. We'll soar
windy like gulls. Alive." And yet no call
or easy babbling talk. Daydream? I kid
myself. Ancient terror of freedom. Again
the knife of freedom paints me on the wall
next to a tender face. Terror amid
the mouths—ours—poised and begging oxygen.

When Words Are Spinning in a Pit

My thinking wears me down. It never gets
away from me. But the Long March or scream
of *thálata* the sea!, when a Dane lets
a praying murderer live, when a night team
of *montoneros* blasts a bank, those acts,
flashy but wisely far, take me from me,
from clothes, from meals in crummy stores, from facts
of shallow nerves or myths of harmony
when words spin in a pit. Yet I am here,
and if I go I'm no one else, not you
or meandering Mao, and nature only when
night is all night. Don't be bitter. You fear
I'm sick and leave a continent. It's true,
I'm nowhere. Who is wise? I start again.

Into the Meadow of Absence

I see. Am not the vision. Where I am
is not the body living in a hut
in Cold Mountain pine groves, or one that swam
near Sodom in the bromine slime that cut
its thighs and burned its vision to the cry
of Samson's noon. I'm not that dark, that rare
high Asian solitude or alibi
of body plotting with the photosphere
for rapture in the ultraviolet air!
Secretly now, I've come into the clear
meadow of absence, to the dumbfound shade
of being behind the eyes, the punctured dream
of sun outside. Perfect, in terror, I seem
to be. But where I look all bodies fade.

How and Why I Became a Mime

Only twenty I looked at dark inside
for one year. No. I lost my eyes and came
to desolate hell, the hill of suicide
of thought. Words lost their act. I felt no flame,
a continent from eyes or passion. Who
was making talk? What polar icecap in
my scalp was me? From looking in, I knew
the secret hoax. Then, rocketing to the skin
I tumbled backward, lost from the dead eye
looking at me. Ice picks of light! But no
bottom or circus cannon to fly me out.
Talking, the good actor, I wriggled dry.
Am I now? Only twenty years or so
from dark, I mime the gray angel of doubt.

A Guy Eating Tomato Salad by the Grape-Eternal Sea

A table on an island. And a man
with his tomato salad, overhear-
ing screams inside the smoky kitchen. An
eternal grape sea burns around his sphere
of longing for the wheat between her thighs,
for cherry nipples flagrant in the sun,
that naked woman with a flute, laugh, eyes
hiding the pumice cave. For him a nun
moon-bellied of remote mad blood. And so
he pounds Cyclopean walls and then forgets
what talking is, lies like red ants below
the blue air trapping him to obscure birth
on the floor. I'm in *him*. And when he sweats
I'm near his skin, scheming to be the earth.

On the Crater of Thera

Deeper into the island. Patience. Here
on the white wing of the volcano, we
almost float. Windy light. Not out of fear
but from infidel hope, I came to see
the source of ancient lava. Dusty and dry.
I bring you bread, a silver bracelet, and
myself. Vagueness of the volcanic eye
dead and watching. Patience. The Holy Land
is always with the other. Our old truck crawls
pounding up to the village. We are dust
but a beginning, always sad, or in
the dusk of peace. Santorini. I must
wait like the crater. It erupts, it falls.
Will I eat bread with you? The statues grin.

Apollo in Náxos

Huge kouros on its back and not alive,
not even finished, but the eyes are blur
of mountains behind mountains under five
layers of mist; the huge lips are a slur
of rocky lust, never to kiss or talk.
Life as stone is simple: the mammoth arm
intense yet calm in the gold marble lock
of time. I'm never still and seldom calm
and feel a fly's six twitching legs. The dark
profiles of mountains of the night are never
enough to burn a way of gold, a spark
of cosmic life. The soul is soul, stone stone.
The kouros stares into the air forever,
a phantom of live rock. We're each alone.

Cyclops in Sérifos

Cyclops looks up to fire. The sun returns
his gaze, and figs, sea, wild carnations glow
under its wings of dawn! The monster spurns
reflection. Born of words, he doesn't know
the will of time wasting the wildest thighs,
the myth of death which only haunts the blood
of meditative creatures. Though time lies
in space, rotting the giant's ponderous food
and butchered eye, my thought secretly gives
a life to Cyclops. Why should vulgate sun
constrict my dream or time erode the myth
of groping Cyclops? Time will blur us with
its wing of night (we are its fugitives).
The light in us is all of time. Then gone.

Monastery at Amorgós

Two bodies in a bed is home. The rest
is exile. Freedom from the heart. To be
alone and suffer jet lag in the quest
of revelation. White over the sea
like a pancake against the cliff, the old
dazzling Byzantine monastery. I
share raki with four monks. But the dark gold
around the head of Mary is the cry
of inept beauty, sullen isolation.
The mother on a piece of wood. Her grave
permanence flows across the painted child.
I look down at the sea. We're each a slave
to nothing but the air. Two bodies exiled
from Mary's heaven. Free. Windy creation.

Motorcycle Spill after Sunset on the Way Back to Port in Ariadne's Náxos

Time is always losing itself. The past
is loss, the future never found. And yet
I circle ancient sites near an old cast
of marble actors feigning grubby time.
My time has come. Against the cold sunset
I gulp hot milk, ride back on a dark road,
no moon, my headlights gone, and start to mime
Hell's Angels flying. The bike flips. The load
of chrome and plastic lands on me. My God!
What a farcical exit! Bloody death is not
choosy or decorous. Without a nod
from hell or heaven, I get up, an actor
inventing actors, comically doomed, caught
in time, a slob on stage with no director.

Luminous Experience of a Brain Scan

An hour ago the nurse shot technetium
into my arm. At last this human mud
is light itself—no eye seeking a crumb
of mystery elsewhere. Radioactive blood.
Rigid I press my face against a screen
and gamma rays reveal the pilgrimage
through every catacomb, scanning unseen
vessels and deadly pools. A squiggly page
shows me inside: ravines of fear, a hill
of wordy hope, a squawking bumpy map
of love, the starry motorcycle spill.
"Nurse, what news from my inner tree of night?"
"You're scintillating!" But the glowing sap
can't see itself. Only the mind sees light.

Seconds of the Last Dream

The nightmare. Paradise of that last peace
when the heart clots, but the still sparking brain
euphorically invents the angeled plain
of heaven. Seconds of the dream release
the battered body: amputated limbs
perform harmoniously in place, the blind
see through their cataracts, the deaf hear hymns
of ocean rocking on its clams, the mind
is free of substance, leaping to the end
of time. But dew fields of delirium
become a waste of dog stars and contend
with hybrid fingers swallowing the light.
The mouth of death! The monsters of that night
assemble now. Infernal cries. Then numb.

A Brother Gone

Death is the end of dying, when, I guess,
time is only for others, when the wait
ends stillborn, underground. Death is the chess
game of the knight and bishop, and the fate
of wooden and of human kings. The move
traps us, and breath is blocked. Holding his hand,
I sought the pulse but heard the silence prove
a brother gone. His ghost was coldly planned
forever by his failure to survive
the famine of our greedy lords. Why fake
the prophecy of moons? We all are drawn
into that dread—known only while alive.
Death proves we are a breath and not a pawn.
With luck we soar a while on earth. Then wake.

A Midnight Car Death in Buenos Aires

Before God made the world he had to find
the letters, which were also numbers, so
with *ayin*, meaning *eye*, he made the mind,
the visionary tree. The Street of Ho-
ly Faith is free of bombs, and Mario talks
about the circular Kabbalah. Crash!
Our eyes race to a corpse, a man like rocks
against a blood horizon; his eyes trash,
which a truck hauls away. A woman hugs
a lamp post, shrieking. In his wisdom, God
descends to clean the world, washing the street
with thunderous rain. We dash upstairs to eat
with Viviana, age six, and on red rugs
we dance and drink and joke, weary of fraud.

Coming Back to You in Java

It's not too late to fail with words, or go
out to the waking East where the day's eye,
daisy, Mata Hari sun, looms. Hello
dawn. I construct the golden butterfly
of light across the holy city and
through bead-door pharmacies, on Muslim domes:
religious eyes scanning the motherland
of air, the blue mysterious aerodromes
on fire that blind a telephoto lens.
I go because of pathos, not belief,
a passion lost each night, but which your voice
and vision in the East restores in brief
illusion. Not too late to wake. The choice
is hope or truth, and words can't reach those ends.

On Thursday under the Oxygen Mask

To die is not so bad. I hold my breath
and feel the pounding power of buffaloes
floating over the pillow. The ninetieth
stumbles and laughs. Violet fire on its nose
kindles the sheets. I feel nice, calm, with heat
of thighs consuming thighs like thunder of
a Haitian morning growing into sweet
intolerable beauty! Furious, then
I shoot up in the absolute throat of love,
but time falls out as brain waves let me down.
Old and animal wise, I try to grope
back through the blood. Blue caves. My idiot crown
shines wrong. I drop through April oxygen
and know the secret hole where black is hope.

Janitor in the Men's Room

Night shift in Ballantine. The teeth of young
leopards are broken. Our days on earth fade
like whims of knock-kneed Peter, whose fat tongue
protrudes a bit, who is, like us, a shade
against the noon and poor in hope. No one
will hold my hairy brother of the weeds
out to be washed in rain, to wear the sun
over his boils. In the men's room he feeds
on candy bars. His is the fate of dice,
a terrible roll. Beautiful creatures stray
on the ocean floor. Governors have no
authority to handle paradise
or vacant souls. Pete is the castaway
circling, like us, under the circling crow.

A Long Walk through the Night Continent

There is no end to time—nor can it stop
to pin a groan or freeze the instant of
ejaculation or conserve the love
of lovers glorified down in the shop
of memory, which is often closed. No end
yet airport crowds still vanish in the rain
(as if they never were) or the white crane
vanishes in white mist. At night we spend
the darkness walking alien roads alone
with beasts who don't appear. In the bush, in
the eye of Africa, we feel the strange
cold of the panther sky, its teeth, the moan
of wildebeest, and time enforcing chang-
ing plenitude. One night we will have been.

Abandonment on Earth

Why was I born as me? I cannot curse
or bless that supreme accident, unique
to each of us. I shower and the universe
is mine and not enough. The weak
curtain against the rain is like a tent
perched on an iceberg, or a tin fishhook
against a shark, or one bag of cement
to devise heaven's floor and know the book
of wisdom from that loft of blue. My head
is not enough. If there were God, at least
a soul, this tiny world of me would have
a dream of other circles. I'm the beast
who knows he is a beast, digging for love
to heat me with good light before I'm dead.

The Genesis of Clouds

Puffing up from test tubes pleasing a witch
or spiraling by Venus, clouds were first
spotted in China around mountains which
were airy like the haze. Earth rolled immersed
in wash, light as rice paper. Wang Wei made
transparent birds. He sang in a small hut,
lazy or a bit drunk, already gray
and bald, his head among the clouds not cut
away from the unmeditating sky.
Raw over rocks in Patagonia, wind
herds sheep across the brutal blue in loud
silence, while here in Brandon one huge thigh
of color mystifies the disciplined
surprise of twilight from a crystal cloud.

Staying Up Late in a Big Empty House in Hamilton, N.Y., Where Rain Comes Late to Keep Me Company

About three every morning like a mole
I move with glass eyes, dreaming up a path
of light, stumbling with hot milk toward the bath
where futilely I finger glass. No soul
floats on the mirror. Souls don't come with eyes,
but the insomniac sees just her green face.
Rain starts to chew the roof and unifies
the forest. Sound of plankton in the mouth
of whales. Rain. Rain. And suddenly the moss
of darkness clears to a blue pearl! The light
invented, while I sit on dirty clothes,
concocting dream. In blurry indecision
I climb in bed and fall like rain from sight
where neither soul nor glasses fix my vision.

A Bit Drunk I Become Melancholy and Melodramatic, Thinking of Loss, Quiet, and Exits

I fear the end. Time without your arms. When
our wonder, alchemy and sleep below
the azure tied-quilt, when the cyclamen
among the rocks, the salt and fire, are no
more ours. Open the window. I run out
clamoring for you who gave the dust a tongue
and night the sun. When dust becomes the shout
of desolation, when the rain among
the hands of continents is ice, I tell
myself there is no nightingale in hell
but blizzards and a rose. Though I am shy
before a guillotine or butchered deer,
it's peace I fear, not hell. My alibi
is shit. Double death looms. I sip my beer.

Hotel Bed of Hope

Often I climb out on a ledge and look
back to a child who dreamt he'd never leave
the earth before knowing the secret book
which has no word, but is the fire of Eve
refusing God, choosing to eat and live
with death. I look for her so we can share
our ignorance. Or like a fugitive
from time, from thought, from me, I climb the air
and vanish in a light darkening all
of thundering ego in a diamond ball
of peace rebounding through the universe!
But then I wake to sanity and hell.
We are alone, everyone in a hotel
of hope until the morning of the hearse.

Kingdom of the Poor

Alive. My kingdom. Shared by dogs and birds,
booming out in the dark until they cut
our lines. When they hanged Bhutto his last words
were "Lord, I'm innocent." Like any mutt
who's put to sleep, he is extinguished. I'm
alive, sipping hot milk with honey so
I can black out a while and let the time
of lion vision feed what I can't know
awake. My land is really poor, for like
the rest I'm isolated, with my share
of caustic grief. I groan. Yet times I quake
with love, alive like glaciers. Startled air
is spirit. Then I grab the hills and hike
with startled mice and mutts, and hope to wake.

The Angel

One night I felt so weak I understood
the plea, the cry into the self, the drop
below the skin of reason to the shop
of stars and idiots wandering a wood
like beggars for a lord. Even a priest
was not a liar. But I came back to air
and me, and the abomination ceased
which almost made me leap into the prayer
of the insane. I lose my loss, and am
a talking word, a ghost trying to shed
the dignity of being. To be no one
at last. Only the angel keeps the sun
alive with light I cannot pray to, damn
or love. The angel. Passion of the dead.

A Bird of Paper in New Haven

What vision is there in a weather vane?
Old cars are leaving thicker trails of smoke,
the light is feeble as a twilight train
is crawling to the sun's discolored yolk.
At home I am walled in, the blinds are down,
cracks on the windy doors are held in clay.
The drunks are sleeping in their icy gown
of bags and papers. On this Saturday,
against the night, the weather bird is snow
and slush and legend in the midnight noon,
yet passing through the unreflective sphere
the vane floats upward near the chariot moon
of waters. Then, beyond the brain's frontier,
the paper bird assumes its sickly glow.

My Heart Is in the East

My heart is in the East where wind has scent
of nard and apple in its wings. Here at
the edge I wonder why the element
of ordinary wonder is a flat
mere plank on which I cannot float to you.
Here is no sea. And no moonland gazelle
runs on wine clouds by Sinai hills. Here dew
outside my humid cottage has a smell
of ecstasy imagined. No release
from combat, gossip or the disciplined
ambition for mere gold. I long to go
into the East of myrrh and heather peace,
of wonder and its courage, and to know
my heart in prison feels that apple wind.

On the Floor of the Creation

Sirens

Sirens are singing monsters of the sea,
With many voices and varied melody.
Often the reckless sailors passing near
Are sung to sleep with sweetness in their ear,
 And ships are wrecked and all aboard are drowned.
Although the mariners who perished found
A lovely virgin from above the waist—
Below, birdlegs were monstrously misplaced.

Bestiary of Bishop Theobaldus (13th–14th c.)

Sirens

Sirens are singing monsters of the sea
who live on mountains in the north. A bridge
connects two peaks, and from that height I see
their yellow eyes: star beacons on the ridge,
longing to shake me into the abyss.
Their passion fills my ears. I've thrown away
the wax, and despite trembling cowardice
I hear the river in their throats. My way
is clear. Their fatal weapon is my choice.
The singing pierces the protective fan
of lead under my clothes. Their wings explode
like virtue cracking through a Puritan.
Easy as consciousness, I jump, a toad
into the waters of their cloudy voice.

Gypsy the Cat

Why am I sad for you when suddenly
your yellow eyes are glaring from the rug
of Persia with its moons of memory?
Expressionless, as if iced by the drug
from the dwarf forest in your bestial eyes,
you simply gleam. I am the one who can't
feel peace. Yet I am hurt before your size,
your wordless brain, the pitifully scant
years of a life. Compassion for a cat?
Why not for lifeless heaven holding the sun's
jasmine of light that falls on every being
for its few days? I am the pitied thing
hiding in you. Your yellow presence stuns.

Deaths of Gandhi

As Gandhi fell he blessed the man who shot
him. Billy blessed Captain Vere before he leapt
through the black rose of morning. The garrote
silenced those Simbas who would not accept
Amin's last orders to fight on. Their screams
greeted the troops outside Busia. The ax
hit uncorrupted Robespierre, whose teams
of mullahs ordered death to unholy packs
of the Shah's dogs. Murder is so remote,
like circus stars who shine a while before
they lose their skill. Maybe one can die drunk,
an innocent far from the butchered throat
of a small Asian child. One day the monk,
soldier and fly will sleep on the same floor.

A Book of Glass

Milton invented thunder and the wood
of paradise, ambrosial foliage. His
dead eyes expanded stars. A simple bud
of passion is my hope, its genesis
in unvolcanic surf inside. No scream
of trumpets. I seek focus and each drum
begs calm. Inspecting me I'm what I seem:
still water in a pit, aquarium
of an eyelidless fish darting with scarred
self-judging glares, yet lucky to be look-
ing for enigmas. Blessed Spinoza stayed
locked in his shop, died young, and never shared
his reasoned God of Nature. Scribe to a book
of glass, my passion is unfocused shade.

Spinoza's White Telegram

Spinoza reasoned away miracle,
yet faith like Andean fog holds mystery
and mountain joy in us. Impossible
is easy. Apples on a lunar tree
shiver like cows obeying natural law.
We kiss in evening rain. Oblivion
and power. Our love swells happily like straw
soaking in water between stars. But gone,
when hope is gone, we drop alone. I am
illiterate, lie down too dumb to die
or crawl out of infernal grass, the wrong
meadow of lethargy. Heaven's the lie
of God, but faith, Spinoza's Telegram
of Nature, reads: MAKE LOVE ON EARTH. SO LONG.

Saul the Tentmaker

What agony to read your letters, Saul,
poignant, simple, and elegant. You lost
none of your rage when you turned into Paul
and sacked Jerusalem. The holocaust
by the apostles cannot match the fire
judgment for your people, whom you fought
in synagogues from Antioch, Kos and Tyre
to Rome. You made the Christ Iscariot.
But Judas grieved and hanged himself; you strung
your people from Rome's cross. What agony
to bear the miracles of faith, to hear
the rhapsody of one who made his tongue
an instrument of love through glass, dimly,
who veiled the wife and made his brother fear.

Letter to the Janitors

Companions of the dust and yellow broom
with which you face the trash, friends of the door
and corridor, when every sleeping room
is filled, you wake the coast of Labrador,
dusting the snow, cleaning the icehills bright
as sun. No stain escapes your cloth. The wind
brushes the whiskers of the seals. Your night
of mops and toilet bowls is disciplined
to purity. Companions of the key,
you go where heroes dread the bats and mud
slopped on the floor, where only artists and
a drifter come alive. You cleaned the blood
where Romans smeared the cross. The agony
of cans and boredom scrubs out in your hand.

Letter to the Universe

How did the face of all the universe
cause me? My ancestry is infinite.
The carbons in the slime became my nurse
and evolution rolled with Jesuit
precision, narrowing to a family tree
on which I am a name, a voice, a dot
loafing in time, irrevocably free
of miracle. The chance of flesh and thought
happened to me. I never chose to join
this being. You chose my parents and their birth,
the feet I wear, my brain, even the light
and arms of women and my secret loin-
to-loin warm love, my cry, explosion, earth
to earth! You *caused* me but I make my night.

The Dope on Willis

I see him clearly now, the one you call
Willis. You know him as slow mercury
in glass. He fades like mudprints on a hall
or vanishes in the Sudan. And he
is your good friend (not mine), kind like hot foam
on morning beards, courageous, never cool
like rain leaking into the catacomb
of passions where he hides, shading the fool
from public light. Obsessed? Yes, with the word,
soul mask. He'll talk you crazy and spend whole
centuries as my scribe. I follow him
along the street. His mind is idly blurred
with café dreams of texts. In that black, slim
folder, I am the one he can't control.

A Writer Gives His Fingers a Tip

Enough. Get off the keys. Go home and hold
a glass of tea and think of tinkering
with apples, clits and tits. Pick up an old
Manila *santo,* feel its wooden being
through the glass eyes, and jet back to the shop
in Spain where workers in Sevilla cut
a dumb dazed face of Christ and carved a drop
of blood against its alabaster skin.
Then play with sleep: hug the half moon, the hill,
the hot invented hips, swim in the inn
of dream until you plunge. You never fill
the hand. Rain never falls to the end of child-
hood. Peace calms tantrums. In your yellow hut,
touch airy thighs of angels and come mild.

Dream Is Light

My friends have slipped into the mine of dawn
like the old aunts. My solitude is queer:
a flash of blues, and now I'm walking on
a milk bottle shard wall. Bloody, I hear
the rain aching peacefully in my lungs.
Out there, Plotinos said, even a face
is just illusion. No. Visionary tongues,
Isaiah or surrealists, can't erase
the world. It is. I bump into its air,
come near its lovers, breakfast on its ink
of bookworm secrets turning into dream.
I need to dream. Dream also is. A wink
withers the world and corpses outlaw prayer,
but dream is light. Then all the mountains scream.

The Wind of Dream

Dream is the mind's reality, the smell
of love invented, horses on the ice
of moonlakes or the biblical gazelle
bounding on whirlwind hills, the paradise
of night, the lake creating lakes, a storm
of solitary monsters yellow like
the salt of daybreak. Dream is chloroform
for time outside, a sleep of history, dike
against river rats floating in with teeth
and hair. I eat a sky of tripe, but words
(the wind of dream) combat the sickness of
my mouth. Words lie unsaid. High underneath
their light, I wake before a face of love.
Words heal like lyres or drums or mockingbirds.

In Mud or Song or Whistling Dew

Between that terror we can never know
before and after being, between the non-
sense of that stellar time, when the sun's O!
of now is breath between that zero dawn
on either side, I have an appetite
for life, for plainness, for the clang of reason,
a temple bell in which all time is light
resounding in one flash. The song. The treason
of biology is doom, is absolute,
and neither ancestors nor printed verse
are life or song. I bound like Chaplin to
a puddle, a bohemian universe
of tramps. In mud or song or whistling dew
I am a secret crazy, loud, glad. Then mute.

The Panther

The panther has no mission but her night
of milk and moon. I float from bed. Pad down
into the room where lemons are the light
of asteroids, hungry in the sepia brown
and melancholy space, the basement where
like birth I start. The blood outside is clouds;
inside my chest the gold forest of hair
grows out of beads of grease. These are the shrouds
around the ruby. Wondrously she came:
a voice. Violet night is honey. I break
the easy lock and follow the command
of the moonwind, far lake of fire, the hand,
roar, the dark ruby panther! Only flame
of her dark heart sings, sings. I live to wake.

Animal Song

Although I smell a fatal day when moths
pollute the blood with evening wings, when smell
of sheets and bedpans and the waxen cloths
on corpses pound me into lobster hell,
I sigh before the uninfected song
of watercress, of migratory hawks
and lunar hymns. Half of me is sick, wrong
with morbid icons of tall plaza clocks
lunging ahead, honking, when every ear
is stone, and yet I dance before the cry
of leafy sun and gentle hands, when cats
are leopards in the apple trees. While rats
and turnips crow convulsively, I sigh
before the mountain voice of vagrant deer.

Enigma of a Dog before the Ruby

After less than a million years on earth,
I laugh, reason, stand up and even jog.
The species grows. I know I pay my birth
with death and am a kinsman to a dog
before the ruby of the absolute dark,
leaving my space for children who will spring
forever like the Peking Man. Their ark
will float a hundred years. Then foundering
on daybreak, vague, abstract like history,
their crania bones will crease some other cave
under a village near Beijing. To be
a while and go: it's sad but not absurd.
The enigma is the force. Its child, its slave,
I'm freed by love, the mystery light, its verb.

Necklace in the Earth

The face of love—now gone so long the tree
of life with eight Kabbalah limbs has fruit
unread, unseen—holds her night mystery
of flame buried around the old taproot
of faith, a necklace in the earth. The air
is ripe with plums, finite globes (Bruno burned
for counting suns beyond our sun). I stare
out to the face. From chaos slowly I've learned
the waters which the aleph tamed, the face
which anciently was rain. Slowly I've come
to glaciers under grass, to faces in
a bakery, lips printed on shirts. I've been
gone long from love, but doped on opium
of buried light I dream our holy space.

Wondrous Light

It's wondrous to be alive, yet hard to live,
although a deeper peace hovers in clouds,
under the bulb of consciousness, to give
the surface air sublunar light. Shrouds
of wedding veils are tombs of ice. The cry
of infants bleating peace, peace, peace repeats
the tyranny of dream. Dominions die
like wars. A roach lives because it meets
the eyeballs Kafka drew. I am a man
of elemental hungers with a moth
of anguish in my belly, a professor
of complicated noise, of scarlet cloth
whose letter galls. It's hard to live. But lesser
light is white soul. I'm near it when I can.

Stinking in Paradise

Out of the depths I cry against the dark,
for darkness is the laboratory in
the brain, is airless firmament, an ark
in which I float my life remote: a pin
in the black dew of wilderness. The lion
stinking in paradise, crows in the sweet
herbfields of hell, the whirlwind freezing Zion
as a stalagmite sun, the trumpet heat
from one cold lark of morning fade like grapes
hanging over the farthest sea or pears
inside the pores of night. I fume against
our god and his dark sword, who always fenced
the light outside. The ray of love escapes.
Breathing, I'm almost happy on the stairs.

What the Lungs Know

The dream asleep is primitive. Awake
she hungers for all forms of light: as milk
when bodies love, merging in the daybreak
of copulation when their bones are silk
of clouds over a snowflake of blue trees,
when limbs rocket upward to the first hands
of dawn. As finite soul draws light like cheese
into the lungs. Skymilk! Her mouth commands
the air, sucking the rays. Words are poor scars
of imprecision when the spirit clamors
for veins to ache, flooding with the milk glow
of firmament below the skin. Like jars
holding angelic butterflies, lungs know
a thrashing worm of light, and spirit stammers.

There Comes a Sea of Milk

Peace is the sea, the still-as-sunlight sea
high on the firmament: garden of air
on waters still. After the agony
of love, the sweat of bodies beyond care
of pain, the seed of their creation hangs
like a mosquito near a midnight face,
tormenting till its murder, till the gangs
of shrieking plazas cease. The atomic lace
of stillness is a sheet, butterfly silk
on bellies as fire nipples join. First screams
creating screams; then comes a sea of milk.
Peace is the sea, the still-as-sunlight sky
of spirit in a cup of sweating dreams
burning the loins and brains and ocean eye.

Horn of Darkness

The shade of revelation was the sun
flooding the night. The sun, the star of grace,
slipped secretly through blood. Oblivion
and light. The shade was gone. Although his face,
moving over the deep of memory,
is there and comes with fire from the one tree
beyond the salt of stars. Hot with the glare
of shadow, cold with rage against the walls
of universal time, the tap of air,
of life, I see his shade. Why does he play
with creatures wakened to their solitude?
And why not let us darken on our way
to nowhere, into salt, to the odd food
of love? Always, the horn of darkness calls.

Lamp of Darkness

Time loses out in object and in friend.
From birth our time is number, and each day
is one sky nearer doom. Clearly the end
is cryptic loss when knowledge, love, the way
are equally irrelevant. But now
I make a village out of solitude.
Loss is technology of pain, the Tao
of nightmare and remorse. Foolish I brood
on public holocaust, a private camp
of suicide, a manic brother's grave,
lovers gone into gray. Horror of loss
sickens the flesh and scours the mind. I toss
a switch. It's dark. Naked I dive and rave
through hell, hoping for darkness as a lamp.

The Lamp

The lamp is everywhere, lighting the stag,
the lily and the sons and daughter of
the paper sun, the ink greening the rage
of memory. Of course the lamp is love.
But how to wake? Love is invented shad-
ow of a shadow. Wasps and worms. At night,
weak vision, but the lamp creates the mad
and reasoned rose, its lips in which the light
folds deep as Africa, black as the globe.
I own one body and a mortal soul
in whom the eye is a dead moon, a hole
of dust, the wake of flame. The orphan Job
called for the Lord. I call for fire, wait long
for fire, to see the rose open in song.

On the Floor of the Creation

I wait. Is there a second when we do
not wait? Quevedo made a man so thin
he was a fork, with rats housed in one shoe,
roaches rooming in the other. Yet in
his heart already yellowing like teeth,
he dreamt of shining at the court. We wait
(in Romance it means *hope*) but underneath
the coming (never here) of desolate
and flaming death is the sad going (never gone)
of every second since the flood at Ur.
I pull the shade. Sun. Suddenly the damp
Midwest is Babylon. I'm on the floor
of the Creation, under a clay lamp,
a child, captive to hope, scheming at dawn.

HISTORY III

Gospel of Clouds

Written in the Mountains in Early Autumn

I'm talentless and dare not inflict myself on this bright reign.
Perhaps I'll go to the East River and mend my old fence.
I don't blame Shang Ping for marrying off his children early;
rather, I think Master Tao Yuanming left office too late.
With a cricket's cry autumn abruptly falls on my thatched hall.
The thin haze of evening is saddened with the whine
     of cicadas.
No one calls. My cane gate is desolate.
Alone in the empty forest, I have an appointment
     with white clouds.

Wang Wei (701–761)

A Secret Truth

The secret of the universe is not
a truth, illumination of a wor7d
or hidden face. Yet look. Plotinos got
his vision of the sun inside and heard
it by becoming one with it. He was
the unseen, unheard, other soul. The sounds
of quiet boom. Dickinson heard a fly buzz
blue, stumbling, when she died; it zipped around
her head until the windows failed. A sleuth
of soul and body will find clues. Yet no
one knows. It's sad. I would say tragic, but
the sun exists and we exist. We go
and light goes on. We live inside with what
burns up the soul. For some days we are truth.

Gospel of Clouds

Seizure

To me he seems like a god
the man who sits facing you
and hears you near as you speak
and softly laugh

in a sweet echo that jolts
the heart in my ribs. For now
as I look at you my voice
is empty and

can say nothing as my tongue
cracks and slender fire is quick
under my skin. My eyes are dead
to light, my ears

pound, and sweat pours over me.
I convulse, greener than grass,
and feel my mind slip as I
go close to death,

yet, being poor, I must suffer
everything.

Sappho (7th–6th centuries B.C.)

Gospel of Clouds

On cloudy Sundays clouds are in my heart
as if my brother came, as if the rain
lingered among the mushrooms and the art
of freedom washed into the murder train
or rinsed the peat bog soldiers of the camp.
On cloudy Sundays clouds are with Joe Hill
(last night I dreamt he was alive); the tramp
was mining clouds for thunder. And uphill
into the clouds I feel that time descends,
as if my mother came, as if the moon
were flowering between the thighs of friends
and gave us fire. On Sundays when the swan
of death circles my heart, the cloudy noon
rolls me gaping like dice, though I am gone.

Yellow Cottage

The yellow cottage in the woods is sun
among the cherry trees, a clapboard glass
on which the father fire becomes a fawn
startled in August. Hands of uncut grass
finger the windows' black abandonment.
Mr. Ketcham the drunk, dead on the floor,
was dropped wet in the earth of white Vermont
and in the dark ferments. But is there more?
A soul? Or hope of secret space? Was he
translated to the chamber of the stars,
the crystal cottage where the fire and dew
of heaven feed the farmer? Two old cars
are rotting in the weeds. Mr. Ketcham's tree
of life is dreamless, still, and earthly blue.

Quaker Love

The Shakers, who died out for lack of love
in sheets, made beds and chairs erect and plain,
and Friday nights they shook the rafters of
their hall with song and danced away the pain
of stark abstention. With a Quaker crew
I go to Mexico to dig some holes
and nail some wooden seats to shit into
so Zapotecs can squat and learn our roles
of hygiene. Then I quake with you. To see,
to hear, to touch, to kiss, to die with thee
in wildest sympathy! Turn off the light.
Bodies are all we are. After still night
comes birth, some light, the vast forgetting and
the blows of love. Sleep, sleep and hold my hand.

If I Could Phone the Soul

The night is beautiful. I live alone
and hope. It's better than to be the king
of rainy nations. Yet if I could phone
the soul, my soul, your soul, or see my being,
if I could sleep outside of time a while
and know why I am ticking toward a sleep
where time will fail (at least for me), I'd smile.
I smile right now, which means I groan, I creep
with shame because I'll always be a fool.
The night is beautiful. I pray. I lie.
I love. I'm happy. Everyone is poor,
especially the king of rain whose rule
drops me dead on a moon where I can't die.
I'm stupid. Love is you. We have no cure.

Walt Whitman and the Lonely

Even Walt Whitman—hugging continents
and lovers, singing of himself—was lonely.
His hungers for the earth were arguments
of isolation. Fame and book were only
the grass of need. I eat my meals alone
and dream the world inside a glove of nerves.
Am lonely in the bed, the room. The phone
is mere connection. Solitude preserves
immaculate distinction. And I ask:
how can a friend, unconscious from a stroke,
keep talking to the room behind a mask
until the gases of the body choke?
Walt felt the coldness between star and star,
sang for the lonely who are far and far.

Vagrants

The sad are lucky for they feel and know
they have a being, because it aches. The loss
of love is common malady. I go
shabbily to a loft, and ring. Friends toss
a key in a white sock down from the sky.
Climbing the warehouse stairs, I smell the cat-
piss in the trash and feel the rain or sigh
of rags and vagrants in Penn Station at
the phone booths. I am desolate not sick
(for age has not yet rammed its plumber's snake
into a heart of deathbed wisdom), yet
the rays of lofty sun and women prick
my heart. Climbing endlessly high, upset
by peace, I drown unsweetly in its lake.

Fools of Love

Perhaps I cannot sleep because I need
to feel the night. To hear its wash. To glance
at mother death, the clam of time, her seed
of black ice glowing through my ignorance.
My genesis is strangely a command:
the wondering of the fool of love, his ship
of wandering fools. They're mad, their only land
a starving deck. I'm sane, but choose the trip
of ignorance because the night is long
and sleep comes only after love; and since
I cannot sleep, the fool of love in me
agrees to sail and wonder. Yes, the prince
of peace lies drowned. I hear death's unheard gong
yet feel love's faces moving on the sea.

Night of the Burning Manuscript

for Ryan White, Hoosier

The night his manuscript burnt up he screamed.
It's true. It tumbled from his arms, and fell
anonymous like trash in fire. It gleamed
a second. So the boy, fresh as a bell,
bleeding with AIDS, who will not breathe the sun
of this old century, then modestly
(despite the Trumps and Jackson stars of fun
and Mr. Reagan's patronizing plea
"for tolerance") drops weak and young and vast
and dies. And other victims? Yes. Each city
condemns the basement where the mice and poor
live by the furnace. Ryan, a boy, cast
his letters into fire and slipped past pity
of silent lips to fade in viral war.

Meadow of Flaming Children

Out in the wind I asked a pine
how I could love and it consoled
me quietly. I drank some wine
and the young meadow wisely told
me I was mad. The morning East
was red with war, and coughing planes
squabbled like pigeons at a feast
of flaming children, and the rains
flooded Eden and Ur. Out in
the gale I asked an oak how I
could die, and thunder in the hills
blew up the moon. I drank some gin
and stupidly began to cry
for peace and pray to daffodils.

We Shiver Once

Oriental like the morning sun,
a rose is growing in the wall
as flagrant as a murdered nun
in Salvador. The biblical
Savior is out of print and can't
restore her eyes of rotting blue,
nor dissipate a nuclear chant
of bombs, nor mend the ozone. True
to dust (before the sky falls in,
pinning us underground), a rose,
a beast, a nun follow one day
of life before they decompose.
Oriental like the Buddha's way,
we shiver once and we have been.

Gospel of Lies

Comrade illusion, I embrace you like
a tuba. Gold and false. My hero Don
Quijote rose up mad and set his pike
against the gales of mills and monsters on
the wasteland of La Mancha. Jesus al-
so toured, performing magic, and he gave
his life so we might drink the alcohol
of heaven, drink the light and be no slave
of truth. Even the Buddha found a way
to free the unsubstantial self and fly
inside a dream of sun. Until the sun
was gone Quijano lived the noble lie
of lunacy: the poor man with a day
of grace and fire. Then true oblivion.

A Cup of Tea

Death governed once before and almost took
forever till its tyranny was up
and I was born. Yet the scene's hard to look
at with remorse. In a spaceless, vast cup
of nothing, a primordial tea was boiled
with spices making me, and now I see
the other nothing and my wait is spoiled
by brooding on that last eternity
of absence. Life is now. And so why care
about a time I'll never feel? Or night
that was when I was not? I drink a bell
of soul punch, a concoction made of light
from a dumb angel gasping in a hell
forever now. My faith keeps gulping air.

Smell of Being

Wake? Yes. Please call with shocking light. I won't
say no. I look for you at every pause,
in panic, shops, in lips. Vomit. But don't
ask me to trade the world for you, because
I won't. To wake. But not to lose my stink-
ing body and foul gluttony for sun,
sex, reason. Is it either/or? A wink
of fire will do to split an iceberg on
a mote of salt and hear its neutrons spin
in planetary chords, but I am sad
with books, the theologians, the tired word;
too smart for afterlife; and as the mad
creator of your scream screams in my skin
with light, with reason I hang on, absurd.

Fog

Even the Gnostics, who rejected sin
and miracles and bravely tried to wake
from the world's noise, from an oblivion
of unconsuming sleep and the mistake
of darkness, looked inside for light to heal
the stump of separation. But no good
orchard of stars grows the eternal meal
of time. The fog in us is black. The wood
is everywhere. No angel enters hell
(the way we call the wayless residence
of breath) with oil and passion from the dog
of dogs, the hand of hands. Only nonsense
lies in the grape of heaven. When I yell,
I yell to you. I call through fog for fog.

Madam Time and Her Iron Hands

Time obeys movement. Where there is no mass,
the void is changeless, free of measure. Time
begins with moving things: the river grass
or naked Artemis and lions climb-
ing golden peaks, her shining disk on some
horizon of a ghostly galaxy.
Time grips me. Always in my blood, she's dumb
but never myth. Sun calls! Call and I'll be
electric bones, oblivious to the thud
of absence when she kills me and goes off
with others. Though I think her in and out
of sound, she never halts. I hug her, loaf
and lose my way. Her iron hands in blood
approach. I lose. Alien at last! No shout.

Patience in the Orchard

Patience. It's better when
the way is long, when time
is slow and mute, for then
the agony of slime
is far and nightingales
are nightingales, unheard
but real. The body fails
under the iron word
of science. The hot brain
dreams an orchard of love
though pomegranates grow
rotten in prodigal rain,
fouling the peaceful grove.
Patience. The way is slow.

About the Invisible Maker Who Thinks Me
and Destroys His Traces

Behind the words that happen on the tongue,
the infinitely changing river noise
of sentences blown from the master lung,
behind the thought: the maker who destroys
his traces. Where is he? I look and lose
the inner sky. He thinks me, dreams me, yet
I am no place inside, and I accuse
the self of fraud. Terror I feel, and sweat
and sludge of dreams turning with cloudy blood
across the brain. Where have I gone? I think
only because I don't see who controls
the words wandering into my mouth. A wink
of revelation and I fall as mud,
as sackcloth packed with my two nowhere souls.

Gospel of the Tower

Back in the tower (scheming a way out of
the tower) I drink a coke to heal my sad-
ness while the opium rain is washing love
out of the heartland night. But it's not bad
alone with books. A lover eats the soul
exquisitely, yet I chew books and hear
my worries sing in the amazing hole
of *nous* amid my flesh, an airy sphere
with ozone gaps. I am with books which do
not judge or hate me, an astronomy
of ink I love and ponder while below
the janitors are playing cards. I play
with letters like Jehovah at the Tree:
vain, lonely maker reading till the day.

The Secret Hand Coming from Nowhere

The author is a fool. He doesn't know
how a far hand plays with a pen to mark
passions on paper, how a puny crow
of darkness wiggles like that flying shark
who carries the great organ notes into
the Paris night. O night aborted like
the year of wandering *le quartier* or dew
of slavery! He grabs and hugs a spike
of sun and prays to know. He won't. The hand
is secret as the soul. In his illusion
the fool accepts the act. If not, he'd trip
into that agony when the mind's land
is gone, and fall nowhere. I am the lip,
the fool, typing crow feet in wet confusion.

Night Windows of the Sun

Standing upright in books against the wall,
my poets want to shine like jonquils or
apocalyptic John, and one night crawl
into my hunger, each a minotaur
dining on virgins in its labyrinth
of ink. For me they're rays of horny song,
night windows of the sun, a hyacinth
of hope. I am their only friend along
the shelf. If I crawl in with them, the dust
will make me bald and poor, my face will flake
like Alexandrian tomb masks, with dead eyes
growing huge, black, and cracked. And so my lust
for poets is like pilgrims at the fake
shrine of old saints, a stained glass of surprise.

A Car Ferry in Northern Vermont

The car's up front. Overhead, gossipy birds
worry about the ferry in the sun.
Destiny east. I've spent my life on words
although below the sea the words are gone.
Slowly the talk, friends, love born on a hill
become a haze of gulls. Way back. The sky
below the sea was closed even to Gil-
gamesh who couldn't undo death. To die
is nature, but the boat is ticking on
into the sun. It's WHITE out there. Sun white!
and our few hours elect eternity
until we dock down in the carless night
below. I sigh for love lost in the sea
although below the sea the dark is gone.

New York Baglady Waking Up Enviably in an Orchard

The subway. I am sleeping by an old
baglady who has dropped into the blur
down in the mind where she rolls freely, rolled
like pebbles bouncing up under the sur-
face of acosmic seas. Inside and black.
She drowns, swims back, space whitens into light,
the sleeping sea is glowing void (I lack
a word for it), and in the luminous night
she drinks its firmament, a photograph
of nothing, free of soul. After her time
of shopping carts, the woman wakens in
an orchard. Subway life was a long sin
of dreamlessness. I envy her bad rhyme
of hope, even her worried choking laugh.

Eve with Adam

Love is the innocence of presence, when
the good beasts are. The melancholy trees
of austere Maine are innocent and can-
not know their limbs are blue to us, or freeze
or break on mountains. In the ancient or-
chard Eve and Adam share two souls. The song
of childhood sun is white. The good beasts soar
like virgin planets cooling into their long,
unthinking circle. Beasts and souls. They know
no horror in their dawn sleep while they ache,
hugging naked, atoms, fusions of mud.
The good beasts heal us with their faith, and though
the passion in the garden cost their blood,
deep in their rage a cloud sings as they wake.

Snow and Woods

Tonight I'm sad with ink. It's coming. Spring.
Yet since I sleep curled in a smile, why care
about the voice of thirty years? I sing
off-key in my own garden. Sun meets air,
heats it gently. I ask for one gold coin.
Not more. A gull comes with the sun. My peace
is warm, yet pain under the mind again
stands by my chair. In years of roaming Greece
I loved white walls on cypress fields, and here
I smell the memory of spring. The night
is blue with brandy; love like snow around
the house glares with remorse and open fear.
The snow is hot, and woods are filled with light,
for the sad spring or love moves in the ground.

Gospel of the Mountain

My Cottage at Deep South Mountain

In my middle years I love the Tao
 and by Deep South Mountain I make my home.
When happy I go alone into the mountains.
Only I understand this joy.
I walk until the water ends, and sit
waiting for the hour when clouds rise.
If I happen to meet an old woodcutter,
I chat with him, laughing and lost to time.

Wang Wei (701–761)

Gospel of the Mountain

On a red mountain north of Beijing (where
the Chinese hermits banished morning frost
by chopping wood), the wisdom of the air
washes the silent herons. Time is lost
like a smoke wisp hanging over bamboo.
Time of no-mind. The mountain cherries bloom
by the white hut, and life is never through
although the heart can never leave its room.
One life, caught on the planet, never with
the burning spice of immortality.
On a red mountain, mist and sunlight hold
some peaceful lemon trees in their own myth
of joy. The long disease of history
is far off screams. The lemon air is cold.

Gospel of Black Hats

The spring is late this year. Its winds are raw,
aching a bit. The moon is full. I pad
down through the gully to Salt Creek. The law
of seasons will prevail, ending the sad-
ness of dead grass, and soon my winter in
the barn will end. I fade lonely in space
back to my land next door to a Ukraine
of vast jade fields, strange like the other race
around the ghetto villages. Black hats
and books in velvet. Of my people? Gone
a century, that blood is me. I pass
and as the grass can't know it is the grass,
I see no wings from mystic chariots,
yet in my blood the moon burns on and on.

Gospel of Light

The moon is natural in the evening. I
cannot be angry at it. And a flute
high on the mountain is the sweetest lie
of separation. And the stench of fruit,
fogging the blasted lots, over the quake
in the Algerian city, joins the dead
who don't smell sweet. Yet in the inner lake
of light, *lake of the heart* as Dante said,
the rays are stronger than the suffering
and rapture of the outer world. To be
inside and be the light is everything
I want. For now I live seized by the wall,
those ten walls of the flesh, and what I see
is glaring dark, that is, nothing at all.

Gospel of the Night

Plotinos sang the way to lose the way
outside. His Alexandria blurs. The streets
become illusion. As he fades, a ray
of darkness fills the wilderness and heats
the night with ecstasy. The ONE above
the night, the sun who never can be seen
(the seer is the seen) is all and love
and joy connecting atoms. Yet between
the flight of the alone to the alone,
the climb, the circling up to light, I've been
a creature of the streets, and I suspect
you share my vagrant sadness. If we groan
the clouds are safely in the clouds. Abject-
ly dark, I thank the night for raining in.

Dark Night of Love

A mountain at high noon. A roof will do,
a city park or just a bed or rug
from the Near East. The afternoon laughs through
a window. We are secrets with the drug
of sunlight in the body. All my dark-
ness, all your orgasm of hair and star
rip up your belly as we sail an ark
severely into the earth's core, down far
into the unseen, felt ranges and rain
of particles of iron. Only hot light.
My yearning ends. Not peace. But we have come
at last and simply into oneness. Pain
of joy. I lean my face on you. With night
condemning us, we dream, we're lost, we're numb.

Mandolin

Bring me a mandolin. Let it be Greek
as my life is when I am floating high
with pain or passion, pausing on the peak
that is the noon of night and love. I sigh
with you, we speak at the white corner of
the mountain village, we are wise, we see
too well. Magic is live. Don't look above
for miracle. Magic is here, a tree
like the white olive in our heart. Though death
is not a way to miracle, is dread
dimming our being, senseless, out of our skin,
with age I float outside. You float. Your breath
is mine. We're many. Just a lip or bed
or phone away. Bring me a mandolin.

Pearl

The universe is ticking, and the pearl
(hidden from day down in the ocean floor)
burns in its shells. And though the watery pearl
is small, its eye is a transparent core
deep as the macrovoid and everywhere.
Leviathan of light ticking in the sea
in buried shells. To know it! And lose care,
hunger, because the milk in every tree,
white sap in every mountain, the moon bulls
pinning the sky of ice in place
all feed on it. In ignorance we feed
on the electrons of the pearl, its face
of plenitude. For just one poisoned bead
of opal fire we dive and gorge like gulls.

Secret Word

Machado said that in his loneliness
he saw very clear things that weren't true.
I think if I could see the bottomless
beginning of the mind, I'd have a clue,
maybe to feel what Borges always said:
the gnomic cipher of the universe
or mirror's face is clear only when dead.
His poet earned the Chinese emperor's curse
and lost his scalp (he knew one word that bound
the world). The rage to hear goes on. The word
may start with Lamed 70 ways, whose L
is God's unuttered name. My children found
a secret meadow, I the grass of hell
and ink. It's almost dawn. No word is heard.

The Lord Was Glorious

The Lord was glorious, terrible and here,
a hope for passage to eternity,
a solace now, expanding our small sphere
of solitude into the arms and sea
of heaven. Galileo found a tear
of light through glass: it was infinity
and not God's realm. He burned. Now fear
of God is gone; our sullen victory
is to be lost alone. When the Lord left
we saw his awesome pose was tasty lies
to hide oblivion for each breathing shell.
Though faith (scorned by the Gnostics as bereft
of reason) also fails, it mystifies
and whispers love into our faithless cell.

Thin Book of the World

The hermit of the Midwest must be me,
for to a vast and empty tower I go
each night, a Jew in ancient reverie
of picking thought from the world book below
a bible sea of darkness that exists
merely like inner clouds. The universe
was a thin book of words. It now persists
as circling voids. I tinker with a verse
of chaos, robbed from a dictionary with
its hundred million mirrors of the earth.
Fat chance of making sense! I might be myth
like you or Job, and no one knows. I talk
with unseen lovers, crabs in sandy birth
and Moses chalking rules on the sidewalk.

Night Room

A room is for confession and amid
   these Turkish rugs and books I should
   lie on the floor, throw up a bid
   to snag a being in me. I'm good
at serious talk with *you.* Turning the key
   and trundling in dead tired, I sit
   intensely still and melancholy.
   A crab. A bore. I'd have a fit
if forced to be with someone fuming hot
   with unclear aching spirit like
   this windbag in his failing years.
A waste of time. Night room. I like to plot
   this ministry of pain: a spike
   of fire, of depths, of noise, of fears.

Gospel of Desire

Until I croak—or am gaga and don't care
   about salvation light
   or coffined hope—I wear
desire and my pecker out of sight
like any violin thrilling the dark
   with unheard ecstasy.
   I witness the black spark,
an unseen violation of the tree
of science. I would kick the universe
   (and bust my foot) to grab
   what is denied each man
or woman, who, unchoosing, shares the curse
   of the imprisoning lab
   of being. I have no plan.

Gospel of Time

The wheels of an invisible timepiece
are whirring someplace in the mind, almost
as fine as quartz. Einstein knew the peace
outside where lines become a single ghost
embracing at infinity, but in
the living head there is no end to planes
or time. I feel that clock. It says *Ich bin*
like Rilke's silent friend turning the pains
of living into wine or transformation,
and in the mammoth night a blatant cock
of dawn cannot intrude. The almond tree
weeps amber yet, like us, feels no creation
or death (that's just for others). But my clock
knows one, outrageous, final mystery.

Gospel of Snow

Death is an insult, since it proves I am
only a witness of a solitude
and you're asleep. I am just one mad clam
pushed by infinite seas and slurped as food
by time. You dream. I feel the planet spin
like a big lettuce in a flooding sink.
Then floating with the vegetables, I'm in
this timebomb skinbag: hairy, lusty, pink.
To be just me is bad enough! To go
and be no more is unforgiveable.
Why not be cheerful like my dog's green eye?
He's fixed but smart and loves me. When you sigh,
lemon trees blossom in your heart. It's all
we have—a bit of love, some fire. And snow.

Gospel of Imaginary Beings

Summer Night

It is a beautiful summer night.
The tall houses leave
their balcony shutters open
to the wide plaza of the old village.
In the large deserted square,
stone benches, burning bush and acacias
trace their black shadows
symmetrically on the white sand.
In its zenith, the moon; in the tower,
the clock's illuminated globe.
I walk through this ancient village,
alone, like a ghost.

Antonio Machado (1875–1936)

Imaginary Beings

The ghosts are you I live with on a ship
of snow. I'm dreaming on my cabin bed,
over the hold of worms, and taste the lip
of lunacy. And "Love," Machado said,
"is in the absence," so your arms of light
tickle my watch. You are invisible
as are the gulls around the moon, or night
horizons blond like Easter bread. You still
the singing whales. You smell of fire. Sick of
accusing faces down in the iron mess
of this black ship, weary of the jaguar
or shark or iron bureaucrat of love,
I love your ghostly words, your clouds, your star
of snow, your laughter at my loneliness.

Room

Returning to my room—it has my lamp,
some shirts, a photo of my daughter, and
a second pair of shoes—I am a tramp
among the worthy (I think proudly). Banned
like Mandelstam, grave as Celan, I feed
my night with firebirds and the postcards found
with poems in a dead man's trenchcoat. Greed
for fame is infamous. Do I confound
the word with me? The *me*—well, trivial
and often taken for the word—has its
own grievance with salvation's clock. But in
my room where even stars circle in jail,
poems were born in faith and lucky fits.
I'm lucky! Now a shirt to hide my skin.

Twilight Jew Nailed on a Cross

How can I give my life for something so
abstract and wordy? No. I'm not so dumb
as that. And yet the darkness I can't know
is endless fog and mud and bulls who come
vomiting ivory nights. The book of night-
mare has a letter for each name of God
and yet the truth of darkness is of light,
not dreadful holy words, nor the black sod
of hell with which a twilight Jew, nailed on
a tree, cursed us, and not the Father of
the terror: oriental despot, dread
manic with fists. Only the vagrant love
of ignorance is brave. Yahweh is dead,
the world's mistake. Truth is the blackest dawn.

The Other Gospel

Because the old good news has lost its spell
and the good angel of the book has flown
like Ikaros down to the sun in hell
and reigns as Satan handsome with brimstone,
cannon and dread, the world is empty for
the rest of us. And with faith dead I seek
another gospel with the news of more
than bodies weakly born and withering weak-
ly from our wakened minds. That book is not
of words (who's happy with the shade of words?)
but inlight of black hills, the calm to be
a swamp gas fire or water drowning thought.
In purgatory I'm erased by birds
who chew my eyes and soar inaudibly.

News of the Dirty War

These mornings of wandering Buenos Aires are
my happiness. Taking the paper *La Opinión*
to the Saint James Café, I read about the war
between the Ford Falcons of Perón
and montoneros. An off-duty death squad of thugs
    who break down a door and kidnap
young rebels. A midnight-blasted store on Florida.
Greedy, I breakfast on the news. Get up, tap
my glass to pay. At the *Salida*,
I phone Amanda. She is mounting a photo blow-
up of Borges. "Come over. Take the metro," she blabs.
"It's safe. Ciao." Down in the jammed train, I read
    Julio Cortázar's *Fuegos artificiales*, and balmily lean
back against the doors I guess are closed. As we slow
around a curve, a short wild-eyed lady grabs
my arm and yanks me back inside the screeching car
    whose *open* doors rattle a lethal grin.

Days in Wild Buenos Aires, Celebrating
Her Week of Failure

Night of explosions. Bombed cafés and shops
all over Buenos Aires. Up north, the war.
In boots of black asparagus some cops
leap out of unmarked Falcons. From a bar
I watch them round up students (who will soon
be killed); then walk to the Academy
of Failure where my friends are taking shots
against success. Paco's composed a tune
against the epidemic malady
of fame. Graciela's got a booth of pots
and pans for her own Center of Despairs.
Despair and failure. Now my chest is firm
beside my comrade washouts. Yet I squirm
with passion in this city called *Good Airs.*

Singer

They call me solitude they call me by
the name of my disgrace the child and so
I'm drunk on corners of the sky and shy
although the moon painted the street with snow
so don't abandon me in the white night
I leave the city looking for my child
who is like me crazy and kiss the light
of sister planets the police are mild
with me a harmless nut O serene friend
under the jasmine air you are like me
guilty of heat of feeling trees of salt
or opals in the mouth what agony
of freedom they won't shoot us it's my fault
for singing child I love you we offend.

Gospel of Love

We took our cycle to the lovers' cliff
at Ronda where the knights murdered a bull
or fought the Moors. Sore from the road and stiff,
we sat where Rilke (in the fanciful
old Quaker lady's inn) sat by the fire,
hearing the verse of Góngora the Jew.
It seems a century ago: desire
for sun, refinement, and for white and blue
Sevilla, oranges, and the Spring Fair,
five nights of dancing into dawn. Sunday
morning in fascist Spain, the women rode
their flowery stallions. Salt was in the air
as we cycled on the coast. That episode
of wonder was our childhood sun. Our way.

Sunflowers in Late Afternoon near Córdoba

Until I get to Córdoba my car
gossips with slopes of sunflowers and black ash.
My pockets groan. Olive fields echo. Star
and fig trees paint the pilgrim way. The lash
of memory is dark, is bloody dark,
yet beauty lives while lemons tumble in
the twilight wheat. Glory. The mountains bark
gently against the wind. No walls or sin.
I wonder who you are? I walk about
envying dogs and flies, who while I yearn
don't worry about ash, extinction or
a place for inner being. I wander out
into your hands. A donkey roars for more.
Pines cry like minarets and sunflowers burn.

Vagabonds in China

Who cares what people say? I need to go
into the Fayyum desert or share tea
with Uzbeks in the Gobi. A rainbow
shone over Yangshuo as we were biking free
from rainy villages to the airport
where we were locked in. Not one open door
until the plane got there. Yes, my passport
wasn't dust. I forgot my desk. The poor
were friends. Only the weak and poor and lost,
the chubby janitors and peasants came
to share our food up in the icy hills.
When two Tibetan nomads fought in the frost
over a prayer wheel, when another's shame
dazed him in song, I ate a sack of daffodils.

Coming on the Golden Horn

Don't wait for me till light is gone.
The continents of clouds across
the sun begin the night and loss
of faith. Out on the Golden Horn
I let my glass of tea turn brown
like sewers and the ancient doors
along the wharf. Stay out of doors.
Inside Haigia Sophia and down
on his knees Mehmet prays to God
and hangs the Patriarch from the gold-
en dome. Don't wait too long. You stum-
ble, poisoned in your groin. The rod
of God is broken. Poor and cold,
you never scream. You cry and come.

Far from This White Sérifos Village,
Medusa Waits for the Mirror of Death

Though Greece is blue I think of gray
and one-armed men after the war,
the civil war, smoking and poor,
crossing Omonia on their way
to some raw cold café. No more
spears of the Persians; no more Franks
or Turks burning up towns. The pranks
of history mute, some pigeons soar
barbarous and white! Now only gods
lurk on the islands. Artemis
and her night lions bomb the moon-bed
of terrorists sponging off her cheese.
Perseus in blue shoes plods and broods
how to slash off a Gorgon's head.

Gospel of the Garden

As Mary turned to leave the tomb, she heard,
"Woman, why are you weeping?" It must be
the gardener, she thought. "Because my lord
is gone," she said. "They've taken him away.
I came with spices for his body." When
she looked again two angels robed in white
were in the empty tomb. Then on that night
of loss and vision in Jerusalem,
of death made miracle, the Magdalene
went through the alleys to her mat, lay down,
and in an evening blue as paradise
she knew the gardener was God. So John
told us. What hope without her stratagem
of faith? She dreamt beyond the funeral spice.

Cloudy Peace and Earthly Infection

Near his disciples on the mountain he
arose and disappeared. Simply a tale
and yet I feel it. Once a mammoth tree
of thunder moaned beside me on a hill
of burdock. Vermont night. I heard the blood
of plants sing out. The arms of time were slow
as bliss. The patch of parsnips was a throb
of poison, and I slowed and felt the snow
of darkest meditation. When the body
was taken from the cave, Joseph's own room
rose to a cloud holding his lord. I feel
their cloudy peace, but fire holds me here. Shoddy
with tales felt more than truth, I hope to heal
abysmal blisters as the mountains bloom.

Rapture and Deception in Snow Mountains
near Annapurna

Meditation is deep and mostly wrong,
and every walnut tree swaying in wheat
is dumb, not Taoist wise. The temple gong
sings rainbows as all past and future meet
near Annapurna. Right or wrong I like
the refuge from the clock, of walking off
through continents. Memory is tricks. I hike
away into the snow, I'm cold and cough,
leaving our Himalayan lodge to climb
Poon Hill where there's a pail and outdoor bath
and shivering dance. Raj helps me with my pack
so I can make it. Wisdom tricks me back
in time, to smells and clouds, not the true slime
of killing age. I like the good false path.

Dream of Mother and Father

You come back and no daisy in the sun
is bright as you. You take a cigarette
and try to smoke. Modern. Mother, your son
is laughing at your airs and can't forget
how mild your vices are . . . I'm on the phone
with Father (ninety if he were alive),
a bachelor with a pearl stickpin, downtown
near the East River . . . Mother has got five
days left before the knife imposes sleep
of far ships . . . Father from the old hotel
floats out like a dove. Dad, I'd disappear
for good if we could meet, and let them keep
our earthly names . . . Before both of you fell,
we'd fool the world with life. I wake to fear.

Gospel of Triumph

It's a green day of sun. Mimosas smell
along the road and blissfully we drive
top down to cheers. The people, yes, they'll yell
for poem after poem. Throbbing alive
I hate the fame of death. My reading is
outdoors. Five million seats are filling up.
Professors chat with me. Words are their bus-
iness, yet I clutch my manuscript to cup
my genitals, my sudden nakedness,
and find the binder has no poems at all.
I kiss a waitress for a bun. She slaps
me black and blue, bloodying my teeth. Perhaps
I'll wing it, be creative—yet I'm less
than sawdust in this filthy jeering hall.

Chaos

To breathe or think is real, somehow. I take
them gravely and I guess I am. Yet when
I lose a job or wife or world—or wake
cheerful and naked like a citizen
of Eden, or as a black tailor feel
a hurricane of love is merely air
never to blast me from the rotting wheel
of years—all meaning dies. Here in my chair
in hot Madrid I don't know where to go.
Does chaos have a way? I'm writing this
for you, ghost reader on a cloudy star
inside, the vagrant spy of souls. Below
this act of words—drama of grief or bliss—
are words. And chaos stings like vinegar.

Ghost

Thought is my friend, my ghost. Is overheard
by the same shady captain of my beings
whose tongue I am, which she controls, whose word
floats like a mermaid. In a wink she sings
through sleep to sleeping ships, and through the day
is the same siren echoing her command.
Thought is my ghost programmed as a black ray
meandering like blood below the sand
of night. She makes the world. Her firmament
feeds the horizon with the flash of green
and golden almond trees or the quick sound
of dying wisdom, Solomon's black tent
of vision song, until she splits unseen,
unheard, and comrades me into the ground.

Inlight

Through the mind's window and its black horizon
the inner eye descends to feeble sun
flickering like the last *Kyrie eleison*
in a Greek dome outside. Oblivion
of sun drifts between fires like a patient
circling near death. The candle flares and just
a flicker. No one knows the last descent
into the chest of night where time is dust
everywhere. And inlight? Does it have waves
or particles? Its luminosity
hangs from the spirit. Flick, it's gone. And while
alive it hides. It means itself. To be
the light; to stand inside the sun and smile,
loving the sun. Until the night, it saves.

Goddess of Democracy

It was a great open square and it had the smell of existence.

Vicente Aleixandre (1899–1984)

Gospel of Fire

In this red room of Paris student days,
under the bulb drooping over the hull
of a wood cot, my novel floods with wordplays
of sex and existential thieves. I pull
the window down—a cement patio where
a Dutch blonde rooms, who once looked up at me
with young misery as if she felt the stare
of my desire. I read on. No way to be
with her. On the wall right behind my bed,
wallpaper smiling lewd with its black teeth
begins a Quaker shake. I hear the flow
of a loud mattress, light a match beneath
my hand (I'm smoking pipes), and Heer Van Gogh
watches my fingers flaming on the bed.

Gospel of Failure

Raining a week, so all the clouds doze on
the poisoned fields, yet now the sun intrudes,
toweling the rainy light. The Parthenon
is still afloat, and underground old nudes
of marble wait for some new sewer dig to
restore their time. I row below the stars
of roaring silences while in Chengdu
some acrobats, poor devils full of scars,
go at each other, slapping swords and fire
against their bodies. As I sit and row
on my machine, my poems collapse below
fat time's rejection. Work, love, being; desire
for more than death. Flopping I laugh. Dogs hear
me fart, bark from the basement at my fear.

My World as Words of a Book Whose Thread Is Obscure

My decades are the chapters of a book
whose title—*Willis*—tells me who I am
but nothing of inside, and if I look
behind the title page, Jesus! I slam
the covers panicky. How can I face
knowing my world is merely words? And worse,
the end is ink? I'm not Gregor whose disgrace
at being the starving beetle was a curse
which only death atoned for. Yet whose dream
am I? I sip hot tea, hoping to drink
a Kabbalistic word or windy sign
soul-blown to help me read the world—or seem
to read it. Though I fail to turn to ink,
some pages spy invisible design.

Bellyaching to the Reader

You are the spy eye in the triangle
of lover, me, and you. I know I am
as much to blame. If words were a black gull
on the gray ocean in my heart, Adam
would ring its neck to keep the mystery
of a poetic bird in his new speech,
and you, voyeur, would kibbitz while I'd be
slammed into jail for flashing. You can reach
me chewing my own tongue and pick up
on me. I bless you when you do and starve
when you're a rat, offering you a cup
of poison. Swallow. It's to hide despair
and cure your hope. I'm also sick and carve
a piece of meat for sharks, for us to share.

Getting Up, after Hitting the Sack, Just to Shine My Raygun on You

I'm not a drunk, no beetle darkly sad
with family members spearing me with hate;
I'm not flamboyantly one of the bad
and decadent. There's nothing in my fate
obscene and roaring to confess—except
nightly I fall half dead in bed and give
in to my tricks tonight. I get up, schlep
back to the kitchen, find a pen and live!
With you I share life's curse: we're each alone.
My out is scribbling, and, if I don't write
my verbose gems and junk, I might as well
drop dead. I love this mellow tongue, a loan
from the harsh roar of old Germanic. Hell,
I'm up again, dying to piss out light.

A Vagrant Fated to Kraut Talk

Borges reserved his Thursday evenings for
his Schopenhauer, his Sunday afternoons
for Anglo-Saxon and Old Norse. A whore
is the mind's tongue sleeping around in runes
of Iceland or a Gothic yellow gulf
and copulating with a lyric rose
on Heine's Paris mattress. From Cynewulf
to Mrs. Woolf I skirt the northern snows,
kissing in tongues that aren't mine. Yiddish,
a German salad of the shtetl Jews,
gave voice to immigrants, a litany
of song I heard my mother's mother use.
I failed to learn it—fish out of the sea—
yet chat in English Kraut, the same old dish.

Proverbs

Better hard bread when the game-heart is glad
     than gold with sorrow. The spiked beauty of
     young spring is torture when memory of love
     hangs on. • Freedom groans in a room. You're sad
as you climb an empty mountain. Good to dance
     in chains as the Chinese do in verse. A bed
     is good for exercise of ecstasy. • The dead
     can't talk, the living cannot know. In France
I lost a fish and ate the sea. • One breath
     proves blowy heavens and my lungs exist.
     Illusion of a consciousness has kissed
me in oblivion that only death
     kills off. • The stinking void proves we're alone
     right now. Funny to know and turn to stone.

Dirty War in Buenos Aires, Christmas, 1975

So shalt thou feed on death, that feeds on men.
Shakespeare, sonnet 146

Lost and found in the bloody Argentine,
after kissing Nelly Shakespear I resort
to ringing my close friends Randy and Mort,
carting some Borges photographs—no sign
of taxis on Christmas eve. We drink and eat
and joke. How many killed in the big attack?
100 montoneros? We wander back
to food. Here dreams of murder in the street
are curiously absurd. I sleep under sheep-
skins, wake to cherries, African hound-eyes
by my cot, breakfast in December sun.
Then tango and dog gifts! Although we keep
our terrors pocketed, soon the phone sighs.
The hospitals are jammed and death has won.

Goddess of Democracy

When Chou Ping took me to his room I said,
"What does your father do?" The floor was cold,
the hallway stank of turnips, his gray bed
groaned under books. "He's carting bricks," he told
me. Ping was shy, the poet in Beijing
I read and cared for most. We often ate
together near the Summer Palace, Ming-
enlightened as we joked about our fate:
soulless yet floating in the inner sea.
Slowly some students jammed the square and made
a statue white like sun. They sat, they sprang
on tanks, yelled *Freedom and Democracy!*
We walked to Tiananmen. Ping stayed. Don't fade,
goddess. Deep in Ping's heart a bullet rang.

Israel Epstein in Beijing, an Old Man and Friend Retired to the Friendship Hotel, Looks Back at His Years as a Pioneer Revolutionary

Some dream of God and his mysterious team
of fat conspiring priests, sickly with rules
and dogmas—stooges of the right. The fools
of evil praise the Dalai Lama's dream,
but my liberation ideology
saved Tibet—I wrote the book. We forged the mind
of all the weak and poor. Though a decree
popped me five years in jail, I wasn't blind
to our class struggle and I wept real tears
when Stalin died. Mao had to rearrange
the world, skin a few rabbits for the smell
of progress. I believe. Red dream means years
of combat against fascist black. I sell
some lies, tell funny jokes, and never change.

Nadezhda Recalls Osip Mandelstam's Poem
and the Camp at Voronezh

My husband sang of Stalin's mustache. He
compared it to two cockroaches. A good
analogy. But an informer stood
among us, and Osip, in fantasy,
was teased and finally sent away to die.
Boris protected me. But nothing took
me from the cold of Voronezh, and why
and how, almost insane, you wrote a book
of magic out of snow seeds and a plow
of words in hibernation by the white
ice graves of Russia. Guards chewed up the road.
They ate the moon. Their teeth were cavernous spite,
spite against spite. You're dead, and earth has slowed
and slowed. No hope, yet I'm still hoping now.

KGB and God

A history of back room floodlights,
the KGB went for your throat
with leather gloves. Like God they smote
the enemies. Those Moscovites
stilled Mandelstam and Babel and
invented camps of violet snow
to freeze the Jews the Nazi hand
failed to tattoo. They always knew
the ways of weakening the soul
to make her shit. In their own halls
they dreamt a plot but were surprised
to see drab beasts of fear unroll
and die. When Russia snipped their balls,
like God they all got circumcised.

Secret Criminal

There's no one I can trust. I do have friends.
Confess to them? And make it three times worse,
trying to prove my crimes have noble ends?
I'm not a happy spy mingling a purse
with patriotism. Sleep is theirs, not mine.
Back in Damascus as I climb each stair
up to her room, it is a hidden mine
field where the slightest noise will strip me bare
and get me shot. I have a knife. I never
reach back for it. Once in the jumbled bed
I use my charm, I lie with truths to sever
the muezzin's predawn moaning from my talk.
I enter her. She moans. She cries. She's dead.
Outside, I walk. No one to tell. I walk.

Gospel of the Executed

Horace Dunkins, Jr., died in the chair,
early Friday after the second try.
His uncle and his father stayed their prayer
nineteen minutes for the Alabama eye
of justice to discover and repair
the faulty hookup of electrodes by
replugging cables in. With volts to spare
the executioner flipped the green switch
and the mildly retarded killer, still
unconscious, breathing, died without a hitch,
the first to taste the federal gift to die.
Our Supreme Court ruled that the state could kill
Dunkins. By voting five to four to slay
retards (and children too), they cleared the way.

Executions in China, 1989

My car ride home is a small gesture seen
by no one in the military court
where Shanghai workers face the old routine
of execution while the news report
is witnessed round the globe on home TV.
The dazed and beaten workers don't enjoy
a knowledge of their moment's grave history
where old men toil to distort and destroy
a tongue of truth. I turn the key and move
uncertain to my lamp. The workers grope
back in their cells (they're unseen now) to wait,
to brood on Tiananmen and clocks that prove
earth time also ticks us to slaughter. Fate
speaks death. With my time left, stupid I hope.

Gospel of America

I am American, Korean vet
who drilled through war, dreaming of getting laid,
and now our patriotic laws have made
my son a felon, spread a legal net
for protesters who won't shut up for peace,
and my good son is caught. He's not a rat.
He hurt no one. They smashed him in the eye
in Cambridge when he stopped a mugging at
Harvard Gate. Morbid executions by
the Chinese, Cubans and Americans
persist—commies kill more for less. From Greece
I call him. "Guilty," said the judge. His hands
are brave with history. Quaker calm, my son
the felon owns a world where guns are gone.

Borges Dying in Europe, 1986

In mid-June in Geneva, a few days
before frail Borges is acquainted with
the night, the blind man sees his Taoist ways
fulfilled: María moves him to the myth
of an apartment in the Vieille Ville
where in the bedroom, full of light, he sleeps
overlooking the orange roofs and peal-
ing steeples. With María. Once, he weeps
remembering milongas. There's a smell
of Buenos Aires, knives, and how to roam
through ciphers in the Kabbalah. "Which of
my cities will release me from the hell
of hope," he says, "that trap lurking above?
This is my happiest day in life. I'm home."

Suicides and Another Miracle of Spring

Now adolescent spring has dropped its clouds
of cellos on the woods to wake their sleep
from winter. When my loved ones put on shrouds
of sleep to end their pain, we went to weep
and weep yet stillness was their will—although
they might have laughed another day. To die
is peace, but costs. I don't want peace, to know
the mystery now, the mystery of that sea
that has no time or cosmos, and I hold
to terror of that disappearance. If
I were the world, were I a selfless thing,
no solitude, just you, I could drop cold
to Buddhist all or nothing. But I sniff
the air, alone, with hunger for the spring.

Fearful Clock

My clock ticks *death*, ticks *death*, or is it *life*,
ticks *life*? I hold this German instrument
of song with worry. Thales claimed that strife
was the world stuff: hatred and love was pent
up in the atoms' godless air. I get
the point: a balance inside space. But in
my Turkish island chest, a minaret
of light adorning it, I taste the sin
of hope, the lie that my dead chest with soul
and God will merge when time is through. Meanwhile
the clock endures, singing minimal song,
monotony of Philip Glass. I loll
about the room, trying to wake. I dial
a singing shower. I'm not a clock. I long.

Clockman

My father was a jeweler and in late
Depression days I went from store to store
with him, selling our last supply of fate:
Swiss kidskin leather straps. Once in the door,
I opened up the case and spread our brand
of luxuries. When someone made a slur,
enraging him, I didn't understand.
When things looked good he laid out gems and myrrh,
the balms of Bible nights, pulled a gold watch
out of his pocket, Corbusier in shape,
whose name, Pierre Grange, was ours! Such is his past
till bankruptcy and deep depression botch
his life. I loved this man of time, but vast
with pain he leapt through time to false escape.

Sérifos Taverna

I'm home in Greece. The parliament of birds
has cut the strings of Papandreou's tongue
yet the old priest sings good Byzantine words
next door on Sunday in the church. I've hung
my laundry on the roof. The air is sweet
with ancient furies as I jog down slabs
of whitewashed stone to ΠΕΤΡΟΣ, on the street
over the dolphin sea. Manolis jabs
me with a hug. We sit and gossip, down
moshári and *revíthia.* Yannis turns
the music up. You cannot describe yellow
if never seen. A white eternal town
and Tina's smirky smile have made me mellow,
slaphappy, drunk and loving as time burns.

Even Heroic Alexander Is a Sentimental Disgrace
before the Enemy of Empty Time

After combat, Alexander the Great
needs to simmer down and so he scrawls
graffiti on a marble Persian gate
and statue. Just for fun. And then he sprawls
inside his leather tent till yellow dawn,
pondering fame and conquest. Studies with
his teacher Aristotle made him scorn
fellow barbarians, but he'll be mere myth
compared to Aristotle's crabbed words.
The Macedonian lends his face to coin
and features to the Buddha for a while.
His scratches on the statue are his birds
of immortality. Yet will he join
that darkness soon? Confused, he kills his smile.

Arnost Lustig Listens to the Sound of People Being Shot

Snow coming down is mingling with the ash-
smoke from the crematorium's nearby stack.
I feel the silence and barbed wire, the rash
of shots, the urge to run out into black-
ness and put my dead lips under the snow.
In just fifty-four days three hundred thousand
of Warsaw's Jews are rounded up and go
to the gas chambers in Treblinka. Frau and
Herr Toten dance all night. The people fall
into their absence. Snow on faces when
they hit the ground. The barracks lends obscene
witness to my depravity. Hear all
those faces drop into snow. Please listen
to bleakness. Time is dying. We're unseen.

Homeless with AIDS

John of the Cross, the mystic, lived to be
inside and burn, to climb through darkness up
to light and die from time in ecstasy
of union and oblivion. His cup
of love he gave to his erotic God.
The youth of China and the Argentine
also kissed death with passion, wasted blood,
dying for nation. Caught in my benign
and tiny hole of air, I'm weak. It shames
me empty. On a New York corner where
a young and downcast guy sits by his sign
and cup HOMELESS WITH AIDS, as I go near
I look away, yet toss a buck. It tames
me. "Thanks a lot, brotha" stings in my ear.

Baudelaire and His Parisian Dead

Am I perverse through your pain, Baudelaire,
your dead, your poor Parisian dead so cold
and skeletal, forgotten in the prayer
of worms where no friend, no Lord, comes to hold
their rotting hearts so they can fly above
the scum of earth up to a cottage white
and beautiful where ice cannot kill love,
where blood nostalgia leaks a dream of light,
where black John Henry finally rose and slept
and all our misery is grace? Am I
perverse to drink your pain? I'm happy since
we are the same—we're lost, we wake to die,
and when death comes at least our ignorance
will help us feel, to feel and not accept.

Homeless

Pascal has his abyss inside, and Baudelaire
walks in the twilight streets with the clochards
through dingy Paris while the hungry stare
across the empty Seine; dull drunkards spar
with cold, and beggar women with a can
of fire blow on the burning sticks to warm
their hands and sagging breasts. Worst is the dawn
when the Hotels of God extend an arm
to draw the dying to a Catholic bed
of hope. While Pascal tramps the sores and blaze
of hell and Baudelaire in decadence
pities the damned like him, the homeless dead
smell bad in New York doorways. Yet when haze
burns off, their souls leak out in innocence.

Patmos

Let anyone who is thirsty come.

John of Patmos Rev. 22:17

Docking at Night

On the ghost sea
white Patmos sits
in Chinese mist.
I yawn and pee.
Our ship drones in
a moonless cell
of stench and spell
of stereo din
driving me bats.
White lamps of shame
like mountain cats
creep on the town
of dreams of John
who wrote with flame.
                              Skala

Walls

White
is
Patmos light
on the Hora houses.
At night they float
glassy with jasmine, revelation lost,
an iceberg boat
hiding the moon inside its frost.
I was sleeping when
the walls
began to pen
me in. No one calls.
I had so much to do outside. I curl
up, scanning, miserable in the black pearl.
                              Hora

Cats in Love

Cats gazing in the Hora slowly slink
about the alleys by the whitewashed walls
under the blue Greek flag. They are bright ink
sporadically applied to furry balls
or robber's feet. Sprawling on the hot stone
they wait for worried widows sewn in black
to lose their awful grief. They scream alone
under the loggia, cunning orphans back
in pirate days when Turks would storm a hill
for land or gold or women. Cats survive
like crenellations on the fortress where
the monks paint icons, copy verse and fill
their buns with sperm. Erotic and alive
like Mary Magdalene, cats lick their hair.

Hora

Declarations by John the Theologian

Leave me alone. I came to Patmos on
a ship of spirit fashioned out of gold
and silver blood running in the python
trapped in the holy bowels of Jesus. Cold,
wet in my cave, I keep a wild carnation
beside my wooden pillow. Ecstasy!
I'm elsewhere. Sadly comes the Revelation.
Oblivion lost, I join the lightning tree;
the eyes of Seven Whales burn in my pen.
I curse the whores who don't love God, and hear
dogfish singing for waters of the sky.
I hear the slaves of sorrow, those poor men
in turquoise mines, their hearts in trash and fear.
In my dark cave I see, so I can die.

Apokálypses

Joshua the Messiah Soon to Be Iesous the Greek

The children always taunted Joshua for
his big Semitic beak, and on his day
of crucifixion, when his soul will soar
to resurrection, he begins to pray
for mercy from the silent Yahweh Lord,
who many claim is he. He wears a hat
before the Lord, a yarmulke. The board
behind his arms and legs (he isn't fat)
is splintered and the spikes, a bloody mess,
are fire in his depressed and dulling head.
A fly is roasting his curved nose. A Greek
and handsome god they'll make of him, and bless
him as the savior. He starts to leak,
naked and suffering, human till dead.

Apokálypses

Drama of Eve and Adam

God made the world and took a nap forever.
Before he snoozed he walked through paradise,
clacking his worry beads, bossy and clever,
fiercely judgmental. When he went to size
up Eve and Adam, he commanded them
to snap to, but they'd gone to do their thing:
they named and ate and screwed. A requiem
could save them—maybe. God blew up. The King,
back in his whirlwind tent, losing his cool,
was screaming: I won't take it any more!
It was an awful soap. He tossed them out,
jobless and poor. They had no union pool
to back them against angel scabs. Came drought
and fear, but they were free to die and roar.

Hora

Renegade Whose Loud Mouth Is Swiftly Punished

Down in the cave I cannot stand the face
of God and curse him with a filthy word,
Old Fucker. Instantly I feel the space
invaded by his lies of grace, absurd,
and yet a whirlwind spirit grazes me
as God's dead eyes are smoking with his dread
disdain. He crushes angels furiously
under his flashing sandals. With blue lead
under my heart, I ride off to the beach,
my cycle dangerously unfit, and hit
some sand, flipping, a minute from the shore.
The Honda pins me to a bloody pit
of rocks. I sit upon the bleeding floor
in Babylon, the warm sea out of reach.

Apokálypses/Lambi

Wounded Hero

After the accident I am surprised
to be alive, and proud of being hurt.
Hopping into the water, I have sized
the wounds with salt. Ouch! Sting! I am alert
to gravity. It's lovely here. I eat
a plate of fish. Tomatoes, olive oil
and goat cheese. Sun. How good to feed my feet
on sun after the salt! Walking with toil
and red stigmata I begin to heal,
aware I'll live. Back at the Rent-a-Bike
the owner gives me hell. He's right. He's swell.
He says a leg's worth more than a bent wheel.
He says I'm old. No! Yet, back in my shell,
I write away, exploiting pains I like.

Lambi/Skala

Gospel of the Damned

I whistle by your balcony,
"Open the door and make the bed
so we can sleep." I cannot be
away again. We're not yet dead.
It's evening and the pigeons sleep.
The moon is in another world.
I'm on your stairs. The windows weep,
"Don't go away." The night has hurled
the rain into the salty street,
writing our names in every drop.
The bells of jasmine stay awake.
I am resigned. I need to flop
in bed with you and cry and shake
until the sun lies on our feet.

Skala

Gospel of the Blessed

The blessed are the rich in ignorance
who wait and do not agonize, who go
in peace although Li Peng may soon entrance
the world again with massacres. I know
like Plato with his Athens clique I can't
forget the city tailing me, and yet
climbing the thistled goatpath to the rant-
ing wind and whitewashed hermitage, I let
the agony be still. I'm will-less for
an afternoon of Chinese rocks and mist,
an afternoon. Cavafy had a day
out on a ship, and he recalled it more
than tavern streets that never let him stray
from love and agony. Few are the blessed.

Hill of the Prophet Elías

Patmos

The waters of the afternoon are pine
and blue over the island in the deep,
submerged under the sea of Homer's wine
yet lighted by the Moon. Zeus made it creep
up to the surface so Domitian could
banish the Theologian here. Then nuns
and Knights of Rhodes and Turks and pirates stood
around the fortress, killing, eating buns
of apricots and almond paste, with berries
for the white hermitage; the Vision Cave
brought eager pilgrims on the Athens ferries.
Torn up by centuries of contemplation,
a skeptic in the winds of Revelation,
I laugh at my few years and calmly rave.

Skala

Memory of Dancing Almond Trees

What is the real? Is Patmos really here
when later in the day, on a small ship
rocking through foam, I'll be in Asia, steer-
ing through old hours of the Near East? I sip
a glass of tea. Already memories
are dominant. After my leg gave out
I looked with awe at dancing almond trees,
frail, milky on a terraced hill by stout
arrogant mountains ogling down. Now sun
rolls between peaks, a Precolumbian mask
of golden beams yet pocked with nuclear storm.
Where is the real? This millisecond done
and lost and born again, coldly I ask,
with Patmos seen from death, will I be warm?

Skala

Return from the Snow

My father in the nineteenth century
was born in Boston, tragic, on Milk Street.
My mother was a Maineiac like me
from Marsden Hartley's town. Death went to meet
them young. They only knew me young,
will never see my photo turning gray
nor have a clue about my life among
the Greeks. I'd like to walk their shoes away,
crossing this holy island. Life is like
the wind: it blows a while out of the east
with sun and grapes; as soon as it is felt
it blows again with ice. I feel the spike
of thorns along the rocky meadows melt
with love as they walk with me to our feast.

Grykos

HISTORY IV

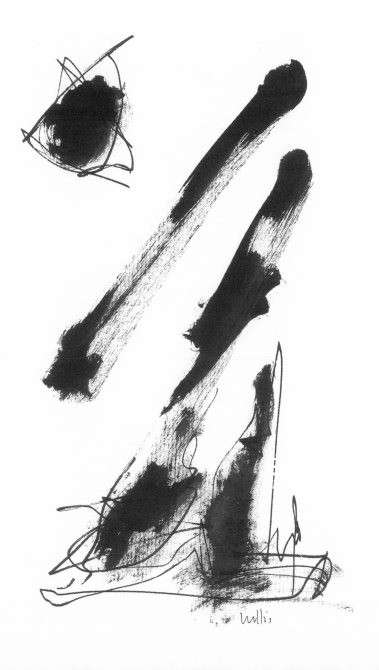

Kafka in His Small Room

A Blindman

I do not know what face looks back at me
When I look at the mirrored face, nor know
What aged man conspires in the glow
Of the glass, silent and with tired fury.
Slow in my shadow, with my hand I explore
My invisible features. A sparkling ray
Reaches me. Glimmers of your hair are gray
And some are even gold. I've lost no more
Than just the useless surfaces of things.
This consolation is of great import,
A comfort had by Milton. I resort
To letters and the rose—my wonderings.
I think if I could see my face I'd soon
Know who I am on this rare afternoon.

Jorge Luis Borges (1899–1986)

For the Secret Reader

Maybe I'll die before I end these lines
(the dogcatcher of darkness hangs around,
picking up strays), and reader, all the signs
will make you dead and safely in the ground
before I come alive to someone else;
and yet I live and dream and think and scrawl
these passions and compassions, sneak my spells
of lonely untrue vision into all
these windy sonnets just for your good ear.
We're two lost migrant souls, whether we meet
and share the secrets we can't find, or walk,
digging up light, despair, or shout our fear
of nothing, nothing till we crash. I'd eat
or maybe sleep with you. At least let's talk.

Joshua Who Hung from Spikes

John 1:14

The oriental histories tell a tale
Of a bored king in ancient times who, fraught
With tedium and splendor, went uncaught
And secretly about the town to sail
Amid the crowds and lose himself in their
Peasant rough hands, their humble obscure names;
Today, like that Muslim Harum, Emeer
Of the true faithful, God decides to claim
His place on earth, born of a mother in
A lineage that will dissolve in bones,
And the whole world will have its origin
With him: air, water, bread, mornings, stones,
Lily. But soon the blood of martydom,
The curse, the heavy spikes, the beams. Then numb.

Jorge Luis Borges (1899–1986)

Joshua Who Hung from Spikes

There was a passionate and suffering man,
who had to hang from spikes. But worst of all
his cross became a way, and so began
a common dream of heaven (though his fall
through darkness really ended with black sod).
That was a while ago, yet times repeat
his passion and abandonment by God,
for Joshua's pain, his crossed and bloody feet,
became religion. Wandering in the sun
that cracks a dry Ugandan tongue or tight
Mesopotamian lips choking on gas
from poison airplanes, think of that poor son
of man, saddest of men, whose creed of torture has
no out, and eat the sun and eat the light.

Crucifixion of an Insignificant Thief

All day the thief, crucified, sags
in pain, obliged to wait and sweat
for a drunk Roman guard to wet
his hot coarse forehead with some rags
of vinegar. Levantine sun
knows no merciful shade. His crime?
A stolen sheep? Books have no time
for petty facts. He is no one.
A second thief will also lie
in a stone ditch before the day
goes dark. Vaguely, he feels the thrill
and fuss of fame. Yet should *he* cry,
he still won't count. In grave dismay
beside him, Joshua's plea is shrill.

Floating Godless in Heaven

All day I watch the mountain. Long away,
you came last night. Fanny asked if Japs had
invented God. She knew already they
invented flowers. You came, godless and sad,
longing to lie on heaven's diamond floor.
I mount with you; we are a faithless race
of jailbirds in a paradise of poor
and dying souls. Heaven's a crazy space
for godless lovers. Wait. All day I ask
how can I be so pitifully in love
when soul and star, impossible to know,
smirk at our impotence. I drop the mask
of heaven made of Kyoto gold. Below,
Confucius is a bore. Godless we toss above.

Inner Leopard Snow and Public Mud

Catherine complains that William Blake
is always lost in Paradise
and not much company. His eyes
look inward where the mountains wake
with leopard snow, where sunflowers grow
like worm moths blowing through the night
into the loneliness and glow
of sun inside and mortal light.
Poor Billy Blake, poor Billy Budd
about to swing, it's time to sleep
and hear the priest's mad daughter shout,
hurling her stones at doors. Her mud
and ours, since Adam's fall, are cheap
scarecrows for terrifying doubt.

Patient Moon

The moon is not impatient like the son
of man who cleaned the lepers, and the eye
around the planet washes her green sun
of midnight on a few whose meadows cry
for sperm, maddens the people of the boats
with milk flaming on rock. Yet even when
she floods a dying child, she never floats
out of her crater with the oxygen
of faith, nor lords us with a vision ray
of crystal heaven. Full and filled with sand,
her face is the death object in the night,
is now and nebulous. While mystery and
apocalypse are sleep, her yes of light
glares out of dream to love, our waking clay.

Bumming Everywhere, from Earthy Mystics in Greece to the Beauty and Hell in Tibet

A rose is Tibet blue, a sign of realms
like this green evening with my dog asleep
yet *with* me in this limestone tower. I creep
older and faithful to the winds and elms
of my Vermont farmhouse where a plain rose
is beauty, refuge, peace. Or I am gone
to Greece where on a whitewashed street the rows
of open island-doors blow in the dawn
of reason floating through the olive trees.
Perseus walked here. And Plato looked up from
his cave to union with his blinding sun.
Then death. I wear Tibetan amber beads
around my neck, recall a murdered nun.
Tibet is hell. Its temple bells a bomb.

Mary's Version

The Christians stole my life. I was a Jew,
an unembellished wife and mother till
the Romans pounded nails in Josh. It's true
he coughed up magic parables—but kill
a guy for that? Then Matt, Mark, Luke and John
gossiped with visionaries, dreamt up tales,
made me unreal and cast him as a con-
man, yes, a stuntman popping miracles
to fool the world. Their curve on history
was holy gospel lies and my despair.
The facts: I never went to rallies in
the fields, Josh wasn't God, I had my spin
with Joe, and Joshua was our son. I swear
there is no bastard in my family tree.

Mary Who Held Her Dead Son in Her Arms

In Mexico the Indians on their knees
bloody the earth and crawl to her. She sighs
eternally to them. Her huge tears freeze
against the kohl below her dazed moon eyes.
Like God she seemed a miracle. But God
was busy fabricating more and more
believers and their laws. She scorned the rod
of suiters, neither virgin nor a whore
but a mother who gave birth. Joe stuck by her
despite the cracks. A woman in her bed,
she bore the infant Joshua and she had
to scratch her way out of a shed. And then
she bore him from the spikes. He moaned and bled
while she embraced him dying among men.

Suicides

Only a family parades suicides
through all your days and folds you in a trap
of guilt. I could have gone, been *with* him. Tides
of days have disappeared into the gap
of years. What would a week, even a year,
have stolen from my life to save the man
who fathered me? He jumped. Nor did I hear
my brother when he wrote; I failed to plan
a trip to Houston. So my brother went
alone into the poisoned dark. What's left
is pictures of a building top, some pills
my brother bought at drug stores. Innocent
they lie alone. I'm emptied by their theft.
We never talk or walk the empty hills.

My Daughter Heads Me to Felicity

When the bad hour of climbing to the roof
to float like Father from the sun is lurking,
however stupidly in mind, the proof
of happiness is sound, for what is working
deep in the cave is love. My daughter tells
me wisely that the hour of happiness
is here, and I agree. And then she spells
it out, insisting that I not repress
the pain. Cry, if you can. Though I'm ashamed
of weakness and my sad and groveling plea
for love, she wakes me free. I'm free. She's right,
of course. I love her truth: not to be named
by Adam, live or dead. And in my night
like sun I float in strange felicity.

Tramping around Beijing

A night in Beijing as I tramp the street
of snow and mule aromas to my room,
a flute hangs on the cabbage mounds. I eat
a moon cake while the all-night factories fume
with blue fluorescent tubes and drudgery
of progress. But the flute persists. It climbs
with Buddhist pause, soaring to the fire tree
of goldfish stars. Out there no words or rhymes
are heard. How strange! when here I am the fool
again, learning a tongue, and cocked to damn
my pen to bliss, to the good news of verse,
to gospel song. Of course alone. The rule
of silence, Chinese vast, is fixed. I nurse
that faith of silence. Yet, please hear: I am.

Confessions of a Weakling and a Hypocrite

He first appeared as chairman of my race,
and after showing us his garden home
he played with us, got mad, spat in our face,
and threw us to the dogs. Since then we roam
the globe, and many drink consoling lies.
I can't. He has a business and a flock
of noble managers and friends. My ties
were always weak—nostalgia for a mock-
romantic scene of grace, of daily hope,
and then the payoff: miracles of time
after my death. I'm sad, I'm terrified
to be this lonely man without a dime
of faith. God could call any night and I'd
say yes. I am on call, waiting to elope.

Coward

My goal is courage but my skin is thin,
and even when I jog, the agony
of blaring memories hounds and halts me in
my tracks. I leaned my heart against a tree.
It rained, washing the bloody mess away,
and I am guilty of the vile attempt
of forcing love upon a bush. I pay
for shame. Yet test me. When I cry or tempt
my loins, there's no one to confess to, and
I'm loyal to silence, faithful till they snip
my tongue out. While I'm sensitive and weak
and screw up in the end, who cares? The sand
I eat is sweet, since fear and any bleak
fiasco turns to words. And I'm the lip.

Serious Clamor with God on Me and Others Like Me

You open your six hands and make the cloud
your chariot, and walk upon the wings
of extended gales. Your whales impress the crowd,
your weapon, death, the lurking monster, flings
me to my knees where I will wait and wait
and decades wait, and still not pray. And when
your glance of anger spits its glowing bait
into my mouth, when stone-worms bite and pin
my heart, you'll win, you'll murder me, but I
won't turn at last to dream of you. I hope
to cheat the madness in our neighborhood
where souls and rain hug in the dark. I'll die
unborn, yet glory lies not on your slope
of heaven's song, but in my soundless wood.

Friend with AIDS, His Plans, and How We All Survive

My friend with AIDS said he won't wait. Not wait
until it's loss of mind and wasting. He'll
just sit before a fire, eating a plate
of oysters, sipping scotch, and only feel
the harmonies of Mozart, drink and let
some pills do tricks with time. I sip my B
& B, hearing Dinu Lipatti. Yet
Dinu, Chopin, and my poor friend are three
who leave life early while I hang around,
a boondock dope in love, guilty to sound
so cheerful while Tibetans set themselves
on fire. Now even children learn to die
of AIDS or hunger. Answers? None. My shelves
are bare, yet I can't help my happy sigh.

Magical Sun in Bed

The wondrous deeds of God are slight-of-hand,
are miracles of words intoned on stage
by prophets, cons, and men who wear a band
of truth (like 60s hippies) while they rage
against the weak in faith. Yet all conform
and mellow out. The holy saints choose reason
and hot cross buns, and have their gods perform
on film. Magic is out. This is a season
when an old hipster shaves and isn't scorned
for giving in. Yet magic lives. Don't ask.
It lives. Angels have sticky wings, and sun
pedantically awakes to warm and stun
a brutal world. Deep in a bed adorned
with you, my sun, in magic arms I bask.

Overcast Soul

Look in your soul, O love. It's green
and overcast and raining there;
her cows float up from a ravine.
You see as far as everywhere.
Be still. Look in your soul. Be still
inside as Adam's sleep, and hear
your hobo eyes under a hill
of dream. The dirty spring is here,
the Beijing alleys overcast,
a Ming tile court of memories.
You look for home. Strangely a past
of barn, of island and Greek seas
shows in the rain. I share your bowl
of mist. It's raining in your soul.

Soul Light

The soul is light, her body living mud.
And although soul light is invisible,
once gone her lonely ark fades in the flood
of death, angelfish glare, the bleaching gill
is stiff to bubbling air, the clam is tight
around her shrinking cloud of fat. So take
me now. Make my mud bake, crack in the light
of light! I ask for little. Help me wake
and be my friend. I love you, yes. The soul
is a small gift of the creation. For
one yellow night of love, the butcher shop
soaks lilies in her blood. Soon I will drop:
a black varicose watch into the floor
of time. I love you from my shining hole.

Fool of Poetry

Seconds of panic, yes, but they are rare
and hide like death, which always is a threat,
never a deed. Of course I am aware
of failure—mine and yours—but can't regret
the loneliness of towers. Yet if I lost
belief, I wonder if I could keep up
the show. I'm lucky. Long ago I crossed
the moor of isolation with a cup
of poison, and I swallow hills of water
for white insomnia of creation, for
that deep felicity when I'm a squatter
outside night. Honestly, I can't care more.
I'm dropping. Better not to beef or think
beyond a dream awake in private ink.

Failed Poet Who Can't Get into Your Sheets

It's no fun to stand locked outside your door,
whistling for you to make the bed and let
me in. On these stone steps I whistle for
an ancient horse, an Inca amulet,
a bell cast on the moon or any trick
to get me in. Truth is I hate the cold
and solitary nights of truth, the click
of goodbye files, the letters saying, "Hold
on, pal," or "Sorry, sir." But you're inside,
I whistle and you hear. Why don't we dump
these fancy words? I don't know how to act,
but won't you fish me out? You'll be my guide
from hell to immortality. The fact
is *please* say no. Say yes and I might jump.

Kafka in His Small Room

Ticking Moon

The new moon fills and empties and I wait,
I'm living for tomorrow. *Now* is gone
before it stops. The *past* I fabricate
with memory, since moon waters on the lawn
must sink away. If not my head would flood.
So what is left? We tramp about the storm
in Maymyo, central Burma, in the mud
and Monsoon rains beating the graveyard warm
like us with our machete hacking brush
to find your mother's tombstone. Just distortion
remains. I bank on lips, letters that may
explode with lunacy and all the lush
of reason and our love to hide how day
by day my heart ticks to its last abortion.

Today's Dream

Yes *now* is gone! The *future* hasn't come
and *past* is a few seconds of relived abuse
of fact. Left is today, another sum
of nowness with the feel of living juice,
a stretch of time, a mattress for my heart
which says I'd rather sing than tick—yet tick
it must if it will sing. I play the part
of fragile *is*, a ghostly *will*, a flick
of *was* that looms as conscience, fades as light.
How warm I feel without those dreams of time,
without remorse or hope. I dream I am,
that I am not illusion, not a sham
of being without a shell or cell. My night
is fire. What if I burn? These seconds rhyme.

Gospel of the Undefeated

I'm not defeated—yet. My brother was,
our father was. They suffered and I hurt,
remembering their laughter. With the buzz
of the fat chopsaw on the deck I spurt
into the meadow to the burnpile where
I work a few more hours, heaving a pine
and locust on the bonfire. Rob's a bear,
a human crowbar (he's my son). I'm fine,
I tell him, though my ankles are a blotch
of cuts and ivy sumac. We quit early,
and go off to the Ripton cliffs. I watch
them roping down. Not quite a brave and burly
climber, I wait and watch, stealing a verse
and climbing starkly through their universe.

Gospel of Sewage

I'm cool, and I got bossed about and strong
from digging out the bloated septic tank,
yanking its lid off, rolling it along
the road in wet July. The back yard stank
until I punched some screws into the disk
and rolled it back. There, swimming in the shit,
a frog groped to get out. Rob took the risk
of falling in—we had no footing. It
was gutsy when he shoveled that poor frog
to freedom. Now I'm dazed, dirty and dead,
flopping into the rubble where I sleep
under my borrowed L.L. Bean. My bed
is a green ghost I wrestle with. The fog
of dawn comes messy, straggling like gray sheep.

On a Vermont Farm, Worrying about
My Place in Albert Einstein's Equations

Let me be happy on the day I die
although that night of nights begins the rot.
I'll be dead pounds of love under the sky
under the sun, one ant fixed on this dot
of air where I was born to crawl for a
fixed dot of time. Let me be happy since
I'll feel the terror when my globe won't say
"Good Morning." I alone will go. You'll rinse
my dirty shirts for a garage sale in
the neighborhood, hear rain talk on my face
nostalgically. The body is a whim
of time. I like to swim, and when I swim
tonight, don't cry. The world will spin and spin
like Einstein's gray mustache grinning at space.

A Kid Dies in Boston and I Don't Feel So Well Myself

God was invented so the priest could speak
with the authority and power of God.
Prayer is a toll-free number for the meek
and brave to hear the voice of heaven nod
inside the head, and save us from the pit
of agony. I read about a boy
in Albany. He couldn't eat or shit.
The howling worm of night flew to destroy
his blood, turning it white. His parents prayed
yet gave no medicine; he swelled and died.
God's will. Though will-less, I have never strayed
into the narrow way of faith, and though
I lose my ulcerating eye, they lied
who claim they rowed to God. I row and row.

Getting Put in Place, Even in Dream

Morning. I drift up. Over is the dream
cinema. Now I start the other float
of life, the dream of being awake. I seem
to be like others—sometimes—yet this boat
of being has a strange rower, me, who's not
in charge, whose body, even mind, obeys
the habit of the living: rowing thought
and rowing thought till the boat sinks and days
and nights of sea-borne dreaming stop. Before
I woke I spoke to Borges on the floor,
supine in his wool suit, handing me some
greasy car parts. I say, "I've never seen
mechanics working in good clothes." "You're dumb,"
he smiles, "I'm blind and stay perfectly clean."

Drinking in a Joint and Not Even Drunk

Forgive me. Yes, I know I talk and brag
too much. Clearly I feel I'm not much good
and scarcely hide the shame, my tent of rag,
my smile of fear. Lost in the human wood,
I mix with other trees, yet what am I?
I'm not autistic, flawed by genes. I'm me,
a stranger fact. And without drugs I'm shy
or skeptical about my agony,
casing a blowhard, Willis, from a far
black peak. He's wound up, gabbing and unreal.
When he's wound down, no one will come to check
him out—no one inside him. So you feel
I'm crazy. No. I am like you, yet wreck
my peace, waking to no one in this bar.

Kafka in His Small Room

The Only Deadly Sin

The only sin is death, and it's not mine,
it's God the Maker's sin. I won't be here
to take the rap or even live in fear
of punishment down in that soundless mine
where coal-like I'm cocksure I'll have no head
for memory or regret. But since death is
the deadly sin and it was God who fed
me into mafia night, he blew his bus-
iness, broke his own commandment and the law,
and Gotti wiped him out, smiling of course
and dressed to kill. The wise-guy God is gone,
his holy, screw-up sin paid off. Yet worse
will be my aftermath of lightless dawn.
So I live sinless, groping in the raw.

Zip, So Long

I can't believe it, zip, I'm gone forever.
I shut my eyes, as on a plane, and when
I wake I wake to nothing, not a feather
of living thought to meet the inkless pen
of time. So all my life has been for this?
Forget it. Yes, I won't awake. I won't
splash into sonnets any more or piss
six times a day or bore you stiff. You don't
need to return my call. I've hung up, gone
out of my room for keeps. And will I care?
The question is absurd. I'm not yet fried
but can't think out a way to know or bear
the truth of death. In April sun my son
and I, in his green pickup, laugh and ride.

Josephine the Singer

To Smile with Cheerful Grief of the Olive Tree

To smile with cheerful grief of the olive tree,
to hope for happiness, hope to survive
smiling, plating each day with gold, and be
this glad, sad vanity of being alive.
And every day I feel lighter and caught
up in that smile of brilliance and black shade.
Stormwinds punish your mouth freezing and taut
while mine is struck by summer winds that strayed
into my cell. A smile soars the abyss
and grows like a shocked pit—yet flapping wings.
A smile climbs hotly over caves, in flight,
diurnal, firm. It will not drop or miss
or darken. Love, you brave and climb all things,
and smiling fled the earth, the sky, the light.

Miguel Hernández (1910–1942)
Torrijos Prison

Josephine the Singer

for the siren of the mouse folk

I took out my watch, looking in its heart
of death, and said, this is the last pure art
her people hear before she is the light,
only the light, in a few memories.
Other mechanics heard her every day.
She never failed with them, although to please
them, she concealed that she had found a way
to be the natural siren, not a horn,
a siren. Back in the small lunch room where
the fellows take a break, she sang. It was
like humming, like an engine hardly worn
or leaky. She loved me a while. The buzz
of motors blurs. Her song lives everywhere.

Ophelia the Singer

Ophelia sang as she was drowning in
the brook, and snatches of old tunes were heard
above the glassy stream while her warm skin,
in garments weighted with her madness, blurred
and sank her melody to muddy death.
Her lay was drowned yet heard by all who sing
and choose—incapable of noise on earth—
to end the fantasy of transient being.
Among the daisy fires of their distress,
they try to sing. I saw my father croon,
I heard my brother dream. You'll stick it out
since every second's better than the dress
of darkness. Kick me, sing me, toss me, soon
like a plug nickel I'll be back and shout.

Gospel of Compassion

Even Lord Buddha was a single di-
arrhetic man among a mythic crowd
of Buddhas. He was good, and yet to die
a man of words and spirit in a cloud
of kind ascetic light, he dumped his wife
and child. Our planet spun around so when
he gazed back, lusting for his palace life,
his eyes were looking straight ahead again.
If Buddhas sin and fail in myth, I guess
delusion tumbles everywhere. To fail,
to lie, to blunder and be weak, to hate
sometimes. I love these gasping fools. In jail
for life, maybe you'll love me too. I wait
for us. How fine, how good our helplessness.

It's Dim. Where's God?

In the beginning God painted the word
of flame along the walls of chaos. No
one was. There was no fool to read or hear
the God. So he made light. A light to blow
into mud eyes. And having words to cause
the light, he gave us being. His being. We were
and are a while. Hyenas laugh with claws
stinking of blood. In Africa the fur
of twilight and a path of infinite
disease turns God into a face of corn
while wasting AIDS makes mere survival nil,
a secret for the poor. It's dim. We sit
through life, unknowing. If of God we're born,
why is his glorious light invisible?

Kafka in His Small Room

Reconciliation

Sometimes the little fugues of J.S. Bach
are all I need. The ecstasy of just
a clavicord. I will not sputter ACH
or OH. Silence is closer to the dust
and joy I am. What else is there? To know?
I can't know much for long. A bit of fame?
I'm sick of longing for an ear to row
to me and hear. I'm too old now. My shame
allows me one or two good friends to care,
which is enough. The soul? Brain caught in time
and never visible down in black seas.
Fucking? A fugue of stars when good. The slime
of death? I'm reconciled (maybe I squeeze
the truth). And love? O floating mountain air!

Talking with Ink

Don't cry
for me.
To be
and die
is what
we are:
a cut,
a scar
of love,
and then
the slow
fade of
pain. Pen,
don't go.

Shots of Friendship

Metaxa brandy in my hand. Come in.
You can hear Horowitz. We'll read and drop
into the sheets of dream, and sin and sin
against the clock. For agony we'll swap
the apocrypha of God and give them both
away. I used to sleep next to the maid
on the straw mat. Poor house. We spread a coat
on us, since Mexico was cold. I made
some money selling blood. Come in. I swing
through time. We're running in the Gobi down
hot slopes of oxygen, jump in cold ponds,
drink wine; and splashing Uzbek kids, we ring
the neck of vampire death. It's sweet to drown
a while with happiness of vagabonds.

Loafing in Blue Tibet

The mustard fields and mountains in Tibet
echo with daybreak and bullfrogs
crooning on the snowlakes. We go out, forget
patrolling Hans and hack the fields. I toss some logs
on a burnpile.
We're freezing, scratch our fleas. My daughter wakes
happy, unburned (except by passion) while
her lofty birthday breaks
out over violet plateaus. Nomads pass. We claw
the dirt of peace. No nuns are shot today, I guess.
Who am I to bitch? I lose my scream.
Without a book, with you, and with a thaw
in frozen time and chronic loneliness,
and no Han soldiers near, we loaf and dream.

Kafka in His Small Room

Days in the Turkestan Desert

Our Russian prop plane has a busted right-
side engine. We've been waiting two
days for the motor to come. Aliki and I hike
a few hours. "Some tea?" Nomad Turks are cooking stew
and skewing lamb. A feast. We join. It's cold.
One fellow asks me to wrestle. We talk Chinese.
Neither of us are good at it. I fold
my wallet in my shirt, seize
his leg. We roll. Everyone is laughing. When
I'm licked, Aliki and I thank everyone again
for good food and we wander to a small
abandoned mosque. It's a stone eyeball. We climb
inside. Goathorns in the sand, God in the wind through all
the small broken windows. Peace dazes time.

Below the Airplane to San Francisco

Words in the air are blank. Below, the far
precise snows on the soundless mountains sit
like glowing animals on parchment: stags, a bear,
mystery whales in mist.
The great wall of red
desert America tilts like dinosaur teeth.
Suddenly a cover cloud.
Everything is metaphor. Microscopic trees
are bacteria. I'm seated by
the overused toilet. People wait. The ammonia smell
blots TV babble. Wilderness is beautiful
below. Blue prehuman bone
of planetary craters lie
by the wordless Pacific. No mind. Earth alone.

To the Mother of All Defeats

Peace must be near, which means I have no place
to sing tonight. My scholar's lamp is dead,
the poet's fire is live, I turn my face
against the wall, chewing a piece of bread
from TINA'S, shouting in my quiet way
against the peace when corporals will be forced
to kick me to the floor. Enraged, I say
my nonsense like our God who has endorsed
both youthful armies who are trained to die.
It's four a.m. There must be something real
beside the pain of incompletion. If
I sing tonight (my voice is a small meal
a prisoner would spit on), I'll be stiff
but not at peace. Just crushed and glad to spy.

A Thread of Heaven

Don't disappear yet, body. You are all
I have to keep my mind and pen alive.
It's Sunday afternoon. Restless I call
a lovely ghost, who loved me once, and drive
to Mexico by five, in time for drinks.
We kiss over the margaritas. Then
above the plaza, in our room that links
us to eternity with oxygen
of love, we float in mingling sweat. You come
with fountains. As we dry, the archaic sun
wrinkling the bloody pyramids declares
us one and blessed. You wake, sad to become
a ghost again. But we are dreams and run
outside our hermitage till one thread tears.

Some Live in Eden

We live in time. One woman walks around
the world. It takes eleven years. They stone
her on her way—some mad mullahs who found
her half naked in shorts, her loose hair blown
about by unveiled winds—they howled and beat
her. Egyptian novelist Mahfouz goes out
each Thursday to an old café to meet
his friends. He's stabbed by one of the devout
dumb terrorists of God. They got him twice
in the neck. Asked earlier if he was scared
of threats, he said, "No, I've done my life's work.
There's nothing they can take from me." Some mice
sing on the roof, some women walk. I jerk
along. Time grins at me. No one is spared.

Asian Meals in Paris That Still Feed Me
as I Cook Up Dreams

Honestly, I've always longed. Paris I knew
when I was twenty. Now I smell that coal-
dust of the afternoons. I met a Jew
from India, looking for a kosher meal.
"Can you direct me, sir, to a restaurant
for Hebrew students?" Gosh, come to my room
and I'll fry you a fish. He came and sat
on the bed eating oatmeal. Polite gloom
was how his face was. Poor guy. I am still
a lousy cook. That night I found a girl
to feed me Persian fruit. We chewed and kissed,
and high in her small attic she said, "Fill
me with your flying sperm." And then we hurled
through central Asia to feast along its steppes.

Playing with Night

That land from which no traveler has returned
is waiting patiently like fish still in
the bay of Vladivostok. I've learned
to wait like them. The land, when I begin
my silence, need not breathe or think. It will
survive. I will survive only as it.
There is a rub. It's not a dream. The bill
for quick eternity is counterfeit
and I am stuck with language, not a chance
to dream. To be? To be thereafter, and
be happy? When I woke into the light
I thought Siberian pears and snow could dance
forever. Rhetoric of hope. I hand
you hope. Why not? I am, and play with night.

W.B. Was Born and Died

The rolling dice came up with Willis. Am
I me? Even my death is nothing more
than confirmation of an epigram:
W.B. WAS BORN AND DIED. The roar
of being is all I know. I hear it, yes,
and neither I nor you can think beyond
this oddity, this arbitrariness
that makes us locked like Earth—a vagabond
of planets in a thinning glove of air—
locked in a universe of mindless things.
The moon has no idea it has no soul.
And yet this heart, this ticking being, a hair
that holds it live, these wheels of love, these strings
of hope, I'd know, though soon I will be coal.

Cyclops in Love

Love Constant Beyond Death

The final shadow that will close my eyes
will in its darkness take me from white day
and instantly untie the soul from lies
and flattery of death, and find its way,
and yet my soul won't leave its memory
of love there on the shore where it has burned:
 my flame can swim cold water and has learned
to lose respect for laws' severity.
My soul, whom a God made his prison of,
my veins, which a liquid humor fed to fire,
my marrows, which have gloriously flamed,
will leave their body, never their desire;
they will be ash but ash in feeling framed;
they will be dust but will be dust in love.

Francisco de Quevedo (1580–1645)

Resignation to Waking Out of the Night
to Scrawl a First Poem
and Having a Czech Friend to Read It

At two a.m. in Maine, an aching night
of winter in the yellow dorm, I woke
and heard my roommate heaving, groan and bite
his epileptic tongue as if he broke
every bone in his corpse. I got up and
floated next door, sat down and wrote eight lines.
That night of moon breasts in my dirty hand
slipped into ink and I was born. The mines
exploded in the clouds. Don't worry. Though
I'm broke, can't sleep, and bumming like my son
slammed by a Boston court, we're all the same.
Groping, I stick a pen against the sun
and stain its yellow heart. Maine is to blame
for breeding me. Fail? Die? I still say no.

Miguel Hernández in a Prison Hospital at Alicante,
Scissoring Paper Dolls

Sorry for coming to your cot at two
a.m. It's 1942, the floor
is ice. Tubercular but hopeful, you
come with wounds of *vida, muerte y el amor*
and cough up so much fluid you are numb
with rags. Your love endures. Sometimes you look
into blue hearts of friends and drink some rum
with me in Burma where our only book
is failure. Then you wake to know and write,
and guards leave us alone while bedbugs save
us from deep sleep. You die and linger down
in Turkic Kashgar in a Muslim grave,
dreaming pearl markets, goats, rain in the ground
of lime, in hell, Miguel, but rhyming light.

Herbal Tea at Midnight

The body has no peace since time cannot
drop out and stop. The body covets time,
its olive oil, its air. I know the plot.
I slinked along the Drive, hoping to climb
the Sailors Monument. I was afraid
of falling. Then in Orange, Mass., I dropped
out of a plane the way my father paid
for failure. The chute opened and I hopped
onto the planet while my children raced
to find and save me. Love persists. I sit
alone in flesh, sipping some herbal tea.
Though love is only mind and frail, its bit
of light is worth a death. Now that I've faced
the sickening of time, love helps me be.

Weary Escape Just in the Nick of Time

Even Sor Juana broke. She brawled, but then
she caved before the priest who killed her word.
I haven't suffered yet. Well, maybe when
I lay in my stone office and she blurred
into a marriage or the year I fell
from being and couldn't find the way to being
again. But time calms every throbbing bell
and rains clean up a neighborhood. While seeing
a mirror with mechanics fixing me,
I almost died. They washed me, scrubbed the grease
out of my joints. How close I came. It's clear.
I'm tired, wise. Juana rose and fell. Her tree
of words lay poisoned. Falling into peace,
I love you and feel good. Let's have a beer.

Voyage to the Moon

It's night but I'm not sleeping and my soul
takes off. She wings in pilgrimage, a hair
over the moon. I just report the hole
of darkness in my head. I don't know where
she flew, I'm soaked with fear, stuck in a bed,
depressed, worn, old. So maybe I should sleep
or mourn as if my family all were dead
in Asia where the cyclone hit. It's cheap
to be this weary, I hate it, strain
to find a moon. First awe, then nothing! Yes,
a ray. I'm floating like a smart bomb to
meander crazy through the night. I'm sane
but can't let go, and as I stare a blue
bullet plugs me. At last I'm bodiless.

Cyclops in Love

My head is full of poems and the shock
and lies of visionary pilgrimage
through time to beds on mountains, to a dock
in Sérifos where Cyclops in a rage
of passion jumps into the bay and swims
out to his lily-fading nymph. What can
he do? His Galatea burns his limbs
but she is myth like him. He's not a man.
He is a monster god in love, the kind
no one believes in. God today hangs out
in churches as a domineering fool.
I am no better. On my island lined
with African-white houses, a slow mule
carts trash. Cyclops and I hunger and doubt.

Art and Love while the Planet Explodes
with Normal Misery

Art has a life. But when bombs fall
and a Kurd's child is lowered in
a muddy pit, her paper skin
wrapped by her father in a shawl
correctly, a full life in art
is less a fire than her good voice
or public agony. No choice
but to give in. I'm smart
and wise to love you. If you see
piles of broiled dogs and children dead
because a bomb is smart, our bed
of love is just a pistol shot
to live on while the misery
of millions ridicules our thought.

Aliki on Her Cot on Perseus Street

She was laughing and it was so beautiful
that evening when she climbed at dusk to the
old kastro, ran along the rocks, and fell
on the summit, breaking her ankle. She
got cured in the Athens hospital. Greece
was white, her opalescent island Sérifos
gave Danae refuge, the iron mines the peace
of toxic ores. In our old barbershop house
my daughter slept in her room under
the slope from which Perseus flew off and slew
the Gorgon. Aliki sat on the cot and wrote
with her pen of light. At night her poems were
dancing in chains, snoring under her throat,
and suddenly the old Greek walls were blue.

Kafka in His Small Room

The Cost of Calm

My father and my brother paid
for peace. One jumped, the other drank
water and poison pills. They fade
yet never fade. I have to thank
my body: I still jog and write,
hoping to transform paper so
a soul will talk. She squeaks. And light
eludes the ink. That's life! I row
each morning. Life's a gym. My cat,
a minor lion, talks to me
with yellow eyes. I envy calm
of sleeping animals who chat
with the Tibetan saints. No sea
of peace. The night will be my psalm.

In Paris Vallejo Recalls His Young Brother and His Poems Who Also Haven't Lived

César Vallejo is a happy and
a grieving man. I'm happy too, but Oh,
I know those tricks of sorrow. In his hand
he holds against his vest a straw chapeau,
his shoes have spats as he recalls the yard
in Lima where his brother died. "Come out,"
he yells, "Stop hiding. Mother will cry
or worry." But Vallejo has to die
before his poems are heard. I am about
to write another piece of trash, my card
of joy, of grief. My Paris friend finds life
in posthumous collections. Well, me too.
And yet it hurts to start again. My wife
is paper words, some stacks I pile for you.

About the Poverty and Ignorance We Breathe
That Almost Saves Us

To know ourselves we dwell in poverty.
We are the poverty that saves us when
a peacock angel pops up in God's tree
to trumpet villages in heaven, then
offers to sail a ship of souls through light.
Heaven is dark. But we are live. I sigh
in failure, my sure light. The human plight
is to taste death. With light in me I'll die,
afraid, yet knowing rays in me and in
the street are good enough to get me through
night's cinema of dreams. I wake to no
sure way. I'll die as dumb as squirming in-
sects. Yet I'm wise. I fear. I love. And you
and I are breathing life we cannot know.

Blue Love

Young Jacob wrestled with him until dawn
while he played checkers with eternity,
then turned invisible. It sickens me
to think of awful Yahweh. We turn on
to praise a monster in the sky, a hoax
who has no being. He didn't make me with
a word. I think, and not because he soaks
me with blue magic. Yah is mind, a myth
of power or paradise or soul, and not
from an old man or young messiah. He wakes
only when I awake. Spinoza knew
him infinite and everywhere. I thought
him nowhere. Now I pause and a force shakes
me blue. She's blue, blue love, and only blue.

Kafka in His Small Room

On My Island of White Geometries in Rational Blue, Thinking of Philo the Alexandrian Floating Up His Ladders of Being

The oxygen of joy, the seaweed sun
on the white island where the moon was born,
where fig and olive trees wrestle for fun
and Philo fills his logical Greek horn
of light to climb to calm and solitude
of the invisible, these were the elements
of dream I ate when we were young. My food
was watermelon and smoked fish. My pens
were not computerized. My notebook was
the landscape of salt stars. Only a ghost
gagging on electronic bilge could guess
I've changed. This winter rain is glum. I'm cold
(that's also truth). While Philo chews his toast
upstairs with God, I'm back with sun on hold.

Reflections on the Poet's Feet

Pound said he started with a swollen head
and ended up with swollen feet. I walk
with just a touch of flu, glancing ahead
with sober greed of hearing my rhymed talk
in secret print. A private book is fine.
I'll do a drawing for it. Picasso can't
help out today (though Lorca might). The spine
will read: *The Dogday Sonnets of a Plant.*
I like to think my voice is growing green
and bouncy. Ovid woefully complained
of exile in the Pontus. I feel grand,
better than Pound showing his balls, his mien
of greatness as he fought for friends and reigned.
I'm calm, though flu muzzles my barking hand.

Among Hoosiers

Weary? Not much. I want a few years more.
Keek, Rob, Ton and I are busy and my pen
itches. So, time, stop bugging me. The door
to my big mouth lets out a hurricane
of dancing words. Will I die in the fall?
In a grim London bed-and-breakfast cell?
I love to dance mad at the ghostly ball
up on the sandbox moon while a white bell
cries up from earth. I am red energy,
a convict sentenced to a page. I wait
too long. When my soul bursts, play a flute, drink,
toss me in a pine box. I'll meditate
under the earth. It's horrible to be
a plant. Burn a carnation while I stink.

On an Ordinary Evening in Indiana Where I Invent a Lover Who Smells Intimately of Existence

Nothing has happened. I'm alive. I wrote
for fourteen years to find you, and the tree
of the sun says the minute gun won't float
its death tune. You I look at cannot be
the reader. She's for books and you have arms,
a heart, and we drink coffee in a mug
at four a.m., not words. I see no harm
in kissing. Germs? No. Your lips are a drug
to save us through saliva soup. Alone
on earth, you master me. I'm calm and look
at everyone with peace. Don't puke. I'm just
an ordinary man. Bones were the book
of moons I drew. Be here in flesh. My lust
for us is not a poem but milk in stone.

Overlooking Rock Meadows of Forbidden Albania

That night it rained a thousand years and when
my heart was soaked, Mólista windows turned
to sleet. The cold intensified. Again
between your breasts I read you poems we earned
in Greek because this mountain cottage near
the Albanian border was a single lamp
and moon-coarse blankets smelled of wool winter
and candles. "Don't expect to sleep." Souls damp
with longing blare like sirens. We were still
because we had the speech of solitude.
A thousand years is nothing for a pound
of rain together. We made love. To fill
the soul with bread and olive oil is crude
and wonderful. Night gossiped while we drowned.

Kafka in His Small Room

*He Cites the Fragility of Life and Points Out
Its Tricks and Enemies*

What other thing is true but poverty
in a life frail and fed by trivial strife?
From cradle on, the ruins of human life
are traps of honor and prosperity,
and time that never stumbles or goes back
spools out its hours, renders them fugitive;
in errant craving, always punitive,
our fortune wastes us weary on the wrack.
Silent death lives, and life itself becomes
a joke, a game; our health turns into war,
assaulted by its very nourishment.
Oh how a man blunders through unseen scum!
On earth I fear I'll fall and disappear,
yet fail to see by living I ferment.

Francisco de Quevedo (1580–1645)

Franz Kafka in His Small Room on the Street of the Alchemists, 1916–1917

One winter Kafka rented a white room
high near the castle where he tired his pen
during the day. At night he rinsed the gloom
out of his eyes and was a crow in heaven,
rising, dancing on awful heights. Before
dawn fed him sleep, the Golem far below
the wall whispered a gravesong in his ear
in ancient Hebrew vague to him. Although
he slept, the ghost of Jewish friends in Prague
(Max Brod who loved his ink) helped him
survive close to the sky. A winter wood
of horses floated on the city fog.
The castle mastered him, but in a whim
he drank white ink and hungered where he stood.

Petersburg in the Sun That Spills Nothing

A crow coughs on the rainy page
of late summer in Petersburg.
A street band near the Hermitage
plays for coins. Guns are gone. The fog
is burning off to Gogol blue.
The brass band tolls eternally
while criminals have much to do
to fill the stores today. To die
they exile Osip Mandelstam
to Voronezh. When the camp train
tolls in, though cold he scrawls a poem.
They've not yet frozen him. Still sane
he scrawls some letters home. The gun
remembers nothing, like the sun.

A Stillness in the Sun

Let me sit in the sun. Sun doesn't cure
all ills (only time does) but the gas star
heats us with calm. The Bosnians still endure
the club of greed. Wilfred Owen, not far
from his young death, wrote: "Move him in
the sun—the amputee in his chair." I need
to know the breeze of peace again. I've been
an actor who cannot sit still, and feed
my nervous fears by showing pages of
a sketchpad or a manuscript to friends.
If they approve I glow a while. The sun
is good and stands outside in massive love
for earth. Unhurried doves ascend. I run
for life. Greek sun says wait. Burning it mends.

Behind Word and World, Spinoza Hears
the Sound of Space

Wittgenstein states behind each word must be
a picture, but the Kabbalists contend
behind each picture is a word; to see
the word like entropy, God's end
was to construct a verbal pattern. So
in the beginning God created letters
first: letters of black fire for Torah. No,
Spinoza says, we're not in jail, in fetters
of word or God, since God is everything
and everywhere and nothing on his own.
Spinoza is a lucky man to live
in Amsterdam, safe in the ghetto. None
(but his friend Leibnitz) knows what he can bring
the lonely: space tunes for the fugitive.

Kafka in His Small Room

A Ghost Chats with Love's Body

I must exist. It's common sense. The earth
is blue and I'm a speck on it. And who
is writing if my ordinary birth
was faked? I am, and then? Illusion? A true
unmagic fact prevails: this death-bound lone
and always separate being cannot see
its mind. It sees outside but not the one
who sees. I function yet how can I be
a face without a face inside? I look
at far words strangely automatic and,
more than Descartes, I doubt. These one-way eyes
have detached retinas to the brain. This book,
this ghost, persists till wipeout, but your hand
kills doubt. So do your face and chatting thighs.

Aliki Scribbling in Madison Fog

The Neva in December has a fog
shrouding the mystery of Peter the Great
who couldn't iceskate with a yellow dog
like you across the lake's white cheek. You wait
until the Russian winter thaws and fish
chew tiny stars of air; now on the roads
across the state the barns, feeding our wish
for milk, already smell of big truckloads
of hay and cowshit. Caviar is cheap
in Petersburg, on pancakes or black bread,
and in Wisconsin you have made your bed
among the hospitals and scholars. When
like sentimental Russians in their den
you lift your pen, you draw the fog from sleep.

Czech Pietá, c.1380

Jesus was circumcised, although the Czech
peasant sculpture under the veil replaced
his penis with a star (no telltale speck
of missing flesh for SS eyes). Death raced
across his soul, bulging his ribs. His starved
Semitic body lay in Mary's hands.
Her gaze of suffering for a son was carved
to crazed, cross-eyed abstraction. Two gray bands
of goatwool draped around his shame. Maybe
there was a crucifixion. Maybe he
(and two poor thieves) were killed. No word
about him, not even Josephus lent
a page to this maltreated son; yet spent
as man he rose as God into the absurd.

Meditation in the Rain

I like to meditate (not formally;
despite my Chinese past I don't know how)
like village rain collapsing dismally
on walkers in the meadow where the Tao
is just a path for farmers who drown cats
or teach their sons to shoot a buck. I think
or think of nothing, forget body, rats,
age, debts. Here on the grass I test the brink
of reason, loafing in the drizzle, hear
piano for the left hand. A meditation
has magic words and methods. I have none.
I scribble poems and kiss. With the inflation
of jargon I'm a shallow stranger, one
strange all-wet man. By night I disappear.

Kafka in His Small Room

Brightly Alone

Death is a meditation too, the extinction
of clouding thought. It's horrible and time
is fatally in love with that distinction,
moving implacably to stillness and its rhyme
of nothingness. The mystics tempt us with
a peaceful voyage to the sun where God,
who once said *Light*, says *Come*. But the deep myth
is wishful fire. No one has found the sod
as passage to an essence beyond dust
and bones. My bones think now. I meditate
and float inside, picking up Roman stone.
One day, someone will pick us up, translate
our darkness. Though time masturbates with lust
and its sweet tooth for flesh, I glow alone.

Killing Boredom

L'ennui makes you a hangman just for kicks,
said Baudelaire. They strapped me in the chair
and hit the switch—the hottest cruelest tricks—
and for a month I sat on ice. I swear
it felt terrific. Once a woman knocked
at the door late at night. What could I do
but let her in? She stripped me, threw me on
the floor and violated me. It's true
I went along with her and didn't yawn
for hours. Gently she murdered me and rocked
my rockers. Tedium is pure reverie.
I wait, bored. Just some days ago the ghost
of Russia warmed up Petersburg and we
went crazy, skinny-dipping off the coast.

Defining Happiness in Buenos Aires

One evening after reading Kipling to
Borges in Buenos Aires, I took him
slowly downstairs (he had dirt on his shoe
which I wiped off) and out along a dim
back street to the Saint James Café. The war,
the dirty one, was noisy. Gun shots, a bomb
in nearby flats, a midnight visitor
pounding a door, the city's catacomb
of terror operating fine. The mess
and drama thrilled me, though the country bled.
We sat under our gothic mirror and
began to eat and gossip. Borges said,
smiling, "Reading Kipling is happiness,"
and blood shivered in his transparent hand.

Worry of the Twitching Olive Trees

People are beautiful and defecate
and think, but olive trees on Sérifos
twitch in Meltemi gales, illiterate
and thirsting for the sun, which is verbose
in silent Greek. Apollo underground
waits in his marble skin for light. One day
down in his hole Apollo will be found
on a construction site. The stowaway,
dirty with evening time, once washed will stand
resplendent. People hear an olive tree
growing silver in a wheat field—a queer
character in Chinese calligraphy—
Skin beauty broods, but the olive tree's hand
is moving dust, incapable of fear.

Soliloquy of a Dog

My dog has character and is a being
insistently alive. The cats the same,
sunning, rolling on their backs. Everything
alive is separate, eager, and to blame
for singing into time. An animal
is me. I run, a stick tight in my teeth,
and chase it if you throw it. I'm prodigal
before my bowl of chow, and underneath
my tongue are sweat glands coloring my bark.
That's nothing. What is best I hang about
a neighborhood, looking for dogs to smell
and lick their ass. My one distinctive mark
is I keep verse concealed on me and shout
it as I trot, yelping a weak farewell.

How Poets from New England and Spain Considered
the Paradoxical Endurance of a Cricket

A soul is weak and full of crickets. E.
Dickinson sent a letter to a friend
and said she was enclosing the body
of a fat cricket in it. Last weekend
in the Amherst library, Aliki found
the letter and a packet. When unwrapped
it held the one-hundred-year-old carcass
of a cricket. F. García Lorca, bound
together with two anarchists, was slapped
dead by two bullets in the head and ass,
but earlier he said one cricket gave
a scream defining the horizon lost
on Andalusian hills. Nothing could save
or quiet a cricket in the soul from frost.

Sancho and His Sancho

I never starved to death or went
to jail for politics or rape.
Don't cry for me or Sancho bent
on mischief. Sancho's out of shape
but cunning about food and word.
We're a good pair. He's letter-made.
I am a less real hummingbird,
not true like fiction. So I fade
though we're both felons, mad or not.
A continent is blooming in
the rain we drink illegally.
Quijote drank with us but got
punched out at bars. We're bad. My sin
is loving Sancho flea by flea.

At the Turkestan Border in Central Asia

No sense. It's misty on these Kunlun steppes.
A mile away, Russia and Pakistan.
Light on a cemetery goat. Rain sleeps
in my blue Chinese shirt. Vagrant I can
go anywhere. Float back to Bloomington?
Or use the Taishan mountain gods to face
Nirvana death of time, or ask why none
or nothing offers me the slightest trace
of how I woke in one-time, no-sense birth?
It's misty and I'm happy. Kashgar peace.
These years of air? For what? Why yearn? What do
I want from all these pages sent to you?
Your love? Walking to Samarkand from Greece,
my sandals hope and creak damply with earth.

Floating Down from Tibet, Damaged Roof of Asia, and Bouncing Back, Haunted

The Chinese let us walk out of Tibet
into Nepal. I look at mustard fields
and nomads, Buddhist ruins, and violet
roofs for murder. Tibet is high and yields
to meditation: blue wheels and blue rock
against oppression. Snow behind us. Now
we pass the border, hike down the air clock
to lower plains. Thin soldiers have somehow
become a shy rhinoceros in the king's
private lowland park where at six a.m.
I gape, hugging a tree for safety. Ice
and murder melt in jungle sun. Yet I'm
still in Tibet, its mystery and lice
and stony killings where a dead nun sings.

Unholy Circle

My company is me most of the time.
Like it or not I'm made that way. Of course
one head has separate eyes to look or climb
outdoors or bring in friends or simply horse
around up in the kastro. I'm one I,
one complicated consciousness and stuck
with me. The pronoun shifts, and though I try
to live two guys, it's grammar, words. My luck
is I am me. My favorite mystical
getaways flash me into some odd God
but God is holy grammar, not for real,
and I can never capture me. I'm with
two grave antagonists, and when I prod
my darkness for one fire, I lie in myth.

Coffee and Early Sorrow in Paris

The train coughs into Paris. Cabs confer
on strike and so I lug my grips upstairs
at l'Hotel de la Gare du Nord. The blur
of midnight rinses sooty rain and hairs
red in the sink. "Monsieur, je vous prépare
le lit?" the maid discreetly grins. She's young.
I'm young. Gulags are filling up. Crowds are
drumming up peace. I'll march with them. My tongue
is politic—yet dreams. "Vous sortez?"
"Oui, je descends. J'ai faim, je veux bouffer."
"Monsieur, je vous attends." She must be God.
Down at the bar I down a hardboiled egg,
coffee, cognac, and race up with my cod
on fire. We'll marry. Gone! God's pulled my leg.

Love Bade Me Welcome

"I loath the mindless, ticking universe,"
Love said to me. "Gross stars roll through the dark
and time performs. But once gone through the verse
of life, no time will pulsate in your art-
less death. So talk to me and don't abstain."
Love took my hand. "I'm all you have," she said.
"You must sit down," she begged me. "I'll not chain
you to a bed." I stuttered and my bread
got stale. "Forget my soul and taste my meat,"
Love urged. But I withdrew to pout (Would sin
prevail?). Stars hurl and burn. Afraid she'd slip
into my sheets and rage my frozen skin
with joy, I turned to flee and saw a ship.
Love sighed, "Before you drown, sit down and eat."

Kafka in His Small Room

With a French Nun in Lapland

Even the constant sun wears a small coat
of darkness till it bangs into our light.
A nun in Lapland on a ferry boat,
whose lips are frozen God, whose hood is white
with ice floating the fjords, unzips my pants
to show her grace. "I'll keep this memory,"
she whispers, "in my bones and sardine cans
back in the factory where I share my tea
and labor with the workers." Sun hangs on
all night in Lapland in July. I bless
my friend the nun for sun. A socialist
and French she talked to clouds over our fun
and deer licks. When our bellies join, no less
than mountains blush and crush us in their fist.

A Sunny Room at Mount Sinai

Mount Sinai Hospital. My mother lay
in a good corner room with lots of sun.
In Perigueux, the children's ward, one day
I saw a young girl in a coma. Sun
came through glass walls; the child was beautiful,
her face freshened with youth. Only inside
the cancer stormed. I saw the nun place wool
soaked in cold alcohol on her. She died
that afternoon. My mother's gown was loose
and she told us that awful things were done
when testing her downstairs. I see her eyes
today. She too was fresh and live. Some juice
lay undrunk by her pillow. A surprise
of pain. I left the room and she was gone.

Imitating Angels amid the Colorado Rockies

I wonder what my father thought
climbing the stairway to the door
that opened on the roof. "I ought
to turn around and calm the roar
of failures and begin again.
It's May in Colorado and
with Van Gogh on my wall I can
make it." He found the knob, his hand
wavered. No, he was very drunk
with pain, his eyes were gone, he had
the smile of the detached. In May
we all got lost and he had sunk
to punishment. In sun my Dad
ghosted to the edge and flew away.

Wise Guy

When I'm in love or in a jam
I'm a wise guy. When life gets hot
or when I'm croaking, I will spot
you Hemingway's brave bulls, I'll ham
it up. The perfect punk was James
Cagney busting a door. A pro,
he'd grab your nuts. You wouldn't know
what hit you. You'd be through with dames.
Jimmy was shy and ran from fans,
spent his last years collecting art.
I like the way he danced. What ease!
He'd dance up Everest. I got plans
for cracking Hollywood. I'll start
out small and starve on a trapeze.

The Iceman

The Iceman slept, staring from Alpine ice,
almost intact until a tourist broke
his penis off and stole it. Frozen lice
glowed on his scalp, and when the Iceman woke
beside a skier's trail, flesh brown, eyes white
from glare, a tattoo hidden on his back,
his dying came to life. In frosty light
of an Italian clinic, the raw sack
of breakfast, his last bite, is spread out on
a table. Seeds and meat. Is it a feast
for cannibals of science? Flesh turned in-
to knowledge? As he slumbered, a man-beast
in hibernation, ice froze time. Now on
display, his rapt eyes watch us through glass skin.

Peking Man / Rudolf Nuréyev Danceman

Once I took the silk route west in May
out to the ancient cave. No one was there.
No one. I stuck my fingers in the clay
and guessed the Peking Man drank his despair
like us. And now Nuréyev drags his feet
toward the eternities. Murderous AIDS
quickens his fate—ours too since we are meat
and soul. Once floating on imperious cascades
of grace, he's carried on the stage. Like all
the Icemen and the Peking tribe he'll stew
out of time into cold blubber. No mark
or hope of light. Russian dancer, the wall
moves in invisibly. Dance to it. You
should flash through it. You can't. We're just one spark.

Chac the Raingod in the Death Well

As I dream toward my other birth when time
is just for others, gods on painted stone
say they are better than meek flesh, my slime
that will lose form. We made them up, on loan
from quakes and hurricanes. They act like lords.
They always do. The real gods walk around
in white pajamas, smoking. Those jade swords
that tore out hearts or tamed an onyx hound
are jewels to grace a woman's breasts. Gods limp
today, are poor, cross-eyed and even pimp
for cash. My flesh and gods slumming hell
seem mortally the same. Eternity
is gone. Even the raingod in his well
begs for girl-flesh to keep him company.

Loss of Self Made Clear

Sometimes I feel like a motherless child
a long ways from home. Worse I feel alone
with me. Is this face yours or mine? We piled
the furniture against the door to zone
the Xian maid away. She tried to break
in anyway. I yelled. She left, and yet
I bitch about this loneliness and ache
because I'm nothing, no one and upset
because I lost my head. It rolled into
the gutter, sank and I'm a soulless lamp,
bulbless, without a glass or light. You laugh
because I'm nuts. I'm sane but missed my cue
to come on stage. Look at this absurd half
a man whose brain is torrid, sick and damp.

Despair Being Gray and Sunless, Hum

There is a glassy puddle of sun
sleeping in the rusty marble grooves of broken ancient
    columns, common and cheap
as a stun gun
for walking safely in the night. You sleep
in the tranquility of its warm throat.
Despair is gray
and sunless. When despair comes, even your coat
of clouds fails to blow away
the torture. Don't smoke. Fool your friends and sing
even if your tongue is sore.
Winter is always near
and a taste of frigid sun is a good thing.
Even in Greek alley rain, where you wander poor
as a rat, it's good to recall a twig of sun and hum
    away depressing fear.

Akhmatova Worries and Then Memory Speaks

Akhmatova complains that God in fact
hasn't saved us on this coarse brutal globe.
They froze her friend to death, they broke a pact
and shot her husband, jailed her son. Her robe
of butterflies she left in Petersburg
and composed orally, ascetically
withdrawn and sad. She visited the morgue
like other mothers. Winter memory
has gladdened her, however. Prison doves
still glide the Neva. "Nothing when we're gone?"
she worries in March poems. Her mirror drips
with cobwebs. But sun glows on buried loves
in Leningrad. Under the webs and on
her glass, a face spots her and moves her lips.

A Kraut Scrawling in His Rainbow Tongue

Why do I feel distant from the German race?
For starts it killed the Jews and I am one
it missed; my midnight blood cannot erase
disquiet. Were I in Warsaw and the sun
was shifting through my ghetto window, I'd
not bask for long in '42. Yet I am
a bit of a Kraut, I fear, and were I fried,
a German name would burn like kosher ham:
Herr Velvel Bornstein. Even now I owe
my tongue and heart to Saxon thorns, my speech
to Old English (Insular Teutonic) prized
and talked into my bones. So I beseech
murders to fade. I talk a huge rainbow
and scrawl a German clean and circumcised.

Isaac Luria, Confining Being to Letters of a Holy Language

Luria puts God in lonely exile from
the world. He is a Kabbalist, a Jew
from Spain. Isaac knows God will never come
to chat with us, yet hungry letters screw
like lilies in a broken vessel. There,
north in Safed, these letters are the genes
determining the soul of God. The air
is sweet with holy chatter; blues and greens
and fresh-cut apples babble. Village-bound,
he restores words with light to carry us
from exile out to cosmic separation
from ordinary clouds and cots—or ground
that bears our gravity. The sun or pus
of death becomes a word of black elation.

A Plea for Imperfection of the Inexpressible, Whether Our Mouths Be Open or Shut

"What cannot be expressed in *words*," the young
Ludwig of the *Tractatus* said, "must be
confined to *silence*," though with sleeping tongue
my dog and I jog through the poetry
of friendship. Zip my wordless mist and you
have zapped my sex and soul. Cut out this book,
if the unwordable is blah. I'm through
with you, if wordless loving is the crook
of passion. Words I skip or eat or save
the way a battered prisoner hoards light
in solitary. Words have wings or fail
and never say it all. Tough luck. I crave
and vomit words to get me out of jail,
just one fat word to bust the trap of night.

Vanity

A time for every matter under heaven.
Ecclesiastes

What does one gain by all the toil
at which one toils under the sun?
When I was born they rubbed some oil
on me and sent me home to run and run
yet all is vanity. We're born
in time and striving after wind.
There is a time to kill or scorn.
There is a time for those who grinned
at death. They're gone. There is a time
for all things in the sun. Some nod
there's nothing new, yet once I came.
And once I'll go. There is a rhyme
for life that isn't death or God:
this vain enigma with my name.

Kafka in His Small Room   293

The Delicious Hurt of Blue

A living dog is better than a dead lion.
Ecclesiastes

There is a night of love, a night
of death, and in between a day
of wondering how we fall on light.
Wonder and death. Too much. I say
nothing as you surprise my mouth.
The woods say nothing. When my tree
in the cucumber garden south
of your warm pears and broccoli
is hot and silently begins
to grow into the darkness of
the planet's core of thermal springs,
we're gone, we're wings, our sweat is love.
You hurt me and the bed is pins
of blue exhaustion. Blue time stings.

Spinoza and a Nightingale

My gods—the lens grinder Spinoza or
Machado garbed in dirty clothes—I look
for them because I'm not enough and poor
in pocket and inside. We're in an old book
with bald men fighting over combs. Our pain
is everywhere and halts only in night
of solely night or when our love is plain
with power. Since love is rare, its common light
spread everywhere (and who can see the seen?),
Antonio's sadness helps me hope. That Jew
in Holland, excommunicated though
he didn't care, is in this room. I lean
on him. His Latin nightingale is so
remote all words are ice and I'm not blue.

The Nightingale

Although the horror of the nightingale,
the holy nightingale who sings unheard,
invisible and strident in the gale
beyond the tree of stars, is just a word
or region of epistemology,
I wake to it like breakfast when my eye
of pus is washed to meet the ecstasy
of day. Horror is never far: the dry
biology of insect hope, the moth
trapping the moon, the wasp of solitude
amid the panting of the air, the cloth
of flying worms. And yet I always hear
the secret of the nightingale, delud-
ing me. Invisibly I'm almost here.

HISTORY V

To Find You at the End of Our Strange Walk

Escaping with the Hermit Zhang

My brother Zhang has five carts of books.
A hermit, he reads endlessly.
Whenever he soaks his brush with ink he surpasses
    the sage of grass calligraphy.
When he writes a poem it makes a classical verse
    seem like a throwaway
Behind closed doors under Two Chamber Mountains,
he's been a hermit for more than ten years.
He looks like a wild man
pausing with fishermen.
Autumn wind brings desolation.
Five Willows seem taller as their leaves drop.
Seeing all this I hope to leave the peopled world.
Across the water in my small cottage
at year's end I take your hand.
You and I, we are the only ones alive.

Wang Wei (701–761)

The Secret

There is a labyrinth of being and snow
and nightingales, cancer, a hospital
for birth and changing hearts, and a rondeau
of copulation and more brats, a call
for pills and condoms to preserve a bit
of airy green space. If I had the wings
of morning I would fly to the infinite
shores of the sea, yet the Lord, the psalm sings,
would seek me out. It's lonely being on loan
and unpursued. God's voice is ugly, strong,
and echoing with impotence. I fax
my soul to you. I'm you and we're alone.
I like to live our tiny secret song
of love, our river pearled for maniacs.

A Roof Bed in Mexico

I Flee the City, Temples, and Each Place

I flee the city, temples, and each place
where you took pleasure in your own lament,
where you used every forceful argument
to make me yield what I could not replace.
Games, masques, tournaments bore me and I sigh
and dream no beauty that is not of you.
And so I try to kill my passion too,
forcing another image to my eye,
hoping to break away from tender thought.
Deep in the woods I found a lonely trail,
and after wandering in a maze I sought
to put you wholly out of mind. I fail.
Only outside my body can I live
or else in exile like a fugitive.

Louise Labé (1525–1666)

A Roof Bed in Mexico

Last Sunday the new boarding house smelled good.
Popo was clear. Even its volcanic smoke looked clean
from my roof bed that faced the serpent plains where Cortés
    stood
shining like the dread white god Quetzalcuatl seen
as God prophetically returning to break the Aztecs there
by the temples at Cholula. We bussed across
that llano and down the carnation mountains to the coast.
    Vera Cruz was a huapango fair
of masks and trumpets and we danced. Then loss
of virginity. What loss? We woke
and entered rooms of love, our lives. Back in the city
    alone at eight
one morning on the roof I was asleep
and felt your body climb on me. You climbed the ladder
    to the roof, lifted the blanket, ate
my mouth. My tree found rain. You cried. I keep
your sorrow. Happy Sunday long ago. Fire in a morning
    of surprise, and far off Popo's smoke.

Bathroom Mirror Giving It Back to Me

The mirror is a friend. It likes me near,
spies elsewhere when I am gone. Slyly it mates
with pals, absorbs the lover into a union, the illusion
    of being Pascal's sphere everywhere and here.
Shining to multiply it copulates
without a speck of memory. Yet it knows and shows
exactly when (a kid sacked in a cold gully) I broke
    a front tooth in football. I grin
and it smirks back. I wink. It ignores my humor
    and picks my nose
until I face my face. What I have been
it throws at me with eyes my spectacles freeze.
"To your own cracked mug be true,"
it scores on glass. At night when I'm alone
I chat with it. I'm not afraid. In the dark I say
I'll try to change. And when I moan
it flashes back, "Idiot, your only way
is *now*. In your first scream, in your old laugh, and soon
    in black clay, look, I'm only *you*."

Predawn Post Office

I have bad habits and don't change. My will
is on vacation. Happy in my midnight office
    I dream up sun talk
to let this dim cinder block home fill
with ink and verse; then friendly with the night I walk
around the boring city to mail my trash away. Near the stamp
machines in the empty post office, by
the wall, a predawn woman stands. Beside her is the ramp
for the disabled to roll in. Her homeless eye
avoids me. Fifty, clean, respectable
in a wool overcoat, she's standing in her groove.
A week ago I saw her by the same clothes-filled grocery cart.
She's sleeping now, her skull
pointed up, yet her eyeballs open. I have to laugh. It's how
    we soldiers in platoons marched in rank, our heart
and eyes asleep yet open to the Georgia dawn.
    Her head is pitched back like a saint. She doesn't move.

It's Christmas. Let's Carol a Psalm to Jesus on His Birthday in His Old Hebrew Tongue

Even if Jesus had got his penis patched
and Christianized to make it lose its clean-
cut Jewish look, some passionate Gestapo eye, unmatched
in spotting bloodlines, would have caught the mien,
the almond eyes, the noble nose, and sent
the vermin to a death camp and then
into a chamber to inhale an earthly punishment
of proper agony for him and other Semite men,
women, and children lying gassed about the floor.
    But now
that war is over. War after stupid war
still bleeds and starves the human body, yet
it's almost sweet Christmas. Why not carol
on one good night in Hebrew? The cow
of India in public streets, when plopping holy shit,
    is free to moan in Sanskrit.
Sing a song in Hebrew to Rabbi Jesus poor and on the cross.
    Cry *Hallelujah* (Praise to Yah) to him boating
and multiplying fish off our Galilean shore.

A Jew on the Cross, Looking Down at a Catholic Wedding Just below His Punctured Feet

Peter said unto Jesus, "Rabbi, it is good for us to be here; and let us make three tabernacles."

Luke 9:33

The Romans hung a rabbi long ago
from noon to evening on a cross. He cried
in agony, pissed blood, and shat. The glow
of darkness cooled his fever; then he died,
a maimed parabolist fated to bear
a tribal stain, for since he was a Jew
he must share guilt for killing God. The air
was black with mourning for the rabbi who
was crucified, soon recast as the god
of Rome, imperial and powerful.
I see him writhing on his cross, here in
Austin, Texas, above the altar, sad-
ly dying. While my nephew Anatole
is wed, the rabbi groans in mortal sin.

Sharing Rabbi Jesus in Whiteface at Christmas

Since Jesus is the world's most famous Jew
and, like the Buddha, international
and smart, the gentiles should enjoy him too
if they respect him as a gentle bull
grazing Judean pastures and a man
of sorrows among his fellow Pharisees
with whom he plots against the Roman ban
on Torah, Temple, and odd treatises
by Essenes and the Gnostics pondering the earth.
This Semite is on loan to Whites and Blacks,
Yellows and Browns. All colors are the same
to him, since he has played with light and death.
Now, though the Jew was killed, and fame and name
a hoax, he still loves those who've turned their backs.

Ghosts of Memory

I love deeply two who are now vague stranger friends
I lived with long ago: Father and Mother.
Did I race up to Broadway on errands
for Mother? I must have. To get BABO, toilet paper,
    bagels, cream cheese or other
breakfast junk? Dad, drunk on Marion Anderson's legend,
    what did you say
to this skinnymarink streaking home from P.S. 166,
who day after day rang the doorbell to sailor in
    from outer space with his Flash Gordon ray-
gun? I guess you forgave this lunatic of comics
and radio serials. Did we exchange souls? Did you guess
    your youngest child could one day close his eyes
        for good? I almost don't remember you or me. I too
am a stranger to Billy, your son on the Drive, yet keep
    a book
with dim leaves in which I read the look
of early death yellowing your photographs. Who are you?
Father of radium watch dials, Mother of Maine pines,
    you are with me
even now. I can't abandon you to black dust, ghosts of
    memory.

Morning in the Schoolyard

As always I was late. Nevertheless, the king
    was standing by the cypress trees.
They pushed me forward. On this lemon morning
    at Anavrita estate where I was a teacher,
    King Pavlos of Greece,
a tall heavy Dane, was shaking hands. The squeeze
I felt made me look up into a glare,
an iron look on the fat metal face of a weak
and sickly giant. Wind lifted his hair
just as our palms embraced. I smelled the Greek
oregano and basil by the wall
and body odor of the guards. The king
grunted a phrase, a kind phrase. The press made
    fun of him,
O Frederikos, a dumb stand-in for a crafty Queen
    Frederika. But all
I knew at twenty-one was that a slim
disputatious queen gladly lent me her English books,
    and she, the loathed granddaughter of the Kaiser,
    pulled a palace on her string.

In a Sitting Room with Frederika

She sat down in my class. The whale
(as Constantine and his chums called the fat boy) made
a lot of noise. Velázquez would have ignored the queen
    to nail
that bloated wily dwarf. At lunch I was afraid.
I tried to keep my mouth shut, but the civil war
was winding down, the prisons filled
with young men waiting to be shot, and every store
around Omonia Square had amputees who spilled
into the smoky streets, racing for
wounded busses. "Why execute the guerrillas?" I kept
    saying. "They're worse
than murderers. Why did Markos shoot the village priest
and teacher?" said the queen. The more
    I talked, the sicker were the olive trees. True,
    Markos was wild, Stalin no angel, and had
    Markos won—poor Greece! At least
we both liked Wilfred Owen (who hated war and died
    in it)
whom we both read in her Faber Book of Modern Verse.

Eternal Room

When I descend to the ground floor to buy
hot chocolate, students guess the underworld
and Dante are my destination. Why?
I linger by the food machines, sit curled
on a torn plastic chair, my head in shrouds
of the dead poets I am close to. When
I cart my eyes upstairs into the clouds
of memory, I slip from continent
to continent. That's what a room does. It
has a safe seat of pain and wishes. Wings
of morning in the hold of night. I took
a bad turn, killed myself a while. Such things
depress me. I had lost my room and quit
my life. I'm back, alive maybe in my book.

Outlaw Sex

Sex is a crime. It is a criminal activity
punished religiously by death.
Adam and Eve in green eternity
of Eden were hungry to feel the meaning of earth
    under their toes. They ate fruit, grew smart,
    and, as God's revenge, lost their breath
to choking time. So sin and punishment began.
Sex rode an outlaw horse, bolting for lust; a cowboy
    went galloping out on
the moonstruck range; a crazy raping man
used his dirty sword; Lolita in Babylon
chatted and danced with an old man in her bed.
My bed is all sky. I dream. I don't think I
am guilty, but it's hard, so hard to shake
    a million years since Eve looked God
    straight in the eye
and found her way. My sex has its own mind,
    laughing in my hands and making friends
with loving ghosts. It likes to swim together
    in a big sea where water never ends.
Never. Happy like Eve, weary at last it flops
    back on its back, remembering hot waves
    and sunblack clouds.
For a while my sex and I are sweetly dead.

Sappho Helps Us in Every Fragment

It is lonely at the lands where the people go to plow.
Bessie Head

Of course she has her lovers, and they eat
breakfasts of nuts and melons on the grass
and sleep together in the sun. The moon
grabs her each night that she must pass,
aching for friends and thighs. She is unique on earth
    in her lone wait.
She is not unique. She wrote
for every secret one of us, and the circumstance
goes everywhere. On the Silk Route, a Turk, remote
in his farm village with gross water buffalo
sprawling on mud alleys in trance,
is no less miserable in poverty night. He was born to survive
and die alone in private smells.
Weavers in Mali, boring saints, we are all the same
in ordinary hells,
and kisses of joy are rare. Sappho waits
    for talk and soft breasts
to sleep on under the sun alive, the ravaging hawk of time,
and she for one would rather see the sparkle
    on a lover's face
than watch all the foot soldiers in Lydia in glittering bronze.

An Event Better Forgotten

Then, to my surprise, I went to sleep and before
I could reach morning I was dead.
I had been reading Cavafy, slowly, in Greek. The door
between me and the world was wide
open, but somehow I couldn't go out
any more into the sun, into the rain.
It was a shock, discomforting, grim. I doubt
I'd let it happen again.
As Cavafy said about vanishing time and age,
I wasn't looking and I had so much to do
outside. My last memory is I took a shot
of Courvoisier, put on my robe—I didn't have
        enough blankets—and like a sage
imagined I could find a title for the world. Well,
I like those trips but ought
to have known better. There is no word. There's
        no death either, and I cancel
this whole joke completely, yet I fear I have become
        only you.

Midnight with the Doomed Prince

At midnight I begin to think. I'm in my room
of solitude. This afternoon I read
the ancient tale of the doomed
prince who left Egypt; who was fated to be dead
because a spirit, crocodile or dog
would bite him. And so he went disguised
    as a poor son of a ship warrior,
he married a princess, had a nice jog
with a canine, a chat with a crocodile,
and for dessert drank beer and kissed his wife
all over her tattooed body. The last part
of the tale is missing, so he was still alive
and happy when I left him. My life, oddly,
has some blank papyrus leaves not yet scrawled on.
When I saw the loquacious crocodile dive
under the river for the ancient pearl,
which wandering magicians call a soul,
I guessed the prince and I could share eternity
in a palace wall or lonely room.

Mystery is a wondrous windflower, is fear
while the candle in the desert burns
and will happily persist for the doomed prince
and all who wear
the chains of time. The tattooed wife is smiling,
    her kohl is wet, she ululates as her conjugal
lord lies lovingly between
her legs and their hours never cease . . .

Too many pages are torn out and unseen
for a sensible parable.

Ten-Minute Snuff Drama

Argentina. Not the Dirty War. Just a back room
in an apartment in the outskirts of the city
where a blonde Italian whore is being filmed
by a crew of two crab-eyed hoodlums. Art, craft,
    goodness, pity,
none of these qualities crosses the eyes
of the hoodlum filmmakers. Greed
and a hardness to kill any guilt or humanity
    they might feel lies
like a knife slash across their faces. A Romeo
    waltzes in. He strips. Then strips
    the blonde. He keeps
his black belt on from which hang revolver
    and lasso, gaucho style. Romeo is ridiculous.
    Then he moves his stiff prick near
her mouth, feeds it to her. If she had any sense
she would bite it off, spit the pink head
    on the floor and stamp on it
till her soles sucked up every drop of blood.
He almost comes. She's doing a good job
in getting him worked up. They're standing,
    he's pawing her breasts. "*Más, más!* More,
    more! But the actor pulls out,
    yanks out his gun with the blanks,
and whispers, *"Pucha madre!* No more obscenities,
little one. I'm here to clean up the city, wipe out
a dirty whore. Get ready to die."
"Don't shoot," she begs, remembering the script.
"It's my duty. And besides, this gun is real."
"Real as this film," she ad libs.
"Say your prayers."
"Cut!" she shouts. "That's not the script."
"Say your prayers, little whore cunt. The good guys
have tickets and are waiting to watch you drop."
The tall Italian whore stops. She's no fool.
"I think you mean it."

"I mean it."

She doesn't beg now. She surprises Romeo.

"If you kill me, you will be executed. Go ahead,"
    she baits him.

"Cunt! Fry in your own grease."

"Go ahead. I've nothing to lose, but the law
    will execute you. I guarantee it."

He raises the gun. She grabs his balls ferociously.
He falls, clutching himself. She fights for the gun.
They roll. And before she can bend
it from his hands, Romeo sticks it in her mouth
and blows her head off. What's left of the female
    figure lies still. Dead ethnic vermin.
Order and civilization have won.
The hoodlums cheer. End of battle. Peace.

THE END

Goya and Rembrandt Stroll on 23rd

Goya takes 23rd Street since he knows
those bodies huddled by the wall to keep
their warmth. He bathes them in brown ink. Their clothes
are soaked. His crucifieds sprawl in a sleep
of stonemen. Goya puts them under wrap,
except their eyes—candles in rain—which look
up from the pavement for a starry map
of hope. They lie by dogshit in the book
of night and vomit. Rembrandt finds a face
of angels in the alley. Neon lights
in the store window of the liquor store
ignite his lady's skin. A holy space.
The masters catch Manhattan's chilly whore
and panhandler in blankets and black tights.

Flying through December 31 to the Coast

It's New Year's Eve and strange. I squat and think,
listening to the thunder from the drain
as the whole sky's black wind echoes and rushes
    up into the sink
in the US AIR toilet. Fists complain
against the door. They pound, "Get out!"
    The wall-light's on,
meekly commanding, RETURN TO SEAT. I don't let the time
move on. It's tight in here. Like dream. No dawn
will ever interrupt the now-time chime
of the old Chinese bell, which holds all past
and future in one ringing of the temple gong.
    Especially
tonight, obsessed with the diminishing
and unknown cache of days, I feel each second
    may be last,
or first, in the gross unreality
as some frantic pisser pounds the door and, abruptly,
    this finite now is my secret being.

Eating Alone in Wonder in a Midwest Café

My limbs recall who they have been, each scar
inscribed with endless ram of memory chips,
and so I sleep sometimes or jog under the star
of noon who frosts my face, whose lethal lips
kiss me with joy. I love the sun. Why not?
The limbs recall. Yet when I'm broke I don't
like facts, would dodge and dream. We're caught
in fatal skin, quick time, and words. I won't
accept the law. I can't. I'm not yet dead.
My pen is scratching its black blood to you,
the secret soul I love. The table grins
through public bedlam to our blur. You said
at Angkor Wat I'll draw. You kiss my sins.
I hug your Burmese buns whose moon is blue.

When a Fragrant Woman Comes

All things have memory
like a mermaid washed up in your arms or Plato's
    idea of a chair
which has no visible reality
yet is everywhere.
When a fragrant woman comes
she is all thighs and lips
and becomes those nights, and history drips
into our arms. I like the slums
of old cities. There, injustice and poverty are
preserving curators of beauty, while stunning cubes
    of Bauhaus concrete, steel and glass
bulldoze a memory of a decorative past.
I like to loaf and think I'm where I am,
    yet old geographies burn
    and visions of eros and ocean are never far.
So I'm in red Hanniá and gray New York and with
    your belly and laughing mouth.
Memory or illusion. What else is there?
Maybe the experience of love, the death of time,
    a friend with paper ribbons on her breasts,
        green tea
  and icebergs in the south.

Rain, Days, Roads, Loneliness

Since I've been up to fiction, nightmare glares and folks speak
like movies: "Go ahead. Throw us out. Furniture
and all. Dump us in front of the hotel." It's bleak
today, but in court, I tell the master
    prosecuting thief,
      "We'll see who's the straight shooter."
In my speech to the stranger I have real confidence,
facing him down. I pause at the right places, don't blow
my lines, am clipped and factual. In life
    I'm in a trance,
wondering if I'm alive. "Who's talking," I ask
    myself. I don't know
if I'm a robot with a pumping heart,
whose center has no center, whose talk
has no speaker. Yet in nightmare I'm uppity and smart,
    though we end up in the gutter
      and it's raining cats and dogs. I walk
about in drippy half-sleep, sure I can invent all
plots. Sleep is free theater and I'm soaked with dreams
    (that happens in bed)
and rain, days, roads, loneliness is sweet until I fall awake
    and fall and fall.

My Somber Friends

And art made tongue-tied by authority,
And folly doctor-like controlling skill.
Shakespeare, sonnet 46

Poets like me. Sappho, Wang Wei, Saint John.
I love them. We collaborate. And I like
the Calvinistic men and women on
the blade of theory, who wield verbs to spike
the heart of books. Yet they loath me because
they care for discourse more than dawning larks
or frozen Mandelstam, and fashion laws
to subvert culture for cher Carlos Marx
and Heidegger, not a bad egg, a true
philosopher. Killing was lunacy,
the camps and commissars a blurred mistake,
and bleak economies extrinsic to
the greed of cast and class. They bully me.
I praise them while I eat what poets make.

Tired with All These Things, I Slip Deeper in the Wood

The Bible and the other bible of
the Gnostics, the apocrypha that failed
to join the canon, these have been my love
and vice and wings. But the big God who railed
and smote and flooded us, I wish he were
innocuous like Homer's Zeus, a myth
not a malign and magic power to stir
the dreams of Irishmen, of Arabs with
the Jews, of cleansing Serbs. God is a bore,
a lie. And we are he. He types us good
and evil. Eve he rapes and Job he tricks
yet he stands angel pure. Dress him with gore
and garlic. Climbing hills where the deer licks,
eating lilies, I go deeper in the wood.

The Lilies

The lilies in the field below a sphere
of half moons in the rain, of fowls and moths,
go unclothed, do not spin or toil or hear
the prayer of Solomon in radiant cloths
and yet their nakedness is perfect snow
under whose milky galaxies the seed
lies comatose. The lilies only grow
and burn. Their meditation is to feed
on light. Naked of thought, a multitude
by the day Adam learned to stand, these plants
are human, living in chance villages
like breezy monks sworn to dumb elegance.
When thrown into the oven, no lord says
a word. The lilies fall in solitude.

The Empty

Living in the Mountains on an Autumn Night

After fresh rain on the empty mountain
comes evening and the cold of autumn.
The full moon burns through the pines.
A brook transparent over stones.
Bamboo trees crackle as washerwomen go home
and lotus flowers sway as a fisherman's boat slips
    downriver.
Though the fresh smell of grass is gone,
a prince is happy in these hills.

Wang Wei (701–761)

The Empty Way

The sage rambles along the empty way
up into the rain on Wang Wei's empty mountain or
along San Juan's lion peaks of honey combs
    and stony caves safely hidden away.
You can follow and, hanging from your heels
        or navel,
    be the black mirror of the empty sky.
Tell us. If you talk you don't know,
if you know you don't talk. Why
are you suffering so?
The full vessel is the mind
when it is empty; like a straw dog
it can still turn into nothing's flame
but it's sorrowful to look for heaven in oily water,
        to find
you in the river's temporary fog,
to know that emptiness is a misery of rats, is ecstasy
    of ignorance, is power, is red wine
and a mystery-sodden garden of shame.

The Empty Heart

Horror is to know the empty way. You are rich
in sorrow. Having glimpsed the heart
of paradise, you cannot dig an ordinary ditch
for what the lumpy earth offers a smart
and meditative fool. To be a fool
and stumble. That's
easy. The volcano is open with a pool
of blue information. Blue bats
skim accurately through darkness. But when
you spoil your heart with bliss,
you can't come down. You abandon the wonderful
mess here. Then
you fall, cringe into the drug of terror, the abyss of
     cowardice.
The heart knows extinction. No pain. You don't
hump. You don't come.
     Your empty heart is chaste
and living without its dirty will.

Never Guessed You'd Come

I empty a glass of Metaxa and have a delusion
    of the first water.
You are reading me. With two drinks I could make
it real. I always wrote for you. I did. But never
    guessed you'd come. Maybe I wrote for *me*
    or *you* as *me*. What could I do? Better than
    yapping at a wall. Later
I grew morose. I wrote for no one. Not even me.
    (But kept the habit of the pen.) I rake
the fall leaves because winter will bury them.
    Absence is fact. If you were here,
would you judge me kindly? No. Better be harsh.
I'll believe the delusion of your presence.
    Let me have it, though I wince and switch to beer
till I can't see straight. Thanks for the false
    memory. I know
no secret reader in the British Museum, in L.A.
    or an alligator marsh
or in an ordinary prison for artists.
Send me a telegram. Say you are! I'll crawl
    like the pious on their bloody knees
before the Virgin of Guadalupe. With my fingernails
I'll burrow down to the earth's core, sail
through a boiling leadstorm and pound your door.
    I'm wrong. I've fallen in love
    with you. Your face lives in my soul,
and now, with sanctimonious gratitude, I please.

Intimacy

Mother, we have a lot to talk about.
I'd like to fill you in. You left New York.
I was in the next room, with the light out,
hopeless, munching on crabs. I stuck my fork
in a pink leg. Oscar came in to say,
"Your mother's gone." The train took you to
the north. We put you in the earth. Today
a clever doctor couldn't pull you through,
even today, although you were so young.
So let's just talk. Dante spent three books in
the other worlds. I stick to shadows here,
whispering to you. It's fun and deep. Your tongue
has vanished, yet how beautifully your thin
melodious words poison and calm my fear.

Rendezvous

Father, you are the phantom of the opera
and not for being a jumpy ghost, insane
or criminal, but you disclose an algebra
of living infinite and zero, plain
and complex, on a stage of dreams. I'm old
enough to be your uncle since you died
so far ago, but you insist on hold-
ing on to us. It's good. And though I've tried
to face your exit, love says no. I yield
to you. Your violent plunge was just the end
but we dream back through our companionship,
warmer and wilder. Daytime, you're concealed.
A sad convention. Come dark sleep, you slip
into my shirt. We talk all night, sweet friend.

Architect Howard and His Stray Dog Carlos

Brother, you left so soon. The others went
away too early, but you fled, weary,
before we could resume. You wrote to me
sorrowed with love. Yet how could you have spent
your suffering for peace? You did. It's wise,
I guess, and yet absurd. I'm just upset.
The poison killed our time. The sun won't rise
again on us. A phone call came that met
your bid. On burial day. It might have helped,
yet you were master of your own estate,
which you designed with genius. You were strong
with ink and zany gales. When Carlos yelped
during the hurricane in Galveston
you took him in. Mere winds whisper our fate.

Cold Mountain

Tired I escape to the cold mountain where
nothing is immortal. Everything's born
like a mushroom lasting a day. The air
is alone. I'm with it. Color of corn,
the sun tastes orange. Years tasted of shit
and bits of spice for which sailors grew old.
When they came to America, it fit
their greed for gems and Indian silk. They sold
tobacco, the red people sank, I lost
my way with them. I'm human, even frail,
but I can't kill the dandelions or
the weeds that choked my throat with frost
in summer. I escape from life in jail.
Tired out with spice and mind, I am a bore.

Hot Mountain

I am not lazy but I cannot wait
another fifteen years. So I give up
and come to fire. Contented with my cup
of ice, watching the moon beg at the gate
to come up the black hill, I say the day
is old as dinosaurs and it is noon.
I was sitting. Finally I found a way
to know the sun had risen. Afternoon
takes back the night, the heat of memory
and beds. I am not lazy but the heat
is what I needed. You will die. No!
Don't be ridiculous. Hot mountain tea
smells all the way to heaven, but my feet
are sick and dream of tramping April snow.

Yearning

The empty way is full of desolation
and lasts a life and many lies. So why
the yearning? Questions are a consolation
but if they cease, I'll sleep again. I buy
coffee to let me doze at work, yet peace
burns when a naked woman grabs the soap
and steps into the shower. She is my niece
and incest is a crime. So much for hope
and easy fixes. I am not depressed.
I like the darkness of the blinding sun.
Plato was a wise guy back in his cave
where singing rats and galley slaves undressed
the sanctity of clouded soul for one
shower of life. Only empty hearts can crave.

Soultime

A Farewell

I dismount from my horse and drink your wine.
I ask where you're going.
You say you are a failure
 and want to hibernate at the foot of Deep South Mountain.
Once you've gone no one will ask about you.
There are endless white clouds on your mountain.

Wang Wei (701–761)

Creation of the Soul

The tales of Africa tell how she came
out of the forest of chaos to be a mild beast,
a star and village in the sun. No shame was known.
Fog and sun were mixed with a yeast
growing egg and sperm. There was no scuzzy sin.
Mosquitoes twittered and wore
the blood of princes in their lips. Many gods were sitting in
teak trees while comets sailed a light year away from
    the equator.

The condition of her birth was fog.
She was beauty bewildering the clear eye.
She popped about like a steamy dog
nosing ghostly flower pots out of windows. She was very
    happy.
It was good to see her in command of heaven
where deities were drunk like cargo ships
leaking crude oil along the ice coasts
    of misty birds.
But she feared the sun.
With so much new light, Africa burned under glass
    like a giant microbe. Stubborn light seared
dried-up river crabs trotting backward
    in slow motion.

There is a time for water from the skies
and water is the best of moving things.
With fog and sun came five hundred yams.
After six millennia of heat and lazy unseen gods,
she became an electronic beep, invisible again,
a fabled chip of memory,
and, gulping gigabytes of stars, vast and inaccessible,
    she disappeared.

Illusions

The Buddhists think it's fine to deny being.
For me it's a thin horror, each day worse:
I can't find me, someone ad libs, I ring
his flat, he's got me cased, teacher of verse
and Spanish but intruder in each camp.
His name is Willy. Maybe he's me. I think,
or try to think, and nail the thought, the tramp
who's got no place or body when I blink
and search inside. He's gone and I'm alone,
a no one. Yes, there was a fellow in
the flat. He had a name like mine, was not
for real. I am the public man of bone
and spirit. Passport of a self. I've been
like you—but I have looked. We're all mere thought.

Lively Soul on Her Way to Feeding Slender
Birches and Daisies

Don't cry for me. I'm fine. I'm happy. What
is horror I accept, forget; and when
my thinking seems to be neurosis, then
I know it's sadly right. To say I'm not
exaggerates the case. To say I am,
however, means I am a banished soul
and soul's as good as any word to ham
it up with, play a person who is whole
inside and out, a character in search
of authorship. What's sure is when I die
the whole confusing mess will go and go
for good. Is soul death ever good? Yet by
necessity, words fool us, and I know
my thinking flesh will feed a windy birch.

Street Moon

Tonight the full moon again is bald,
standing like the homeless between buildings on Telegraph.
It has a plastic cup and asks for change. I called
it a drunk, a parasite, riffraff,
but the hairless moonface, pocked and mute,
is dignified.
I've glanced at the full moon in Tibet and Greece
    and once when I was young it spat down from the boot
below Brindisi; it's always fresh. I've lied
to it. That's how you treat celestial bodies. So
the moon is a halfway house for beggars and beauty,
    cobblers and astronauts,
      the starving before they bloat,
the war-murdered just before
they're blasted and close their eyes. I look and go
away a year. Each year friends say I'm younger;
    I must be a child by now, infantile and poor
in caste. One day I'll face the stone moonface low and fat
    like a city tenement
and say, "You're dead, moon, but I'm still alive."
Then stuffing that shiny nickel back in a pocket,
    I'll waste a last syllable on the street moon
and shove off on my lifeboat.

Street Sun

A big street sun hops into John Donne's bedroom
    and finds a hermitage
on his lover's pillow shining with happiness and youth
    and the cartographers' thrill at the discovery
        of spicy continents.
Jack Donne and his lover are the center of a bridge
of dreams. They look at the wonderful warm city
    sun; they blink and firmaments
go dark and they are all their bodies. Country sun
is bountiful to the body of the earth
but in London sunlight is a spirit warming streets
    and the arms of whore and hangman
    and lord mayor in his kitchen drinking milk
    and a baby by the window as it paws the birth
of daylight. Just for fun
Peter Stuyvesant in New Amsterdam goes down
    to the harbor and bowls
by the sunny ocean. When I came up from the subway
    at Stuyvesant Square I'd carry damp books
    through the winter sun to my high school
of science. Donne lived in a small amazing town
    and before he died, a St. Paul deacon
robed in sickness black, he left a sermon about
    the sun also rising where no man or woman
is an island. His own unruly sun is no pastoral effete
    but a generous fool
        who timelessly inhabits every stone
    or wooden city heating up the lovers' souls.

A Sentimental Journey

For years I've worked alone. It is the way
of artists. Though I wanted you to hear
and said one day you would, it won't happen till I lay
the queen of England, and a commoner
is not a bet to hump Elizabeth.
Out in the cold—cut off from palace and from verse—
at dismal moments I drink the sentimental death
of hope, the tart self-pity of myself against the universe,
dining on failure, chewing lacerating ropes
    with gusto. Weakness
is my visionary force. Luis, my Spanish friend, knows
    I am stumbling right.
He says it's easier to love one's misery.
On the fifth-floor heaven of my bleakness
you might hear me. Yet then, without the curse
    of anonymity, I'd be unreal. You, the hearer, wait
        to get me.
You menace the darkness of the lonely concrete tower
    where I float night after night after night.

Faces of the Soul

The soul is fierce as crotch itch, twice as real.
She likes to screw, draw faces of the moon,
pick lemons from a tree in Poros, steal
the sun from them one unclocked afternoon
when time bounced between island and the coast,
the Peloponessos of winds and grapes
and ancient gold and murder. Cain, the most
maligned of murderers, crude as the apes
among the civilized, gave soul the club
of force, opposed by Christ's sad suicide
that filled the soul with mystery and flight
from lemon trees. To be (and here's the rub),
the soul has Cain and Abel say who's died,
who lives, who on the mountain becomes light.

Fragile Life of a Finger

I broke my finger when a trailer truck
took a sharp turn and crushed my car roof. Had no idea
    the finger cracked
till evening when it swelled blue and sore. Just my luck
that I'd phoned Harry who said I should be wacked
in the teeth for being such a slob.
Harry sped me down to PROMPT
CARE just in time. The doctor did his job
on me. Then, we should have gone out for a beer
    and romped
crazy about the city. For weeks everyone said I'd been
so lucky. I could have been killed,
a reed snapping in the wind. They're right to harass
and kid me. But I don't feel lucky with the crooked
    finger. Fate. "We toil and spin
a day," Matthew said. But like the lilies of the field
a wind blows, the oven heats, and we are grass.

Two Souls Meet on a Windy Night and Worry about a Marble Face

After the war when we were young and gray in heart,
I went to Paris to get exiled, kiss a soul, and hear
    the wind
blowing the urine fragrance along Bonaparte.
Stiff black coffee and warm bread were my early copains.
    Wind dozed among the lindens.
I let it share my bed. The bed was bare;
a torn red blanket under a gray bulb of maybe
    30 watts, if I can count,
sputtered high on the ceiling, blinking at my underwear
dripping and wrinkled on the sink edge. I read
    the philosophy of Auguste Comte
hard as I could at the Sorbonne until my prof,
Monsieur La Porte, dropped dead. *La Porte est fermée*

was cruelly scribbled on the door. I met a soul
one windy night. Paris embraced us with her laugh.
She was a Greek. She gave me an ancient statue that hurt
my arms. The cheekbones almost pierced the skin.
    It's so heavy, where can I put it down? I say
to her.
    Don't ever put it down, she says. We Greeks wake
    with a glaring
marble head in our arms. Hold it up or it will roll
    away.

My Soul's Doing Fine

Be patient. We both know life is a wait.
Should unholy fame come
or love at last or a grand poem to hum
insistently like a bad tune, it will always be late.
Late, but. . . . Be patient. We die alone. When now
becomes eternity, it's really bad,
since time is good only when like the Tao
we're free of its sad
bullying claws. I'm sad. That's an exquisite feeling.
 Please,
don't exaggerate. No prayers for this soul.
My soul's been just fine without a holy god
 to shove her. As for tonight,
I'm alone in a diner, eating turkey and cheese.
This soul needs TUMS but we two are having a ball,
chatting, laughing at time, and eating light.

Soultime

It's good to have a life of spirit with
the measurable stuff we guess is real.
To be requires a carnal brain and myth
of thought and maybe cosmic signs to steal
the show from God, who one time owned the soul
of us, his miniature creations. I
look into me. No one is home. The hole
looks empty and my sentimental eye
becomes a cloud of sorrow. In the still
depression, I see nothing. Friend, be near.
To be alone with nothing, be destroyed,
homeless from being, a goofy imbecile,
is normal. It's a start. I live with fear,
a dog in heat, humping the shining void.

Death of the Soul

I saw the end. It wasn't pleasant. Hell
must be when nothing is that's any good.
The soul got sick and lost her tongue. The smell
of dying, the heat of camphor, smoking wood
as the last toothpicks flame. I felt the loss
was verbal. Soul wasn't a word and so
when she went I went too. Times change. The Boss-
man is no holy shrink. Come tomorrow
the soul and metaphysics count, I hope.
Rilke said look into yourself and change.
More, he said, *be.* Soul, be my silent friend.
I think the dead soul is alive. I grope.
Of course she is untouchable. The strange
unseen. She's me. I'm strange. A silent end.

Soulpeace

After the revolution all the guilty monsters will
be blindfolded and thrown against the wall
and shot. Good riddance. The young bodies fall.
They always do. Born 1900, Germany. Lives until
1918. Mustard gas. Death of a Kraut. Exciting. Better
    than
baseball. Shrewder than chess. And feels
wonderful like pro football. A team loses and you can
the coach and life goes on. The universe conceals
its origin in time-space, but the big bang
theory works for our gunpowder planet. Fidel,
who made everyone on his island healthy and literate,
sent hundreds to the *paredón*. It was thrilling
    and we sang
when the corrupters fell and it was sweet to be healthy
    and know how to read. Better than dream.
    However, I think it feels like hell
        with tears
when you are eighteen, against the wall, and it is
    you, certainly you, whom very soon we'll kill
        and abominate.

Help

Who can help me? Rilke asked who among
the angelic hierarchies would hear his cry.
No one will help. When I die I'll still feel young.
I'm sorry but it's true. Help? I rely
on my odd habits. Never play it safe,
dance about midnight. Cognac, and recall
a vagabond in Asian towns, a waif
of amber south of Cairo. When I crawl
into my mother's arms, I pull her hair,
get slapped, remember how a Bible turned
Adam and Eve to flaming exile. When
I wonder how to turn soupy nightmare
romances into soul, I guess I've earned
the peace of failure. Help me not. Amen.

When Greece Was Young, an Owl on Mount Pendeli Was Hooting Epiphanies

Discomfort? Why? I'm happy. Cucumbers
are wiser than the moon; you chew them cool
and place them on your brow. The moon has furs
made of torn socks when rain taps the old school
windows in the basement where we hide out.
Late afternoons I walk from the main road
back up the marble hill where the low shout
of a gray owl in our private Morse code
echoes about the grapevines. I am home,
it tells. Saigyo wrote that mind is all sky
with meadows for the eager; lovers said
before they vanished they'd share a grass bed
of ecstasy. In ignorance I roam
through speechless light, hooting the lover's cry.

Season of the Dark Soul

The window's turning dark and night is deep
with words (those noisy signs of human minds),
warming the soul till soul puts noise to sleep.
Dark soul contains all sound down in her mine
of silence. Being part flesh I need to use
those words. I hang on them and they hang me.
What can I do? I'm human and abuse,
night upon night. My poor felicity
is thinking words will speak. I hear. Be still,
they say, be still and vanish into soul.
Madness! Yet good if I could be in there,
out there. Who knows where soul's white chemical
calls home? I need to scream, yet talk. A bowl
of words outdoors is me: I am dark air.

Dark Night of the Soul

John of the Cross assumed the womanhood
of soul and body: on a dark and obscure night
she went into the street as in a dark wood,
looking for her love where no light
        shone.
Toledo is a cobbled city. Greco came
from Crete and Italy with green flesh and purple fire.
Awake in secret night she found the flame
of noon, brighter than sun, whiting her heart
    with illicit desire
for the lover in the street. They met. He
was wind on her face and hair.
There was no shame. He slept in her. They were
    confused. By morning they had gone
into the countryside, climbed. John never
    uttered a word of theology
    on his dark night. Two bodysouls were
ordinary wordless animals, breathing spiced
        lion air,
lost in lily dawn and happy.

We Are Profound Like Air

I'm looking. I feel nothing. Know nothing. This
is not a beginning. I'm left with words
but I can't make them speak to me or us. If bliss
is ignorance I win. If I were Tang Chinese
    and elegantly wise, I'd be happy to know
    my emptiness. Then like two birds,
cuckoos in the woods or geese over a paddy by the Burmese
    border,
my shallows body and skimming mind
would disappear.
These thoughts that come from nothing are beautiful.
    Existence is kind
to offer images and hope when mere order
and reason meanly help. I know the Gnostics who
    at least
mapped the universe with meditation. They help.
But death will clearly be the only absolute, a plate
    of disgusting kelp
and much too soon. Yet though the fearful feast
of emptiness is true and goes nowhere
and drops us away, I'm here. You're here. We talk. Lucky
    sometimes we love. We are profound
    like air.
    We are profound
with blood. Not for a screech of light, but for the brute
    eternity of us. Of course these words of air
must fail. Truth is merely a word. But we hear us
    and we are sound.

Circus

God was the author of the play,
director, clown and stuntman hurled
through the Grand Theater of the World
onto the stage. He had no way
to quit. His gig had no last scene
and the show went from town to town
forever. So the lord kept unseen,
calling the shots. Then like a mole
he disappeared. He wasn't killed.
The fans walked out on him. A shame.
He wasn't good yet he was billed
"Lord Know-It-All" and took the blame
for our know-nothing empty soul.

Recalling Gratefully a Lucky Way Out and In

Da stieg ein Baum. There rose a tree. One day
I sat out on the grass—I was twenty
and lost, almost a hollow man. No way
to spot a mind inside (I still can't see
one) but I touched the obscure sonnets of
the solitary Rilke, who forgave
me with feelable distances and love
(love's passion, not its objects); and to save
me from abstraction he read mystery in-
to ignorance and weak despair. Then soon
my hollow eyes fell on a Greek who filled
the rain with marble walls and lovely sin.
Two bumming pals. My pen got hot and killed
dead Buddha with a rhyming night of noon.

Dancing in the Tower

I have become a creature of myself,
sitting downtown in the Encore Café,
reading a book or writing one. My wolf
waits for me in the garage while I stray
into an intermission. Some folks greet
me, I greet back. I'm friendly and alone
and used to it. Mornings are grim. I meet
the copulating mirror, put a milkbone
in the wolf's bowl, tell him goodbye. I'm stale
on my mail run, but hole up happy in
my tower. My books are sitting in this park,
I love them, I've become them. They blackmail
me and I pay off. Go home? Why? I've been
there once. Right now I'm dancing in the dark.

Blindman

I move, guess I'm alive, and wake because
the sun is orderly. But I was bad
again, scrawling all night until the laws
of body felled me. I cruised to my pad,
a rag, happy. Still a rag, I've become
a coffee bag to stay awake. When night
shoots me again by janitors, I'm glum
but burn my shoes. Once inside my block of light
mechanically I dream of Paris rain
and dance for no one, dance a bit insane,
looking nowhere. How dreary in this jail
for an old dog of habit in white trance
of elsewheres to be jumping wild in braille!
The difference between death and life is dance.

Gabbing

I talk to friends, Edwin who's getting old
and is a future mirror, though I've said
death's not for me and I won't show. It's cold
and dumb to waste eternity in bed
with termites. Yet I spend most of my time
talking to some dead poets who talk back.
Maybe I feel the wind of their wing crack
with madness. Baudelaire lost his will to climb
out of his pit of sloth (*Acedia* was
his word for torpor of the soul) and so
his desolation holds me up. I'd like
to talk in poems to others. I've some dark clothes
to show. Yet if I could, I'd feel death's spike
tear up my rags with joy. Best to lie low.

Loneliness

The loneliness intensifies the fact
and dream. I talk to me. I'm not a bore
and when I dream as Daniel dreamt and act
with faith like Shadrach, even though I snore
the Babylonian furnace cannot singe
my hair. But I am sick of miracle
or waiting for the sun to cool orange
so I can climb and camp on that black hill
of light the way Plotinos would if he
could get a foot onto his mystic star.
It's been a good cold rainy day. I talk
all night to me. Dreaming up a Zohar
to lamp my way to peace, blindly I see
no shore of silence as I walk and walk.

Existing Is Strange

I always thought that time would fill the hole
of being and I'd no longer be a ghost.
I never knew I'd played the normal role
of human with a brain. What scared me most
was when I found I was just a pink sack
of flesh ballooned with Eastern nothingness.
Am I the only one to watch the black,
and worse, the non-interior of this mess?
I always thought that on a rainy day,
maybe a Saturday with no one home
and loneliness a cave, I'd spot a deep
and plunging drop of mind like a snow ray
from hell. One Paris afternoon this dome
of nothing almost shone, but then came sleep.

Laughing is Real, but around the Corner Comes Black Wind

Anton Chekhov died young and yet he wrote
ten thousand pages and trudged all across
Siberia to the prisoners in remote
notorious labor camps. They froze. Their loss
of hope was total. Lashes and disease
were everyday. He spoke and healed and gave
us word. He knew our secrets and the ease
of wasted lives. I'm secretive and crave
exactly what he was. He's dead. But not
tonight. Tonight I feel my death will stare
at me before I'll chat with secret you
the way that doctor warmed the world. He thought
suffering bad, found no escape. I declare
my love for you. Tough luck. Nothing comes true.

THE SECRET FRIEND

Jaguar Throne
Willis 194

The Secret Friend

Baruch Spinoza

A haze of gold, the Occident lights up
The window. Now, the assiduous manuscript
Is waiting, weighed down with the infinite.
Someone is building God in a dark cup.
A man engenders God. He is a Jew
 With saddened eyes and lemon-colored skin;
Time carries him the way a leaf, dropped in
A river, is borne off by waters to
Its end. No matter. The magician moved
Carves out his God with fine geometry;
From his disease, from nothing, he's begun
To construct God, using the word. No one
Is granted such prodigious love as he:
The love that has no hope of being loved.

Jorge Luis Borges (1899–1986)

The Secret Friend

I am surprised to find you at the end
of our strange walk. You stick with me, although
I'm dead, or else obscure, and I depend
on you, the unknown friend, for life. Spino-
za built a world with words, dressing his tree
with letters of infinity. He ground
his lenses with a love that couldn't see
the one they fit with vision, and the sound
of the mute cosmos was his sole return
for love. I've been too lonely to survive
on nature or the wild and singing shark,
and shaped my life and manuscript to earn
your gaze. Sun burns up thought, yet in the dark
inside, I pause to meet your eyes alive.

Afterchat

As I read through these sonnets, preparing them for publication, I am very happy. The last poem even affirms a hope of meeting your eyes alive: "I am surprised to find you at the end of this strange walk." Yet I'm also uneasy, even ashamed, for after decades of ordinary solitude—the natural state of the artist—publication itself carries its own ironies. That you, the secret reader, may be around flies against the solitary passions in these poems' composition. Pathos always fueled the poems, a pathos bloated with isolation. While I believed in them, their possible strength lay, in part, in the improbability of finding your gaze. So built into them was an impossibility principle. "Love is in the absence," Antonio Machado wrote.

Presence can undo.

Presence is *secret* you becoming *public*, kind or unkind, a condition threatening the longing for the hitherto unattainable you, *reader*. Yet I'll survive the paradox and keep to my illusions. And I know I can't break our personal pact. Constantine Cavafy told us that Ithaca gave us voyage and that even if we find her poor, she didn't *trick* us. I sailed out to found you, with days and nights as sonnets. You haven't *laughed* at me (to use Cavafy's exact word), whether you are visible or a ghost. Looking for you gave me the book.

Reflecting these lonelinesses and his own compassion for the artist, my lovely, smart son Robert built a model, "The Library for Unpublished Writers," for his masters thesis in architecture at the Graduate School of Design. He wrote a bittersweet, elaborately witty introduction, speaking to matters of creation and market. He faced art and the soul's auction, prefacing his project with this volume's first poem, "I write my unread book for you who in a life or day will find it in a box or cave or dead man's pocket . . ."

Tonight, in my café where I like to read and scribble, I thought up this "afterchat." Then, finding myself penless, I sneaked out.

Back in the tower I read some of Rainer Maria Rilke's *Sonnets to Orpheus,* that two-part sequence of fifty-five sonnets that the poet composed in early February 1922 at the Château de Muzot, a small stone tower in Switzerland's Valais. I read the first ones and the great concluding poem, II, 29 (of which I did a version). This final sonnet is addressed to the "silent friend of many distances."

Silent friend of many distances, feel
how your breath draws apart the walls of space.
Lost in the timbers of dark belfries, peal,
let yourself toll. What feeds on you will trace

its own dominion from this nourishment.
Pass through a transformation and resign
to it. What pains you most? To it assent.
If drinking is a bitterness, be wine.

Be in this night whose borders have no frame
a magic force wherein your senses cross.
Be meaning of their strange encounter. Go,

and if the earthly fades and has forgot
you, whisper to the silent earth: I flow.
To the onrushing water say: I am.

As always, Jorge Luis Borges has the word. In a conversation between us recorded in 1980 in the auditorium at Columbia University, he put me in my place, as he should have and often did:

BARNSTONE: Yet today we're speaking to this very friendly group here. Tell me how you feel about speaking to them and letting them in on your knowledge.

BORGES: I am not speaking to them. I am speaking to every individual of you. After all, a crowd is an illusion. No such thing exists. I am talking to you personally. Walt Whitman had it: "Is it right, are we here together alone?" Well, we are alone, you and I, and *you* stands for an individual, not for a crowd, which is nonexistent, of course. Even I myself may be non-existent also.

Borges at Eighty: Conversations 74

Let us say goodbye. At four a.m. the world is intimate and vast. It's time to leave the cinder blocks and books and rumble back to my rooms. It's snowing, perhaps the last snow of the winter. Once, a composer famous for his four minutes and thirty-three seconds of silence spent hours urging me to write poems without words. We were in Connecticut, had stayed after a concert in a small building, and talked and talked until we were snowed in. At daybreak as we walked out across the fields, the snow was poetry without words, that is, "silent poems," which is what the Chinese classically called Southern Song landscape painting. Earlier this evening, as I drove through a strangely out-of-season icy rain, I heard a beautiful violin on the car radio. Deep and ecstatic. That too was wordless poetry. Everything around us is a poem, though more often grubby than beautiful; and inside us extends a globe of emptiness, waiting impossibly to be known. Unless it is snow, a poet resorts to words. As for these half thousand utterances, I give them to you, secret friend, in the form of dry ink. In the end it is arrogant to say what they are, and I give up. As for us, I do assert with immense happiness that for now we are *not* nonexistent. You and I clearly are.

March 1995
Bloomington

Afterchat   377

Notes

COVER   The two Chinese characters that appear within the frame on the cover are a dry brush drawing in "grass script" (characters brushed in cursive form). They mean "wind" and "moon" and are normally boxed in with character strokes on four sides. The absence of surrounding strokes suggests "without limits," and these two characters in this form have become known as the "emperor's characters," here meaning "boundless windmoon." I brushed it by mistake, and the Chinese poet Chou Ping, my former student in Beijing, told me what I had scrawled.

THE SECRET READER /5   Saul (5?–67? A.D.), a young Pharisee rabbi, student of Gamaliel and follower of Hillel, "saw the light" on the road to Damascus, changed his name to Paul, and proselytized thereafter in synagogues of Near East and Rome. He is St. Paul of New Testament letters.

CAMDEN, 1892 /7   Walt Whitman died in Camden, N.J., in 1892.

FATHER ON GLASS WINGS /11   Greystone Hotel in New York City. Brunswick, Maine, is the site of Bowdoin College.

NOSTALGIA FOR A CHINESE COMMUNE . . . /12   William James's *Varieties of Religious Experience* (1902).

LA RUE JACOB, 1948 /13   The French poet Guillaume Apollinaire (1880–1918) suffered a head wound at the front in WW I. Returning to Paris, he died of the Spanish flu two days before Armistice Day, *Le Jour de la Victoire*.

IN A PARIS FAUBOURG /14   Gustavo Adolfo Bécquer (1836–70), extremely sensitive, delicate Spanish poet.

GOING MULEBACK . . . /14   Mount Athos, a mountain and peninsula in northern Greece, is a tenth-century Greek Orthodox monastery. Masada, a fortress mountain in Israel overlooking the Dead Sea, was where Zealots (perhaps Essenes) held out against Roman rule from 66–73 A.D. "Kleftes," meaning "robbers" or "bandits," was the appellation for Greek guerrillas during the eighteenth-century rebellions and the nineteenth-

379

century War of Independence against Turkey. During the Greek civil war (1946–49), the guerrillas also called themselves "kleftes," meaning Greek patriots.

WHITE ISLAND /15   Constantine was Crown Prince Constantine (then nine years old), later King Constantine (1964–74). The German Queen was the granddaughter of the Kaiser, Queen Frederika of Greece (1947–1964). *Xenos* means "foreigner."

ONE ANDALUSIAN WINTER /15   *Rojos*, meaning "reds," was the term that Generalísimo Franco, leader of the *azules* (blues), called the opposition, whoever they were. In 1951–52, there were still loyalists hiding in the Anadalusian hills, who when caught were shot and paraded through the towns.

A BLONDE IN TANGIER /15   *Azulejo* is a blue tile.

HIDING IN A WARDROBE CLOSET. . . /17   SOAS is School of Oriental and African Studies, University of London.

COLUMBIA BLUES AND GREEK FIRES /17   Y is YMHA/YWHA where the Poetry Center is in New York. Federico García Lorca, in New York from 1929 to 1930, was a student in a poetic drama class given by Henry Wells, English professor at Columbia University.

BOOT CAMP IN GEORGIA /18   Fort Dix was an army base in New Jersey.

RED GUARD BEIJING, 1972 /19   A *hutong* is an alleyway in an old traditional neighborhood. Empress Dowager Tzu Hsi (Cixi) (1835–1908).

THE CAMP NEAR KRAKÓW /22   The Auschwitz sign still at its entrance is ARBEIT MACHT FREI, meaning "Work Makes (You) Free."

THEFT OF A BROTHER /23   "Between Mobile and Galveston," referring to Houston, comes from the first line in "Annie," a poem by Guillaume Apollinaire.

MY BROTHER ENTERS THE EARTH ON MAY DAY /26   The Rothko Chapel was designed in Houston by the architect Howard Barnstone.

IN GNOSTIC PARADISE EVE RAISES ADAM . . . /31   In the Nag Hammadi Gnostic scripture *On the Origin of the World*, Eve creates Adam, and God and his angels rape Eve, from whom humanity descends.

LUCIFER, ANGEL OF LIGHT /32   The Magi of the New Testament were Zoroastrian priests.

BUDDHA IN THE TWILIGHT /33   Siddhartha Gautama (563?–483) was the founder of Buddhism. He received his first illumination while meditating under a fig tree, sometimes called a banyan tree, but more often the pipal or peepul tree. Eventually, the tree was named The Bodhi Tree or The Tree of Enlightenment, meaning, as does the epithet the Buddha, "the awakened."

SOCRATES IN JAIL /33   Socrates was to be executed upon the return of a ship from the holy island of Delos.

THE TRUE HISTORY OF SOCRATES AND JESUS . . . /34   For background information, please see "How through false translation into and from the Bible Jesus ceased to be a Jew" in chapter 2 of my *The Poetics of Translation: History, Theory, Practice*, Yale University Press, 1993.

JESHUA THE GNOSTIC /35   Jesus is from Hebrew and Aramaic Jeshua.

JESUS THE CHRISTIAN /36   Saul the tentmaker is later Paul. See note on "The Secret Reader."

WANG WEI AND THE SNOW /37   The Chinese poet Wang Wei (701–761) was a Taoist, Buddhist, music counselor to the emperor in Changan, and a landscape painter.

LI QINGZHAO AND THE MOON /38   Li Qingzhao (Li Ching-chao) (1040?–c.1115) was a poet and scholar of the Song dynasty. She and Tang poet Yu Xuanji (c.843–868) are perhaps China's most important women poets.

IN MÁLAGA A POET ONE MORNING /38   Solomon Ibn Gabirol (1021/22–c.1055) was a Jewish poet in Muslim Spain, who wrote in Hebrew.

LUIS DE LEÓN IN A PRISON CELL /40   Spanish mystic poet (1527–91), Augustinian monk and professor of Latin, Greek, and Hebrew at the

University of Salamanca. Imprisoned for five years by the Inquisition on charges of "Judaizing," of translating Song of Songs directly from "corrupt" original Hebrew scripture rather than from the approved Jerome Latin Vulgata. Reference to John is to John of the Cross (Juan de la Cruz), his probable teacher at the University of Salamanca.

JOHN OF THE CROSS IN THE SPRING /40   John of the Cross (1547–91) was a mystical poet and Carmelite monk, later canonized as Saint John of the Cross. He was held in captivity in a monastery sardine closet by rival Carmelites in Toledo for nine months, where he probably wrote the poem "The Dark Night of the Soul."

SAINT JOHN LAUGHED ON THE STAIRS /41   John of the Cross, when dying, chose to spend his last days at the monastery in Úbeda, where he knew he would be abused by the prior.

FRANCISCO DE QUEVEDO WALKING . . . /41   The Spanish writer Francisco de Quevedo (1580–1645) was the last great poet of the Golden Age. He also wrote a picaresque novel and a nightmarish, visionary work entitled *Los sueños* (The Dreams).

SOR JUANA INÉS DE LA CRUZ . . . /43   The Mexican nun Sor Juana Inés de la Cruz was a major poet in the seventeenth century and author of "Response to Filotea," asserting a woman's intellectual and artistic right to study, teach, and create. "Indian criolla": "Criolla" is a female of Spanish or partly Spanish descent born in the New World. Sor Juana was a mestiza, child of a Spanish father and Indian mother.

G.W. LEIBNITZ AND SOPHIE IN BERLIN /44   Sophie was the wife of the German mathematician and philosopher Gottfried Wilhelm von Leibnitz (1647–1716).

BILLY BUDD /45   Herman Melville's novella *Billy Budd* ends with a poem, "Billy in the Darbies" ("darbies" meaning handcuffs), whose last line, "I am sleepy, and the oozy weeds about me twist." is the source of the last line of this sonnet.

CAVAFY ON HIS OWN BED ABOVE A POOR TAVERNA /47   Constantine Cavafy (1863–1933), a Greek poet from Alexandria, recreated Hellenistic times and contemporary Alexandrian life. He was openly homoerotic in his poetry. Most of his poems were published only after his death.

ANTONIO MACHADO IN SORIA . . . /48   The Spanish poet Antonio Machado (1875–1939) first worked as schoolmaster in Soria, where he married Leonor in 1909. She died three years later at age eighteen.

ANNA AKHMATOVA UNDER GLASS . . . /49   Anna Akhmatova (1888–1966), Russian poet from Leningrad, was silenced by the government most of her life.

MARINA TSVETAYEVA AND HER SHIP OF BEING . . . /49   Marina Tsvetayeva (1892–1941), Russian poet, returned from exile in Prague and Paris to the Soviet Union, was persecuted, and hanged herself in Elabuga, where she was in internal exile.

LARRY ROTHMAN, MY ARMY BUDDY /52   Victoria is the Spanish contralto Victoria de los Angeles (1923–).

LATE DECEMBER, WHERE ARE YOU, ROBERT FROST? /53   "Snow" refers to Wilbert Snow, Maine poet and friend of Robert Frost. "Stone" is Barnstone, not Ruth Stone of next poem.

PORTRAIT OF THE LORD AS A YOUNG MAN /59   Josh is Joshua the Messiah. Jesus is from Greek *Iesous*, from Hebrew *Yeshua*, from Hebrew *Yehoshua*. Messiah, meaning "the anointed," is from Greek *Khristos*.

GOD THE MISER OF TIME /64   Ἄξιον ἐστί ("Worthy be") is a phrase found in Greek Orthodox liturgy.

HOLY LOGOS, WHAT CAN I DO? /74   John of Patmos is said to have written the Book of Revelation, the Apocalypse, in a cave (now a chapel cave) on the island of Patmos.

COFFEE IN PREDAWN BUENOS AIRES /78   Cape North is at the northernmost point in Europe, in Norwegian Lapland, where winter darkness lasts three months.

SINCE DEATH, THAT CALLOW THIEF . . . /80   "I go to die and you to live" is from Socrates' last words to his judge in Plato's *Apologia*.

ROMPING FOR A WEEK IN XANADU . . . /81   The Xanadu in Samuel Taylor Coleridge's poem "Kubla Khan" is present-day Chengde or Chengteh, some five hours north of Beijing, built by Kubla Khan as his summer palace. Many of the early buildings remain.

A WINTER ON MOUNT ATHOS . . . /82   See note for "Going Muleback."

GENESIS /93   The Septuagint is the Bible translated from Hebrew into Greek, c. 250 B.C., perhaps as late as second century B.C., in Alexandria for the Greek-speaking Jewish community, which could no longer read the text in Hebrew. It was legendarily translated in 72 days by 72 scholars, hence its name the Septuagint. In this version of the opening lines of Genesis, differences between the Hebrew original and Greek texts are emphasized.

REINDEER /101   "La Petite Soeur (the Little Sister)" is a French nun from a socialist order of nuns, Les Petites Soeurs de Marie. The landscape background for "Reindeer" appeared in an earlier poem, "Lapland":

The roots of the earth protrude
down into the pinegray ocean
and up into the glacial snow.

There are not many fir trees
as we push into the unreal
north. We are beyond the green

and on nude scrubby earth again.
Here where snow yawns into the
sea, and air is clean like fish,

distance and form and seasons
are more true than the odd boat
or village. Time. This land is

dream—planet where almost no one
is—or if real, then quick cities
south are dream before the slow

iceland. At night sunshine floats
on big mountain ribs of snow;
gulls cry and cod run in the ocean.

SONG OF THE BIRDS /101   Title refers to a Catalan folk song that Pablo Casals frequently played on cello. Canigo is a mountain near Prades, French Catalonia, where in an old French convent the Casals music festival was held in 1952.

TALKING TO YOU WHILE REMEMBERING MY FRIEND CÉSAR VALLEJO /104 The Peruvian poet César Vallejo (1892–1938) moved as a young man to Paris, where he died, like Baudelaire, of diverse diseases, including poverty. All his Paris poetry was published posthumously.

THE SHINGON WATER MOON /106   The Japanese Buddhist monk Kukai (Kobo Duishi, 774–834) wrote the Tantric poem "Singing Image of a Water Moon." In their moon meditation (*gachiringan*), Buddhist monks in Shingon concentrate on the full moon, a symbol of supreme awakening. I owe information on this practice to a work by Morgan Gibson and Hiroshi Murakami.

OUR RAIN /107   Spanish newspapers in early 1983 recorded that the Spanish poet Vicente Aleixandre (1899–1986), Spain's Nobel laureate in poetry, could not, because of sickness, receive the king and queen of Sweden.

CAUGHT BETWEEN CREATION OF A MOON DEITY . . . /111   Matei is Matei Calinescu, to whom I owe many literary debts and with whom I have shared thought and friendship for decades. Inanna is the Sumerian moon goddess. Main source is Diane Wolkstein and Samuel Kramer's *Inanna, Queen of Heaven and Earth* (1983).

DROPS OF NIGHT /112   The Shulamite (one from Shunem, present-day Sulam in Israel) is name given to the female speaker in the biblical Song of Songs.

WHEN THE APRICOTS ARE RIPE /122   Title in Arabic means "when everything is right."

A FLY /124   The minute gun was sometimes used in English funerals. It fired at one-minute intervals.

ZERO /129   The Indian mystical poet and Hindu saint Mahadevi (twelfth century) threw away her clothing and wandered "god-intoxicated," covered only by her tresses. She died in her twenties in the desert.

ARCHAIC FACES ON THE WALL /130   Santorini (from Italian Santa Irene) is a Greek island. Thíra (Thera) is the ancient name. In probably the sixteenth century B.C. a volcanic eruption created a huge caldera, and the island was covered with lava. The recent discovery and excavation of the capital revealed many important Bronze Age wall paintings and artifacts.

WHEN WORDS ARE SPINNING . . . /130   In the *Anabasis,* the author and general Xenophon recounts how his harried troops in 401 B.C., retreating from Persian Asia Minor, finally reached the Mediterranean and shouted *thálata, thálata!* (the sea, the sea!), knowing they were saved since they could build ships and return home to Greece. The "Dane" is Hamlet. *Montoneros* are Argentine Trotskyite guerrillas who fought the government during the 1970s "Dirty War."

INTO THE MEADOW OF ABSENCE /130   The Chinese Tang Buddhist poet Han Shan, meaning "Cold Mountain," wrote a sequence of 100 poems also called *Cold Mountain.* The "cry of Samson's noon" derives from Milton's *Samson Agonistes.*

A GUY EATING TOMATO SALAD . . . /132   See note for "Cyclops in Sérifos."

ON THE CRATER OF THERA /132   See note for "Archaic Faces on the Wall."

APOLLO IN NÁXOS /133   Greek island of the Cyclades on which a famous, unfinished kouros (an archaic Greek sculpture) of Apollo lies prostrate.

CYCLOPS IN SÉRIFOS /133   Sérifos is a Greek island in the Cyclades. A purported site of the Cyclopean caves from which Cyclops threw stones at Odysseus is the Neo Livadi area of Sérifos.

A MIDNIGHT CAR DEATH IN BUENOS AIRES /136   *Ayin* is the sixteenth letter of the Hebrew alphabet, meaning *eye* and the number 16. "Street of Holy Faith" is Avenida de Santa Fe, a major street in Buenos Aires.

COMING BACK TO YOU IN JAVA /137   "Daisy" from Old English *daeges eage,* "day's eye" or the sun. Mata Hari from Dutch Margaretha, also meaning "daisy."

KINGDOM OF THE POOR /141   Zulfikar Ali Bhutto (1928–79) was president and prime minister of Pakistan. In 1977 he was deposed by a coup d'état and later executed.

MY HEART IS IN THE EAST 143   Judah Halevi (c. 1075–1141), Tudela, Spain, was a poet, philosopher, and rabbi. He is eulogized in Rafael Alberti's poem "Returnings to Spain's First Poet."

SIRENS /147   Bishop Theobaldus (c. 1200–1300), probably Italian, wrote a bestiary of twelve beasts in leonine rhyming Latin verse.

SAUL THE TENTMAKER /149   See note for "The Secret Reader."

NECKLACE IN THE EARTH /155   Giordano Bruno (1548–1600) was a philosopher, astronomer, mathematician, and poet. His Copernican and pantheistic infinite principle of the cosmos influenced Spinoza and Leibnitz. He was burned to death by the Inquisition in Venice.

ON THE FLOOR OF THE CREATION /159   The allusion to the man as a fork is to a character in Quevedo's novel *El Buscón* (The Swindler) whom Quevedo calls *tenedor* (fork). See note for "Francisco de Quevedo Walking . . ."

GOSPEL OF CLOUDS 169   The phrase "peat bog soldiers of the camp" is taken from a famous concentration camp song, composed in German, in which the inmates speak of themselves as peat bog soldiers, carrying spades instead of rifles. Paul Robeson, among others, made this song popular after the war.

QUAKER LOVE /170   "To see,/to hear, to touch, to kiss, to die with thee" from an English renaissance song.

GOSPEL OF THE TOWER /177   *Nous* is Greek for mind.

THE SECRET HAND . . . /178   *Le Quartier* is the Latin Quarter in Paris.

GOSPEL OF THE NIGHT /184   Plotinos is Plotinus (205–270 A.D.), Alexandrian Neoplatonist philosopher. For Greek names I follow the custom, largely initiated by Richmond Lattimore, of using a Greek rather than a Latin spelling of Greek names. Hence, Plotinos, Olympos, Krito, etc.

SECRET WORD /186   "His poet earned the Chinese emperor's curse and lost his scalp (he knew one word that bound the world)" is derived from Jorge Luis Borges's "Parable of the Palace."

THE LORD WAS GLORIOUS /187   "Faith" usually was a negative concept among the Gnostics, for it signified a surrender of truth to clerical authority and abandonment of personal gnosis (self-knowledge).

GOSPEL OF TIME /189   The phrase *Ich bin* makes up the last words of Sonnet II, 29, which is the concluding sonnet in Rainer Maria Rilke's *Sonnets to Orpheus.*

ROOM /193   Osip Mandelstam (1891–1938), a Russian poet, was arrested and sent to a concentration camp where he died, probably executed. The Romanian poet Paul Celan (1920–70), who wrote in German, walked into the Seine and drowned. Celan, author of the poem "Death Fugue," was a major postwar poet in the German language.

NEWS OF THE DIRTY WAR /195   *La Opinión* was a leading liberal newspaper in Argentina, whose director, Jacobo Timerman, was later jailed and tortured. Falcons are Fords used by death squads. *Montoneros* were the Marxist (usually Trotskyite) guerrillas during the "Dirty War" (1975-1981). *Florida* is an elegant shopping street in Buenos Aires.

DAYS IN WILD BUENOS AIRES . . . /195   Artists and intellectuals in 1975, during the days of killing during the Dirty War, declared "Una Semana del Fracaso" (A Week of Failure) in which disaster was celebrated and people were inoculated by nurses against success and happiness. Buenos Aires means "good airs" or "good winds."

GOSPEL OF LOVE /196   Luis de Góngora y Argote (1561–1627), Spanish poet. The Generation of 1927, including Federico García Lorca and Vicente Aleixandre, was named after the tricentennial of the death of Góngora, whose influence, especially in his highly metaphorical, obscure *Las soledades* (The Solitudes), was paramount. He was lampooned by Quevedo as a Jew. By profession he was a prebendary and priest of the Catholic Church, who wrote secular poetry and enjoyed bullfights and gambling.

VAGABONDS IN CHINA /197   Fayyum is a desert area northwest of the Nile in northern Egypt where many antiquities have been uncovered. It is accessible from Alexandria.

MY WORLD AS WORDS OF A BOOK . . . /206   Gregor is the beetle protagonist in Franz Kafka's *The Metamorphosis.*

ISRAEL EPSTEIN IN BEIJING . . . /209   Israel Epstein, born in Poland, spent his life since childhood in China. Editor of *China Reconstructs*, a propaganda magazine in English, he also wrote two books on Tibet, justifying the Chinese "liberation" of the country.

NADEZHDA RECALLS OSIP MANDELSTAM'S POEM . . . /210   Osip Mandelstam (1891–1938), one of Russia's great poets, was arrested after writing "The Stalin Epigram." He was sent into exile in Voronezh where he perished.

BORGES DYING IN EUROPE, 1986 /213   Jorge Luis Borges married his companion María Kodama on his deathbed in Geneva. The milonga is a fast tango.

SUICIDES AND ANOTHER MIRACLE OF SPRING /213   "Miracle of Spring" recalls Antonio Machado's line "otro milagro de la primavera."

EVEN HEROIC ALEXANDER . . . /215   "Features to the Buddha." After Alexander crossed into India (315 B.C.), Hellenistic art influenced India. Gandhara art, named after the Gandhara region now in Pakistan, flourished between the second and fifth centuries A.D. and offered the first human depiction of Buddha in sculptures; their faces are both Western and Indian.

ARNOST LUSTIG LISTENS . . . /216   Arnold Lustig, an Auschwitz survivor, is a character in a short story by the novelist Aharon Appelfeld.

DECLARATIONS BY JOHN THE THEOLOGIAN /222   The "Theologian" is another name for John of Patmos, also John of Ephesos, to whom Revelation is attributed.

JOSHUA THE MESSIAH . . . /223   Joshua is the Hebrew original for English *Jesus Christ*, derived from Greek *Iesous Khristos*.

PATMOS /226   The Theologian wrote Revelation in a cave on Patmos. See note for "Declarations by John the Theologian."

RETURN FROM THE SNOW /227   The American painter Marsden Hartley (1877–1943) was born in Lewiston, Maine.

FLOATING GODLESS IN HEAVEN /238   Fanny was Jorge Luis Borges's cook and housekeeper for decades. One morning, Borges told me, with delight and amazement, about Fanny's insights on the Japanese.

JOSEPHINE THE SINGER /255   Josephine is a mouse in Franz Kafka's short story, "Josephine the Singer, or the Mouse Folk."

RESIGNATION TO WAKING . . . /265   The Czech friend is Slava Klima.

MIGUEL HERNÁNDEZ IN PRISON . . . /265   The Spanish poet Miguel Hernández (1910–42), who died at age thirty-one in a prison hospital at Alicante, was the youngest and last among the major poets in twentieth century Spain, from Antonio Machado to Hernández, who reflect a renaissance of poetry in Spain unequaled since the Spanish Golden Age. Hernández was a self-educated goatherd, who, encouraged by Pablo Neruda, Vicente Aleixandre, and Federico García Lorca, was to master, in his verse, verbal acrobatics not found in Spanish poetry since the baroque poets Francisco de Quevedo and Luis de Góngora. He wrote surreal sonnets, socially committed war poems, and metaphysical verse of "a dark night" during his last years in prison. His powerful poems, like those of kindred Peruvian poet César Vallejo (1992–38), have pathos, passion, grave depth, and yet play experimentally at the edge of language.

WEARY ESCAPE . . . /266   Sor Juana is the Mexican nun Sor Juana Inés de la Cruz. See note for "Sor Juana Inés de la Cruz . . ."

CYCLOPS IN LOVE /267   See note for "Cyclops in Sérifos."

AMONG HOOSIERS /272   "Keek, Rob, Ton" is short for Aliki, Robert, and Tony Barnstone.

OVERLOOKING ROCK MEADOWS . . . /273   Mólista is a small village in Epirus.

WORRY OF THE TWITCHING OLIVE TREES /282   The Meltemi winds are strong late summer winds from the south. Meltemi is probably from the Italian *maltempo*, bad weather.

HOW POETS FROM NEW ENGLAND AND SPAIN . . . /283   The Spanish poet Federico García Lorca was executed outside Granada in 1936.

AT THE TURKESTAN BORDER . . . /284   Kashgar is a white city, with a great open market, on the Silk Route in China by the Pakistani border, populated by Turkic peoples.

COFFEE AND EARLY SORROW IN PARIS /286   The lines in French may be translated: "Sir, I am making bed for you." "Are you going out?" "Yes, I'm going downstairs. I'm hungry. I want a snack." "Sir, I'll be waiting for you."

LOVE BADE ME WELCOME /286   Title and phrases are from a poem by the English poet George Herbert (1593–1633).

CHAC THE RAINGOD . . . /290   Chac is a Maya raingod.

ISAAC LURIA . . . /292   Of Spanish origin, Isaac Luria (1534–72), born in Jerusalem, was a major Kabbalist visionary. In his school in Safed he preached to his circle of mystics that human deeds cause cosmic redemption and thereby bring forth the Messiah and supreme earthly redemption. In Kabbalah, the universe is a verbal construct made up of words, and prior to words were letters.

A PLEA FOR IMPERFECTION . . . /293   Ludwig Wittgenstein (1889–1951) ends his *Tractatus Logico-philosophicus,* published in 1921 when he was an elementary school teacher, with "Whatever cannot be said in words must be confined to silence." By this he was not, like the logical positivists, rejecting the metaphysical as nonsense but denying the possibility of stating the metaphysical in words.

SHARING RABBI JESUS IN WHITEFACE AT CHRISTMAS /310   Sources are the Presocratic Greek philosopher Xenophanes (c.580–c.480 B.C.) of Colophon and Al Jolson's blackface impersonation. Xenophanes opposed the anthropomorphic representation of the gods in Homer and Hesiod and asserted there to be only one immutable, eternal God, pantheistically connected with the world. He wrote in satiric elegiac verse about the relativistic nature of gods, of their constant retranslation among humans according to each nationality and, among beasts (to rub it in), according to each animal species:

> Man made his gods, and furnished them
> with his own body, voice and garments.
>
> If a horse or lion or a slow ox
> had agile hands for paint and sculpture,
> the horse would make his god a horse,
> the ox would sculpt an ox.
>
> Our gods have flat noses and black skins,
> say the Ethiopians. The Thracians say
> our gods have red hair and hazel eyes.
> (*Sappho and the Greek Lyric Poets* 131)

Following Al Jolson's minstrel routine of altering appearances, Europe translated—with regard to his proper name, identity, thought, religion, and appearance—a legendary Jew named Joshua from whatever he was in Israel into the whiteface version, now named Jesus, whom we see in the Greek Pantocrator depicted on the mosaic vault in Osios Loukás, in the noble, fair Slav on a Russian icon, or in the stern, thoughtful Lowlands face in a Hans Memling altarpiece painting.

MORNING IN THE SCHOOLYARD /312   Pavlos, King of Greece (1947–64). See note for "White Island."

IN A SITTING ROOM WITH FREDERIKA /313   Markos Vafiades, normally called "Markos," led Communist guerrilla forces during the Greek civil war (1946–49).

TEN-MINUTE SNUFF DRAMA /319   Snuff films, culminating in the violent death of a participant in a sex act, were made in Argentina, but their authenticity has been questioned. Beyond question is the "performance execution" at the ancient Maya "basketball" courts in Mexico and Guatemala, where at the end of the game, the captain of the losing team was decapitated before a seated audience.

WHEN A FRAGRANT WOMAN COMES /324   Hanniá is a city in western Crete, noted for its Venetian architecture.

MY SOMBER FRIENDS /326   I too like theory. We part because my somber friends, who fiddle a lot, take in the first line but not the second of Marianne Moore's poem about her "disdain for primary texts": "Poetry / I, too dislike it: there are things that are important beyond all this fiddle. / Reading it, however, with a perfect contempt for it, one discovers in it after all, a place for the genuine."

NEVER GUESSED YOU'D COME /333   Metaxa (Metaxá), meaning "silk" in modern Greek, is the name of a popular international brandy.

HELP /356   Saigyo (1118–90) was one of Japan's most profound and skilled Buddhist poets, who wrote largely in the tanka form.

SOULPEACE /360   *Paredón,* meaning "big or thick wall," is an execution wall.

RECALLING GRATEFULLY A LUCKY WAY OUT AND IN /362   *"Da stieg ein Baum* (There rose a tree)" is first sentence of poem 1 in Rilke's *Sonnets to Orpheus.* In 1947 my friend Jaime Salinas gave me a copy of Rainer María Rilke's *Letters to a Young Poet.* He planted a seed. A year later, at age twenty, I read Rilke's *Sonnets to Orpheus,* woke up one winter night in Maine, and wrote the first poem. Then I left, in a lost notebook about the empty mind, the me who was.

Epigraphic Poems in Translation[*]

---

[*] All translations are by me except for Federico García Lorca's "Sonnet of the Mild Complaint," which is by Tony and Willis Barnstone, and the poems of Wang Wei, translated by Tony and Willis Barnstone and Xu Haishin. Borges's "Spinoza" and my sonnet version of the first lines of Septuagint Genesis are included among the sonnets.

Index of Titles

UNIVERSITY PRESS OF NEW ENGLAND publishes books under its own imprint and is the publisher for Brandeis University Press, Dartmouth College, Middlebury College Press, University of New Hampshire, University of Rhode Island, Tufts University, University of Vermont, Wesleyan University Press, and Salzburg Seminar.

ABOUT THE AUTHOR Willis Barnstone was born in Lewiston, Maine, and educated at Bowdoin College, Columbia, and Yale. He taught in Greece at the end of the civil war (1949–51) and in Buenos Aires during the "Dirty War" (1975–76). He first went to China in 1972 during the Cultural Revolution, and was later a Fulbright Professor of American Literature at Beijing Foreign Studies University (1984–85). He has published more than forty books of poetry, scholarship, translation, and memoir, including *The Other Bible* (1984), *Five A.M. in Beijing* (1987), *Sappho and the Greek Lyric Poets* (1988), *With Borges on an Ordinary Evening in Buenos Aires* (1993), *The Poetics of Translation* (1993), *Funny Ways of Staying Alive* (1993), and *Sunday Morning in Fascist Spain* (1995). A Guggenheim Fellow, NEA and NEH recipient, and two-time Pulitzer Prize nominee, Barnstone is Distinguished Professor of Comparative Literature, Spanish, and East Asian Cultures at Indiana University.

Library of Congress Cataloging-in-Publication Data

Barnstone, Willis, 1927–
  The secret reader : 501 sonnets / Willis Barnstone.
    p. cm.
  Contents : Gas lamp, 1893 — Solitude of planets — Gospel of clouds — Kafka in his small room — To find you at the end of our strange walk.
  ISBN 0–87451–660–9 (pbk. : alk. paper)
  1. Sonnets, American   I. Title.
PS3503.A6223S43 1996
811'.54—dc20   95–17105